FOREST OR FARM?

Forest or Farm?

The Politics of Poverty and Land Hunger in Nepal

KRISHNA GHIMIRE

MANOHAR
2026

First published 1992
Reprinted 2026
First eBook edition 2026

ISBN 978-81-7304-213-3 (hardbound)
ISBN 978-93-7451-252-4 (eBook)

Published by
Ajay Kumar Jain for
Manohar Publishers & Distributors
4753/23 Ansari Road, Daryaganj
New Delhi 110 002

Printed and bound in India

To my parents

Contents

List of Tables, Figures and Maps

TABLES

FIGURES

MAPS

Preface

This study explores the experiences of the landpoor and the landless in seeking title to land in the Nepal Tarai. It is suggested here that the unequal distribution of cultivated land, the fact that extremely small units of land are held by the majority of the farmers, declining yields and population growth have resulted in the phenomenon of 'landlessness'. At the same time, the overwhelmingly rural economy, the seasonal nature of agricultural wage-employment and low wage rates means that the notion of being a self-sustaining 'peasant' has become quite attractive. However, maintaining effective control over land and securing legal ownership is an extremely painful experience. Because of the growing official concern for forest protection, settlers are not only constantly intimidated by forest guards, the police and government officials, but they are also regularly evicted from their settlements. Their houses are often burnt down, crops are destroyed, they and their family members are beaten up and arrests are often made. This study describes the hopes and frustrations of these people with respect to their aspirations to land; it also examines the rationality of present land-use policies and the vested interests of socially dominant groups which coincide with official forest protection measures, but which are totally contradictory to the subsistence needs of the landless. The main argument which runs through the book is whether a poor country like Nepal shtuld not maximize social benefits by promoting small-holder land settlements in areas most suitable for agriculture (i.e. the Tarai) instead of pursuing a 'luxurious' policy of forest conservation which frequently entails letting productive land lie idle whilst hungry people in the area multiply.

This book comes out of a doctoral thesis submitted to the School of Development Studies, University of East Anglia, England. In the course of researching and writing the thesis, I was guided by Professor Piers Blaikie and Mr John Cameron to whom I am most obliged. Within the faculty, I am also grateful to Dr David Seddon, who initially invited me to the University and provided me with many useful suggestions.

In Nepal, I owe much to the settlers themselves who answered the questionnaire with great patience and offered me their hospitality, yet expected nothing in return. During fieldwork, my old friends, Ravimohan Sapkota, lecturer at Chitawan campus, assisted me in establishing initial contacts with the 'settler-community' and Sukdev Dhungana helped me in the data collection. In Nawalparasi, I am obliged, amongst others, to Mr Mohan Prasad Adhikari of the NRC project office, the Director of FASC and the officials of RDRO, who supplied me with much useful information.

In Kathmandu, I am particularly indebted to the Director of the NRC who kindly provided me with a letter of introduction allowing me to get administrative approval for the fieldwork. The staff of APROSC, CEDA, RD, NPC and FD offered me their publications.

Two colleagues and friends whose occasional comments I greatly value are Beldev Sidhu and Richard Sexton. I am also grateful to Kurt Marisa who proofread the manuscript. Finally, I must especially thank my wife Véronique who has courageously supported me all along during the preparation of this book.

K. GHIMIRE

Series Editors' Preface

The accelerating pace of environmental degradation in South Asia has highlighted an area of research gravely neglected by historians and social scientists, viz. the interactions between the human social world and the natural world that humans share with other species. The environmental debate is rapidly making social scientists aware of this neglect, and a small but growing number have begun systematic research on different aspects of the human-nature relationship. In recognition of the importance of the field, the Oxford University Press has decided to start a monograph series entitled 'Studies in Social Ecology and Environmental History'.

On both intellectual and pragmatic grounds, the convergence of ecology and the social sciences is especially appropriate for South Asia. From an ecological perspective, South Asia is unique in its diversity of environmental regimes. More strikingly, this ecological diversity is matched by a comparable cultural diversity in which one can find representative examples of every form of natural resource use in human history—from Stone Age hunter-gatherers at one end of the spectrum to thermal and nuclear power plants at the other. The interactions of these different modes of resource use, in the present and in the past, are of keen interest to historians, social scientists, and ecologists. Again, the wide range of nature-based conflicts in contemporary South Asia has given rise to a vigorous debate on the relationship between economic development and environmental sustainability. Questions of scale, of traditional, modern and 'appropriate' technology, and of the socio-environmental costs and benefits of development options are likely to be of vital significance in the intellectual and political agendas of the countries of the region.

The primary goal of this series will be the publication of thoroughly researched and theoretically informed monographs under the broad rubric 'Social Ecology and Environmental

History', whether written by historians, anthropologists, geographers, ecologists, or others. Although some of the studies may have policy implications, that will not be a major focus.

This second book in the series focuses on the forest–farm frontier in the Nepal Terai. In many Third World countries the state's response to 'illegal encroachment' by landless groups on government forests has been to use the law, and occasionally force, to evict the settlers. Very rarely are the structural causes of illegal settlement investigated. In this work, the author takes a historical and diagnostic approach, locating the problem in the highly skewed pattern of landholding in the inner hills, from where most migrants to the Terai come. The study will be of wide interest both for its skilful integration of several intellectual traditions—regional analysis, rural sociology, and political economy—and its incisive critique of narrow conservation strategies.

MADHAV GADGIL RAMACHANDRA GUHA

Abbreviations, land measurement and currency equivalent

Abbreviations

ADB	Asian Development Bank
ADB/N	Agricultural Development Bank/Nepal
APROSC	Agriculture Projects Service Centre
CBS	Central Bureau of Statistics
CEDA	Centre for Economic Development and Administration
CDO	District Chief Officer
DFC	District Forest Controller
DSP	District Police Superintendent
FD	Department of Forest
FASC	Forest-Area Strengthening Commission
HMG/N	His Majesty's Government/Nepal
LDO	Local Development Officer
LRMP	Land Resources Mapping Project
MP	Member of Parliament
NPC	National Planning Commission
NRC	Nepal Resettlement Company
RD	Department of Resettlement
RDRO	Department of Resettlement Regional Office
SFDP	Small Farmer Development Project
TCN	Timber Corporation of Nepal

Land measurement

Ropani	0.05 ha
Bigha	0.68 ha

Currency equivalent:

Rs	Nepalese Rupee
Exchange rates (in June 1989)	\$1 = Rs 21.90 Indian Rupee 100 = Rs 165.15

1

Introduction

Landlessness and Pressures on Forest Areas

This research deals with the phenomenon of 'illegal' settlement in Nepal's West Central Tarai (alluvial plains) and concentrates on the Nawalparasi district in particular (see Map I). In recent years, as in much of the Nepalese Tarai, the Nawalparasi district has been a destination of in-migration for landless and landpoor migrants (known popularly as *sukumbasis* in Nepal).[1] These people have been seeking land for cultivation in the area, especially as this is one of the Tarai districts where large tracts of agriculturally suitable uncultivated 'forest' land are present. In this work, these peasant settlers are the central focus of analysis and their aspirations to land are examined within the wider socio-political, agricultural and forestry contexts. The following are specially emphasized as key elements: (a) the origin and the evolution of the process of landlessness in source areas,[2] (b) the connection between unequal access to means of production and landlessness and 'illegal' settlements, (c) the nature of struggle for land in the Tarai on the part of the landless populations and (d) the effects of the State's changing forestry and land-use policies on access to land and the implications for the future socio-economic and agrarian positions of these people.

'Illegal' settlement by landless and propertyless migrants is clearly evident in the Tarai. A traveller passing through the Tarai cannot help but notice settlements consisting of clusters of small, poorly constructed houses located on the fringes of forests and on the outskirts of villages, and on the roadsides. Many of these settlements appear overcrowded and the people living in them have a shabby and undernourished appearance. Although, as shall be shown later in the discussion, these people are fully

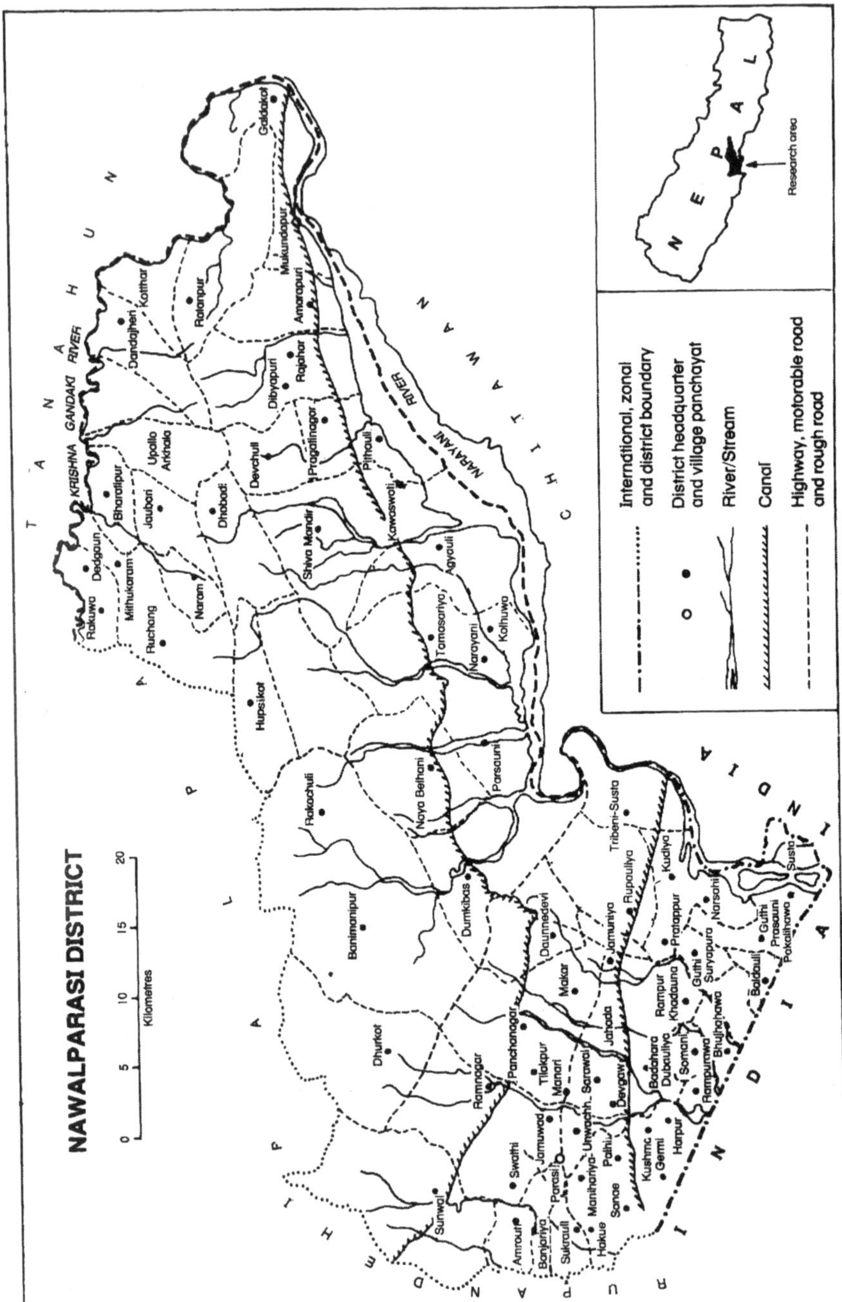
NAWALPARASI DISTRICT
0 5 10 15 20
Kilometres
International, zonal and district boundary
District headquarter and village panchayat
River/Stream
Canal
Highway, motorable road and rough road
NEPAL
Research area
KRISHNA GANDAKI RIVER
NARAYANI RIVER

integrated within the wider economy and are important to labour relations in villages closest to their settlements, their settlements are not usually considered as parts of villages. The larger settlements are called *sukumbasi tol/tola* (the sukumbasi section), or very accurately *syauli bazaar*—the market made of forest twigs and bushes. Indeed, many of these settlements give the impression of small market, shanty towns.

'Illegal' occupation of land, principally land gazetted as protected State 'forest', by migrants and local landless people is widespread in the Tarai. Out of the twenty outer-Tarai districts in Nepal, sixteen districts have experienced substantial land squatting (see Map II). Siraha, Saptari, Dhanusha and Mahottari are the only four districts where the above phenomenon does not occur to any great extent for the simple reason that there exist no significant forest-frontiers in these districts. Amongst the inner-Tarai districts, the Sindhuli, Makawanpur and Surkhet districts host a considerable number of landless settlers. Although the intensity of illegal settlement in these districts differs greatly, this phenomenon is not simply related to the physical presence of cultivable land but to varied factors such as the concentration of early migration and land colonization, malaria eradication, road-construction and the initiation of official resettlement schemes. These and other underlying issues specific to the development of illegal settlements in the Tarai will be expounded upon in chapter three.

There are no reliable figures on the total number of 'illegal' settlers in the Tarai, although some estimates have suggested that, by the mid-1970s, between 70,500 to 130,000 people had settled 'illegally' (Rieger et al., 1976: 18; Ohja, 1982:48–53). Given this range and, on the basis of the average national family size of 5.8 persons of the period (CBS, 1984:18), between 12,155 and 22,414 households could then have been involved in the process. However, this figure is likely to be a great underestimate, as the settler-census undertaken for this study showed that by 1977, the number of households settled in the Nawalparasi district alone reached 7,465. Details of this census will be discussed in chapter three.

Because of the significant numbers of people involved, the sukumbasis over the last thirty-five years or so have come under increasing scrutiny. The Nepalese newspapers frequently report

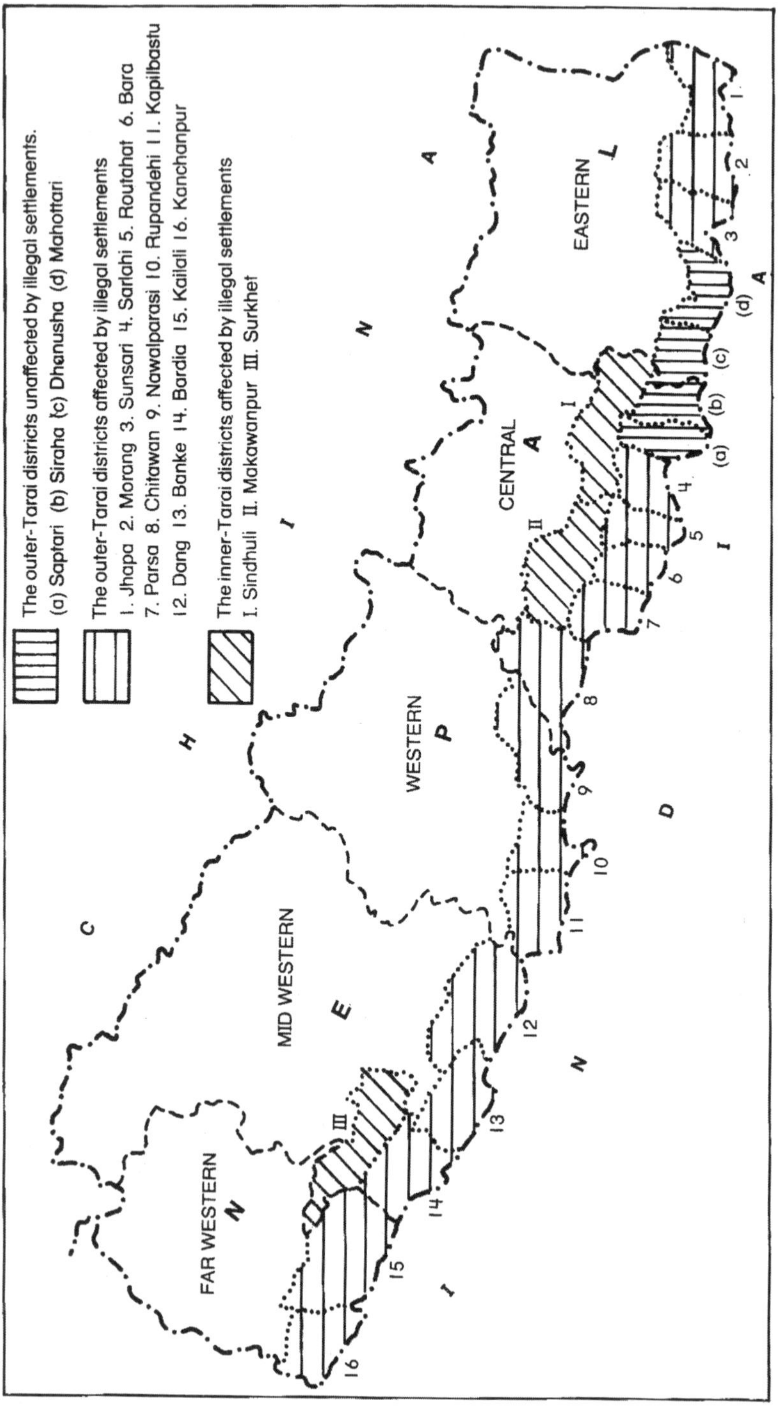

Map 11. THE MAGNITUDE OF ILLEGAL SETTLEMENTS IN THE TARAI NEPAL

cases relating to hardships and repression faced by the sukumbasis in the frontier areas. Government publications refer to how 'large and growing illegal settlement is causing problems for law and order' (Department of Resettlement, 1974:2) and how such settlement 'threaten(s) the remaining forest areas' (ADB/HMGN, vol.I, 1982:51). International aid agencies have also recognized the phenomenon of illegal settlements in the Tarai. For example, FAO, in evaluating criteria for land allocation for agriculture in Nepal, acknowledged that a much larger unauthorized settlement sector existed, as compared to the planned settlement sector (FAO, 1974:46). Another UN agency has stressed that the process was 'the result of a southward movement of impoverished villagers, who lost their land through fragmentation and land pledging' (ARTEP/ILO, 1974:IV:26). The agency also observed that 'frequently the official response to these "illegal" settlers is to contain them rather than accommodate them. They have been expelled from certain areas without any alternative arrangements made for them' (ibid). Similarly, sukumbasis have been mentioned in economic and sociological studies carried out in the Tarai. Some have viewed the development of the 'illegal' settlements by the landless as 'the search for ownership of the means of production' (Blaikie, Cameron and Seddon, 1979:62), whilst others considered them as politically significant 'movements' (Conway and Shrestha, 1981:226). Some have even gone so far as to describe the sukumbasis' attempts to obtain land as being like the 'fire from below' (Kaplan and Shrestha, 1982:75).

From the above conceptions two dominant views can be identified. The first is that since the sukumbasis' attempts are to bring forest area under agriculture, their actions are seen as producing deforestation and environmental degradation; thus, they must be restrained. The consequent arguments for forest protection are based, in the first place, on the view that uncontrolled access would lead to the depletion or disappearance of common property resources such as forests. Secondly, the increasing losses of tropical forests elsewhere in Asia, Africa and Latin America have caused concern about the steady deterioration of the world's ecosystem amongst conservationists, academicians and planners (Manshard, 1974:187). Specific forest protection measures in Nepal also gain support from claims that 'Nepal is the most ecologically endangered country in the world' (Eckholm, 1975:764–70), and, therefore, 'destroying the Himalayan forests means destroying an entire ecosystem and thus removing the natural foundation for life' (Martens, 1982:93).

Contrary in many respects to the above perspective, a second view situates actions of the rural poor within the context of poverty, economic inequalities and their lack of access to the means of production. Within this perspective, historical processes and class relations are emphasized in order to indicate how certain groups of people in society become resourceless and are thus forced to take actions that may be ecologically unsustainable, i.e. forest clearance, over-grazing and cultivation of erosion-prone areas (e.g. Blaikie and Brookfield, 1987). With respect to the global process of deforestation, ranching interests, particularly in Latin America, and the international timber business are recognized as more significant than the actions of the poor. It is estimated that in the early 1980s, in Latin America alone, the cattle raisers annually burnt down 20,000 sq. km. of forest, and as much as 50,000 sq. km. of forest in Asia, Africa and Latin America were cleared each year through commercial logging (Myers, 1984:109–24). In examining the Latin American situation, Myers argued that, 'the forest farmer deserves to be regarded as an unwitting instrument, rather than a deliberate agent, of forest destruction. He is no more to be blamed for what happens to the forest than a soldier is to be blamed for starting a war. The root causes of his lifestyle lie in a set of circumstances often many horizons away from the forest zones. Far from being an enthusiastic pioneer of forest settlement, he finds himself pushed into the forest by circumstances beyond his control' (ibid:150).

This study will largely work within the framework of the second perspective. As will be described later, Nepal in the 1980s in fact maintained one of the highest percentages of land-surface under forests in South Asia; an even more important fact is that the Tarai forest areas, where demands for land are made and the 'illegal' settlements have grown, comprise only a small part of the country's forest area. It should also be noted that since the Tarai is a flat plain, ecologically it is not as fragile as the Hill areas. The warnings such as those Eckholm and Martens have made about the ecological vulnerability of Nepal as a whole do not take account of this difference. Given exhaustion of land, declining crop yields and the high level of soil erosion in the Hills, and the bright prospects for agricultural expansion in the Tarai, a rational and sustainable conservation policy would be to grow trees in the Hills and food crops in the Tarai. Owing to the high rate of population growth, landlessness and the rising demand for food, a poor country like Nepal would need a carefully designed strategy and could not afford to adopt a sweeping, undifferentiated policy in pursuit of the 'luxury of conservation'.

In terms of using this study for comparative analytical purposes, it might be mentioned that 'illegal' settlements (principally on government forest areas) by landless people are by no means unique to Nepal. This process is occurring in many Third World countries where, in order to meet food and other basic requirements, a large number of people are compelled to move to forest frontiers where 'virgin lands' for agricultural settlement are available.

This process is occurring in Latin America, particularly in Brazil and Peru, where large-scale, and often politically organized, land squattings by landless and poor migrants have taken place. In both countries, the construction of highways accompanied by land colonization schemes attracted thousands of rural poor to the frontier areas. In Brazil, it is estimated that the construction of the Transamazonian Highway resulted in an influx of more than two million settlers to uncultivated frontier areas in a period of little more than ten years (Caufield, 1982). But more fundamentally, this process seemed to have been associated with high levels of national landlessness: the Brazilian countryside, in the mid-1970s, possessed as many as 7 million households without any land, whilst 1 per cent of the top households cultivated as much as 43 per cent of the country's productive land—generally as export-oriented estates (Lappé, Collins and Fowler, 1977:42–3). A similar situation existed in Peru where, out of 80,000 sq. km. of cultivated land, in the early 1980s four-fifths was owned by large farms and 'because of this poor distribution of land, nine farms out of ten have become too small to support a family in the long run' (Myers, ibid:148). As a consequence, 'during the past two decades or so, the population of Amazonian Peru has increased from just a few tens of thousands to 1.5 million' (ibid: 150).

The coastal countries of West Africa with forest frontiers have also experienced unplanned settlements of the 'poor'. Here, too, the highway provision seemed to have given initial impetus. For example, in the Ivory Coast and Nigeria, it is estimated that, between 1976 and 1980, 600,000 hectares of broadleaf forest areas were cleared annually after the logging roads penetrated the forest (Foley and Barnard, 1984:47). But it was poverty, drought and famine which led many people to abandon their previous place of residence and move towards these more fertile areas (Myers, ibid:154).

In Asia, the Philippines and Thailand face this phenomenon on a massive scale. It is estimated that, in the case of the Philippines, '4 to 5 million people, representing 10 per cent of the national population are now illegal occupants of public forest land' (Gibbs, 1982). A similar situation is observed in Thailand. Because of the high demand for land as a result of export-oriented rice growing, a large number of subsistence farmers are squeezed out of one area and forced to move to another at the frontier. As a result of this and other factors such as commercial logging, between 1960 and 1980, the forest area in Thailand declined from 53 per cent to 23 per cent of the national territory (Myers, ibid:146).

Many of these unauthorized settlements have remained permanent, leading to the establishment of a stable type of cultivation. But in Thailand, and in Indonesia to some extent, 'illegal' swidden cultivation is a widespread phenomenon (Kunstadter, Champman and Sabhasri, 1978;UNESCO/UNEP, 1983). In India, the occupation of forest or wasteland areas by landpoor and landless people has been common, but given general population pressure, there is competition for every piece of vacant land; hence prospects for further settlement are minimal. But even India still has large swidden cultivation populations; and the government intervention measures to change land use and control in the past have frequently led to social unrest (Gupta, Banerji and Guleria, 1981; Fernandes and Kulkarni, 1983). Given the growing restrictions on the use of forest land for agriculture, in many countries whole groups of people can find themselves illegally occupying land which they had been periodically cultivating for centuries. The response of the governments concerned commonly has been to pursue 'regulatory', as well as legalistic and punitive measures.

This phenomenon also appears in Nepal as swidden agriculture is widely practised in the Siwalik Hills, adjoining the Tarai. For example, in the Siwalik region of the Nawalparasi district, my fieldwork showed that, out of a total population of 5,975 households, over 75 per cent (4,531 households) relied on swidden cultivation as a major means of subsistence. But despite such reliance, the official forest policy has been to discourage the practice of swidden agriculture without providing any alternative sources of survival for the people involved. However, as the government's recent efforts have centred upon the 'plain-forests' where there is the greatest occurrence of 'illegal' settlements[3], the present forestry 'protection' measures with respect to swidden cultivation have so far played a minor role.

This examination of stable and swidden, or of migratory and non-migratory illegal land occupation, suggests that there exist many similarities between the global processes and those in Nepal. Given the high economic benefits attached to the control of land, economically better-off elements are involved in the 'illegal' occupation and use of large tracts of forest/State land (i.e. cattle ranchers and large estates producing cashcrops for export in Latin American countries, land speculators in African and Asian countries), but the vast majority of people seeking access to small amounts of land for subsistence in these countries tend to be resourceless and economically poor; and they are the ones who especially find themselves in conflict with the State's forestry intervention measures. These conflicts are structurally unequal in that in many of these countries, political power is exercised by or on behalf of those owning property and by interests of socially dominant groups, which inhibits the possibility of formal political representation on the part of these propertyless and powerless people. This situation is relevant to the Nepalese case. Nepal's most significant particularity is possibly the lower level of industrialization in the country and the lack of prospects for the rural poor to escape to the cities.

Unlike in Brazil, Nigeria, the Philippines, Thailand and India where a certain level of industrialization has been achieved to absorb at least a proportion of the urban migration of the rural poor, Nepal so far has experienced insignificant industrial growth. In 1981, the industrial sector in Nepal employed only 81,050 persons, whilst the population of the country reached over 15 million (CBS, 1986:140&11). Between the period 1972/3 and 1980/1, 33,412 more people were employed in the manufacturing industries (CBS, 1987:456), though between 1971 and 1981, the urban population itself grew from 461,935 to 956,721 (ibid, 1982:16 and 1986:18). However, the rural population rose by nearly 3 million (ibid, 1987:3). This indicates an insignificant contribution of the manufacturing sector and of the urbanization process in terms of providing employment to a rapidly growing population.

Short and long term out-migration to Indian cities and employment in British and Indian armies as mercenary soldiers have remained crucial sources of employment and income for many rural households. But at the time of this study these prospects also were diminishing.

The lack of industrialization and a limited scope for temporary employment outside the country had already had a most profound impact on patterns of rural-rural migration within Nepal. The last thirty-five years have seen a significant level of out-migration of people from the Hills into the Tarai. This trend continues. In addition to this, there is an equally strong trend towards increased rural-to-rural population movement within the Tarai both in search of land and wage employment. It is logical that as long as a large proportion of a growing population lives in rural areas and their livelihood depends upon agriculture, the search for land will be an overwhelming priority. Pressures on land for settlement are particularly exacerbated by the high birth rate and by immigration from India, together with the failure on the part of the State to provide means of production to the landpoor either through land reform and resettlement schemes or by improving the production base inside or outside agriculture. Hence, for many rural poor, seeking access to land, through 'illegal' settlements within forest areas in the Tarai, has become both self-perpetuating and attractive.

It is important to note that the increasing physical pressure on the remaining land resources is not merely induced by the inability of the industrial sector to provide employment to the country's rapidly growing labour force and the subsequent concentration of people in rural areas but, in large part, it is brought on by the increasing numbers of the population within the landpoor and landless categories who possess very little or no land. It will be shown in the text that, whilst the socio-economic structure and the demographic characteristics of the peasantry give strong impetus to a process of landlessness, it has also become increasingly difficult for landless people to gain access to new land.

Agrarian Relations in Nepal: Some Conceptual Issues

Figure 1 shows a simple model of the agrarian position of sukumbasis in which their socio-economic relationships appear transitional and highly complex compared with conventional and more static models of agrarian relations. The sukumbasis can be theorized as a group of people who maintain barely a *de facto* possession over the land they occupy but nonetheless are not simple wage labourers or slaves. Chayanov defines peasants as

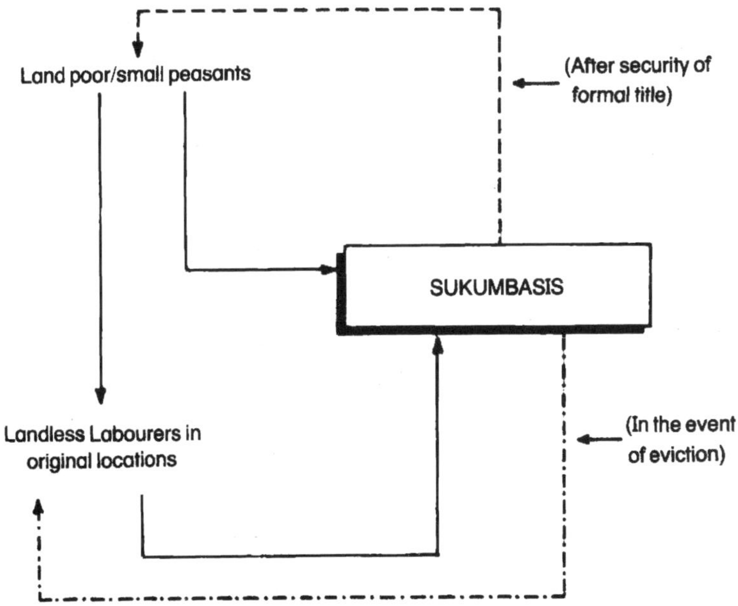

Figure 1 THE AGRARIAN POSITION OF THE SUKUMBASIS

'those whose ultimate security and subsistence lies in their having certain rights in land and in the labour of family members in land' (Chayanov, 1925, in Shanin (ed), 1971:105). Although the sukumbasis have no legal ownership of land, their present control over land is socially recognized within the village community in the sense that once one occupies a certain area of land a moral right is established and generally no other member of the village would make a claim for the same piece of land. Galeski has asserted that the access to land is 'a necessary and generally sufficient condition to enter the occupation' of a peasant (Galeski, 1963:48). Within this context, sukumbasis can be seen as small peasants. But sukumbasis are at greater risk of being removed from their land at any time by the government than other rural people. In such circumstances, they would not only lose access to cultivable land but they would also lose their peasant status and would become totally dependent on agricultural wage labouring. Indeed, the agrarian position of the sukumbasis constantly hangs in the balance between that of the small peasant and of the landless agricultural labourer; their class position thus remains ambivalent. Nonetheless, most sukumbasis are from previously landed populations who lost their land in the past and they have a tendency to see themselves as dispossessed peasants rather than natural wage labourers. Here a question may be asked: what processes have led to the landlessness of the sukumbasis? To understand the processes of generating and reproducing landlessness and to provide a framework for empirical analysis, it is useful to look into general theories of agrarian and social relations.

Small peasants become landless as a result of a complex socio-economic process; and in studies on peasant economy and agrarian change this phenomenon has been a major focus of analysis. One predominant view, led by Lenin, is that the penetration of capitalism into feudal agriculture results in an increasing differentiation of the peasantry in which a small group of peasants develop into 'capitalist farmers' at the expense of 'middle' and 'small' peasants. Examining the Russian peasantry before the Revolution of 1917, he asserted that 'the old peasantry is not only "differentiating", it is being completely dissolved, it is ceasing to exist, it is being ousted by absolutely new types of rural inhabitants–types that are the basis of a society in which commodity economy and capitalist production prevail. These types are the rural bourgeoisie (chiefly the petty bourgeoisie) and the rural proletariat—a class of commodity producers in agriculture and a class of agricultural wage-workers' (Lenin, 1899 in Harriss, 1984:131) Thus, according to him, in Russia the impact of capitalism led to a situation whereby the smaller producers lost control over their resources and effectively became rural proletariat.

It should be noted that capitalist development in agriculture in Nepal is quite limited. The overwhelming majority of rural households in the country are essentially subsistence farmers. The existing level of agrarian technology is extremely low. Everywhere in the country, even in the Tarai, agricultural techniques and practices have remained largely at the level of hand-tools and animal-drawn implements. In fact, the country as a whole has one of the lowest levels of consumption of chemical fertilizers, improved seeds, modern tools and mechanization in the world. It is estimated that the modern inputs–fertilizers, improved seeds, tractors, pumpsets and agro-chemicals–contribute only one per cent of the total agricultural production inputs while land, labour and animal power account for 99 per cent of the total cost of production (Chapagain, 1983:7).

Although some have noted a limited degree of involvement of large landowners in innovative activity (McDougal, 1968:101–20) and in agricultural business and inputs such as ricemills, tractors, pumpsets (Feldman and Fournier, 1976), the surpluses appropriated by large landowners have not, for the most part, been reinvested in agricultural production. Agrarian surpluses generated have mostly been used in buying urban properties or in conspicuous consumption, buying luxury goods, organizing election campaigns, financing family feasts, arranging expensive marriages and other social ceremonies. Substantial sums of monies are also invested in education for children in view of salaried job opportunities that exist within the bureaucracy.

As the supply of educated manpower from the large landowning classes has increased, and as their prospects of paid employment in the bureaucracy in urban areas have remained favourable, a tendency amongst the new generation has been slowly to sell their share of agricultural land and to settle down permanently in urban areas, preferably in the capital city.

As there seems to be a general lack of use of modern inputs, little reinvestment of surplus within agriculture, limited or no land-consolidation process and a subsequent failure of the landed upper classes to transform themselves into capitalist farmers, no concentrated alienation of small peasantry from their land can be expected. At the present moment, such developments are occurring only in an isolated manner.

Contrary to Lenin's arguments, another view, primarily advocated by Chayanov, claimed that in Russia it was possible for peasant farming to continue to exist despite capitalist development. According to Chayanov, the household size of a peasant was positively correlated with the amount of land and other means of production held by the household as, over the family life cycle, increased consumption requirements of the household as a result of population growth were met by the increased labour supply within the household which had to acquire more land and capital to increase output; this 'naturally changing cycle' of the ratio of producers to consumers was such that the survival of the household was ensured (Chayanov, 1925, in Shanin (ed), ibid:152–9). However, if one looks at the Nepalese case and, given the small and declining size of plots and the rapidly increasing population together with the lack of off-farm incomes, the survival of the small peasantry appears increasingly questionable.

One of the important factors in terms of the creation of landless people in Nepal has been the gradual, piecemeal evolution of land as a highly sought commodity. This is because the vast majority of the farmers hold extremely small units of land and there is a high population growth within these households. These processes undermine subsistence farms and produce a landless class. Evidence reveals that in 1981/2 in the country as a whole over 50 per cent of the households owned less than 6.6 per cent of the total cultivated land. The average land-size of this category of farm households was just 0.15 ha (see Table 1). Concurrently, the demographic pressure within this category has been building up very rapidly. In fact, between 1954 and 1961, 1961 and 1971 and 1971 and 1981, the population of Nepal grew at an annual rate of 1.8, 2.07 and 2.7 per cent respectively (see Miyan & Poudel/APROSC, 1986:20). Since the

TABLE 1 *Number and area of holdings by tenure and size in 1981/2 (in Nepal)*

size of holdings (ha)	number of households	%	area covered (ha)	%	average households land holding (ha)
no land	8224	0.4	—	—	—
0.0–0.5	1099677	50.1	161999	6.6	0.15
0.5–1.0	355420	16.2	264930	10.8	0.74
1.0–2.0	379051	17.3	490413	19.9	1.29
2.0–3.0	156961	7.2	379590	15.4	2.41
3.0–4.0	77228	3.5	266513	10.8	3.45
4.0–5.0	42441	1.9	189159	7.7	4.45
5.0–10.0	60082	2.7	388679	15.8	6.46
above 10	14872	0.7	322434	13.0	21.68
total	2193956	100.0	2463717	100.0	—

Source: CBS, *National Sample Census of Agriculture 1981/2* (Kathmandu: CBS, 1985a, p. 2)

marginal and small farmers combined together represented over 66 per cent of the population in 1981/2 (Table 1), population growth has resulted in more people within this category, whilst their proportion of land has remained the same if not declined.

Theoretically, it is possible that, given the increasing population, higher inputs of labour per hectare would take place, thus leading to increased total output. However, in so far as the land per household itself is below the size required for subsistence, no such increased output can be expected. It is widely recognized that in many parts of the Hills (as well as in some parts of the long-settled Tarai), existing techniques of production plus higher inputs of family labour have already resulted in over-use and degradation of land (FAO, ibid:6, Wye College report, quoted in Macfarlane, 1976:207) and there existed little or no prospects for productive labour intensification, particularly in terms of realizing increased yields. Furthermore, given the apparent ecological limitations (e.g. steep slopes, stony soil, long winter), it is not always easy to increase agricultural output with the introduction of different technology and production systems in hilly environments. Therefore, the assertions that with the use of increased family labour, small peasants can raise agricultural output and maintain output per capita (Boserup, 1972:118) as well as continue to maintain their peasant status (Chayanov, ibid) do not appear to be universally valid. Indeed, such may be possible only in a situation where peasants have a flexible access to land.

Furthermore, the existing social system of equal inheritance of land amongst all sons has created fragmentation and increased sub-division of household plots to the extent that land-sizes are progressively decreasing and unable to provide subsistence. Because of the meagre size of land and the small margin for economic safety, many households become extremely vulnerable to indebtedness. In many cases, even the illness of a family member or the death of an ox would be sufficient to break down the precarious economic balance of the whole household and would lead to the eventual loss of their land.

Similarly, the increasing pressure on cultivated land due to rapid population growth can lead to a situation whereby land-prices escalate (see Table 2 for land-prices in Nawalparasi). As this is the case, in the event of land loss, it also becomes difficult for small peasants to regain control over land. Furth-

TABLE 2 *Existing prices of registered land in Nawalparasi district*

land type		year	
	1965	1975	1987
	(price of per *Bigha* in Rs)		
accessible:			
irrigated	5,000	30,000	70,000
non-irrigated	3,000	20,000	35,000
inaccessible:			
irrigated	3,000	15,000	40,000
non-irrigated	2,000	12,000	22,000

Source: own survey;
(The sample was taken in seven Panchayats, i.e. Pragatinagar, Kolhuwa, Dumkibas, Daunnedevi, Tribeni-Susta, Narsahi and Tilakpur; and the above prices represent average figures of responses relying on recall by local people).

ermore, the demographic pressure has reduced availability of land to rent and also reinforced higher rents on land (often 50 per cent of the total produce).

It is therefore quite understandable why there would be a great desire for the possession of new land amongst the sukumbasis and landless populations. It is clear that the possession of land allows them not only to grow staple crops for subsistence but it also provides them with much needed security for house-building and shelter. It should be noted that, having their own shelter and thus not being dependent on the employer for a 'housing-plot' gives a considerable amount of freedom as to the choice of employer, and as to when and under what conditions they would work for the employer. In particular, this is very important as wages are already low and stagnant (Blaikie, Cameron, Feldman, Fournier, Seddon, 1976:4, 45–7). With respect to wage rates, Kaplan and Shrestha write that: 'Despite rapid inflation (25–30 per cent per annum) the actual pay level has remained constant over a considerable period of time. The main reason for this is the "buyers' market" for such labour power' (1982:77). Evidence suggests that between 1968/9 and 1976/7 the wage rates of agricultural labourers in the Tarai declined by nearly 30 per cent (Islam, 1984:178-9). As a result of the unfavourable conditions for wage-employment and, for the reasons mentioned above, for all 'rural poor' the notion of becoming a self-sustaining peasant has remained highly attractive.

It needs to be said that the agrarian theories developed by both Lenin and Chayanov for Russia are both conceptually inadequate in explaining the complexities involved in the parallel, interrelated processes of landlessness and re-peasantization. More specifically, with respect to Lenin's theory of 'differentiation' of the peasantry, it primarily describes a one-way process of the reduction of the 'middle' and 'small' peasantry into wage labourers as the development of capitalism in agriculture advances. It does not give attention to the fact that the peasants who lost access to land will continue to try to gain access to new land and seek to 'repeasantize' themselves. Landpoor and landless households may secure land in resettlement schemes and through programmes relating to land-reform. Historically, in many parts of Africa, Latin America and the

Pacific, colonial authorities and the owners of large capitalist farms provided small plots of land to labouring households in order to secure a reservoir of labour (Wolf & Mintz, 1957; Paige, 1975; Cameron, 1987), which attached these people to land. In addition to this, many landpoor and landless households have regained peasant status by voluntarily migrating and settling in forest frontier areas as well as by invading and squatting on large estates.

But, when it comes to an effective analysis of the dynamics at work among the Nepalese rural population, Chayanov's logic of continuous survival of the peasantry does not appear valid either. For many peasant households, population growth, declining land holdings and the lack of outside employment and incomes have meant a steady economic decline and the eventual loss of the family land. In fact, much of the criticism of Chayanov's theory has been made along the line of argument that it ignores not only situations of marginalization and underemployment (Hunt, 1978:58–85), but that it also ignores the constraints on access to land and other resources that the peasantry often faces (Harrison, 1975).

Indeed, individually both theories (the transformation of peasants into wage labourers as a consequence of capitalist development in agriculture; and the peasantry's ability to survive through its family labour), can at best only partially explain the dynamics governing Nepalese agrarian relations and the future of the peasantry. In both theories what has not been appreciated are the geographical or ecological and interrelated political processes. What is implied here by geographical or ecological processes is the existence and the availability of productive resources such as the land in forest frontiers. And, by political processes, I refer to the regulations and policies restricting the use and appropriation of these resources. Such restrictions may be customary or formal legislative measures introduced on behalf of the State and sanctions may be moral or coercive. As long as potential arable land remains physically vacant and uncultivated in and around their areas, the landpoor and the wage labourers will continue to seek access to it, thus possibly repeasantizing themselves in the process; for many households, surplus family labour and the discouraging wage rates would be further stimuli to such endeavours. On the other hand, where political constraints preventing access to new agricultural land exist, household land may become steadily fragmented and over used. Under such circumstances, the maintenance of peasant status becomes extremely difficult and migration in search of new land and wage employment becomes increasingly a part of the survival strategy. This research examines the proposition that access to land and the subsequent repeasantization process for sukumbasis and landless households will depend upon both the availability of cultivable land in the forest-frontiers in the Tarai and the State policies and interconnected interests governing the use and the appropriation of these resources. This study documents the origins and nature of tensions between the sukumbasis' aspirations for land and their limited success in gaining access; it also looks at the constraints to longer-term maintenance and extension of landholding and the implications of these constraints to the sukumbasis' future economic and agrarian position.

METHODOLOGY

The empirical evidence advanced in this study includes secondary and primary data. The existing literature on the political economy of Nepal, particularly on agrarian relations, migration, resettlement and forestry and land use policies provided an important part of the data. But, the nature of this study is such that much of the information had to be collected by me through interviews and personal observations in Nawalparasi district. As indicated in the beginning of this chapter, Nawalparasi was chosen because, for a long time, this district has been the focus of in-migration, both within government resettlement schemes and 'illegal' settlements. The district has both a forest frontier and a long-standing cultivated area and thus is representative of both the growth of 'illegal' settlements and of the broad, long-term social and agrarian changes that are taking place in the Tarai—partially as a result of such growth. The major part of fieldwork for this study was carried out in the late 1980s.

The first stage of data collection involved a census of the sukumbasis. Through this method, it was possible not only to determine the total number of settlers, but also to collect overall information on different groups of sukumbasis, the timing of the establishment of various settlements in the area and other settlement-specific characteristics such as the problems relating to the registration of land.

During the fieldwork, the bulk of the information was collected through interviews with sukumbasis. 160 households were selected on a simple random sampling basis, though in questioning, careful attention was given to regional variations and caste/ethnicity as possible stratification factors between groupings of sukumbasis, as well as to different times of arrival in the settlement. The interview schedule for the sukumbasis enquired about their origins, economic situation before migration, reasons for migration and illegal settlement, present economic condition and political participation. In addition, information on their relationships with the landed classes and the State and perceptions about their own future were sought.

Participatory observation was the third method of fieldwork. During the field survey, I, together with occasional enumerators, spent most of the time living in the sukumbasis' settlements. In Nawalpur, a considerable length of time was spent at Karamghari (Naya Belhani Panchayat), Dumkibas (Dumkibas Panchayat), Bagkhor (Narayani Panchayat) and Sitabas/Rambas (Devchuli Panchayat); whilst in Parasi, Tribeni, Narsahi, Daunnedevi Panchayats and Shankarpur (Sunwal-Amrout Panchayats) were the main sites. In the beginning I felt that the sukumbasis were suspicious and somewhat hostile about the research. But when the acquaintance developed, in most settlements, sukumbasis became friendly and open. Indeed, by being able to 'integrate' with the sukumbasis and by staying in the research area for a considerable period, it became possible not only to observe closely the day-to-day activities of the sukumbasis but also to cross-check and verify the accuracy and validity of the information collected through interviews.

Lastly, some semi-structured interviews were conducted with forestry and resettlement officials, politicians, large landowners, school teachers and with other key informants. The questions asked in these interviews were in check-list form and thus interviews were informal—often carried out during teas and snacks. Nonetheless, information collected through this method was vital in understanding the views of external agents about the sukumbasis and their actions, and about many political and administrative issues which were so intricately connected with the pattern of growth and the restriction of 'illegal' settlements in the district.

It is important to note that, although sufficient empirical material was gathered through fieldwork, the nature of data employed here has remained largely qualitative rather than quantitative. Additionally, my own personal exposure to and understanding of the problem (i.e. coming from the Tarai and having been brought up in forest-frontier areas) has constituted an important part of the information used in the study.

Notes

1. The expression *sukumbasi* is a Nepalese word popularly used in the rural areas. Literally speaking, *sukum* means possessing nothing in terms of shelter and land and *basi* means an inhabitant or a settler. Turner defines sukumbasi as a person 'remaining without work or food' (1980:611) and Pokhrel et al. interpret sukumbasi as a 'subject without land and other properties' (1983:1355). Some definition of the word and the societal position of the sukumbasi are also expressed in the following Nepalese song:

   Jam bato Kasiko
   chhaina gharbar ma sukumbasiko

   [let us depart to Kasi-Banaras (perhaps the ultimate and final holy retreat for elderly and destitute Hindus), as I sukumbasi have no house and land].

   From the above, it appears that the sukumbasi is a person who possesses neither shelter nor any apparent means of production. However, in recent years, a sukumbasi in the Tarai is viewed as the 'illegal' occupant of public land, primarily government forest areas, rather than simply a poor or landless person. In this study, the term sukumbasi refers to a landless settler seeking to secure the legal right to cultivate the parcel of land which he and his family occupy.
2. No reliable nationwide figure on the rate of landlessness is available in Nepal. In the early 1970s, Zaman estimated that about 8 per cent of the country's population was landless (1973:83). But as within this figure those living in urban areas were included and there was an over-representation of Hill-areas as well as of the large farmers (cf. Islam, 1984:176), the reliability of this survey is questionable. Nonetheless, during this time, a National Planning Commission survey suggested that over 10 per cent of the sample households were landless (K.C., 1984, quoted in ibid). In 1974, an ILO mission claimed that 23 per cent of the sampled households in the Tarai were landless, whilst in the Hill areas only 1 per cent of the population was found to be landless;

but it indicated that as much as 59 per cent of the households in the Hills held land less than 0.2 ha and 10 per cent of the households in the Tarai were identified as equally marginal (ARTEP/ILO, 1974: Tables 1 & 2). Similarly, a survey covering 15 Village Panchayats in two districts suggested 16 per cent of the sampled households were landless (Pyakhuryal, 1978:62); and another study of the eastern Tarai reported 22 per cent of the people as being landless (Sainju et al., 1973).

On the basis of this evidence, it seems that the percentage of absolute landlessness in Nepal is not as serious as in some South Asian countries, notably India and Bangladesh. But what is crucial to recognize is that a large number of peasant households in the country possess extremely small holdings and are in the process of becoming landless. As indeed Islam writes, '. . . during mid Seventies between a third and half the households in rural Nepal were either landless or possessed only small pieces of land insufficient to ensure even bare subsistence. The operation of the demographic and economic pressure suggests that this situation is probably the result of a continuous process' (ibid: 177).

3. The irony is that the plain forests in the Tarai not only represent the last tracts of virgin land suitable for agriculture, but these are also the only areas in the country where hardwood (e.g. *shorea robusta*) is grown and where commercial logging is most viable. The conflict of interests arising from this situation will be examined in chapters six and eight.

2

The root causes and the reproduction of landlessness in Nepal

The phenomena of landlessness and illegal settlement and the present socio-economic position of the sukumbasis cannot be understood without reference to Nepal's historical, political and economic development. As a prelude, a brief review of the relatively recent history of the Nepalese political economy is provided, followed by an examination of the present political power structure and of agrarian intervention measures involving the State.

Historical Legacy of Socio-Economic Inequalities up to 1951

Prior to the arrival of Hindus from the northern plains of India during the period of Muslim invasions in the eleventh and twelfth centuries, the territory which is now called Nepal was divided into numerous sparsely populated (outside the Kathmandu valley) tribal chiefdoms. Nearly all these chiefdoms were located in the Hill areas and on the higher altitude valley floors, predominant amongst them being the Kathmandu valley. This was partly because the earlier inhabitants in these areas constituted Mongoloid populations (i.e. Magar, Gurung, Rai, Limbu, Tamang, etc.) who had entered Nepal from the high altitude north (i.e. across the Himalayas); and partly because the low population density meant the availability of sufficient land and other resources to allow subsistence at an altitude above the threat of malaria. Most of these people practised swidden cultivation using very simple tools, and relied on pastoralism. There existed a relatively simple social structure, with the division of labour and status being largely organized along the lines of age, gender and military performance.

The Indian immigrants, who entered the Hills of Nepal, possessed a better technology both in the field of warfare and in agricultural production. The local warfare technology before their arrival was limited primarily to the use of light bows and arrows, whilst they brought swords and other metal weapons (Sanwal, 1965:14). Similarly, they brought with them the latest technology of wet rice cultivation, combined with an extensive use of bunding, ploughing and irrigation (cf. Seddon, 1984:4). Their superior warfare technology made possible the forced subordination of existing Mongoloid society; and the changes in crops and methods of cultivation allowed the rulers of the newcomers to develop a stronger economic base than that which existed among those who did not belong to the artisan and trading economy of the cities of the Kathmandu valley.

The immigrants formalized this subordination through the introduction of a complex form of social division based on the caste system. Within these immigrants, the ruling elements were high-caste Rajputs (Chhetriyas; known as Chhetris in Nepal) and Brahmins. But, accompanying them also were a large number of low caste people, who had left their previous place of residence probably for fear of religious persecution. These low caste people continued to serve as artisans, labourers and tax-paying peasant producers, alongside poorer Brahmins and Chhetris. Once the tribal areas came under control, the Hindu rulers swiftly extended the caste system into these communities and successfully replaced the prevailing less complex forms of production organization with a more extensive form of division of labour and extraction of surplus. In this process, the bulk of the tribal populations were generally given a low caste status and were subjected to paying taxes and providing free labour.

The Hindu rulers established their control over much of the Hill areas within a relatively short stretch of time. By the end of the seventeenth century, most of the petty states (counting over 50 in total) were already under the firm control of Hindu princes. The Kathmandu valley was divided into three 'city States': Kathmandu, Patan and Bhaktapur. Here too the rulers, known as Mallas, were migrants from India and Hinduism was established as the ruling ideology. Around the middle of the eighteenth century, Prithivi Narayan Shah, an ambitious king of the State of Gorkha and the founder of the present line of monarchs, gradually conquered the Hill areas. His ability to create a strong army by subjugating and then persuading the Mongoloid populations of Gurungs and Magars to form the core of his army and, very crucially, his access to the latest type of fire-arms brought by the British to India (Bhandari, 1981:172) further strengthened his position. By 1770, he occupied not only the Kathmandu valley but he had also extended his control over large areas in eastern Nepal and parts of the Tarai (e.g. Makawanpur). The annexation of and political control over larger areas resulted in a situation parallel to that created by the British East India Company to the south whereby increased amounts of land tax could be spent on war-efforts and a larger army. Furthermore, after the conquest of the Kathmandu valley, he virtually controlled all the lucrative trans-Himalayan trade. As he bequeathed a relatively stable economic and military base, the campaign relating to territorial expansion continued after his death. By the early nineteenth century, his successors occupied the whole of Nepal's present territory and, because of the weakening Mogul authority and the disruptive European presence (Moore, 1981), they were even able to control considerable areas in the present northern Indian States of West Bengal, Bihar, Uttar Pradesh and Himachal Pradesh as well.

However, from 1790 on, the Nepalese ruling classes found themselves increasingly in conflict with British imperial power which had consolidated its power in Bengal and was also in the process of expanding. The interests of the British in Nepal were primarily associated with the control of trans-Himalayan trade routes and of land tax revenues, especially from the Tarai. Yet these were also the major sources of income for the Nepalese ruling classes. The conflict of interests over economic issues between the Nepalese ruling classes and the British colonial power eventually culminated in the 1814–16 Anglo-Nepalese War. This war and the Treaty of Sugauli (1816) which followed brought almost a century of territorial expansionism to an end and turned political energies inward, resulting in bitter and continuous internal conflicts within the ruling stratum (i.e. members of the royal family, the nobility and religious and military establishments).

In 1846, the continuing power struggle was resolved when the Ranas (a previously relatively weak section of the nobility/

military force) came to power; they then maintained a century-long family rule based on a loose hereditary form of power inheritance. During this period, the monarchy linked with the initial unification of the country remained only as a symbol and the Ranas maintained total control over the affairs of the State and its king. Their policy towards British India was that of reconciliation and survival. The Ranas agreed to supply Nepalese manpower as soldiers for the British Army. They also began to export agricultural products and timber from the Tarai to India. In return, the British guaranteed them minimal political support and non-interference in internal affairs.

By the twentieth century, stagnation had set in within the Nepalese economy as surplus was extracted as tribute by the State and dissipated in conspicuous consumption. Very little economic development took place before 1951; broad processes conducive to the increased impoverishment of whole sections of rural society were set in motion and continued to play a role after 1951. In this respect, the following specific aspects relating to the historical development of the Nepalese political economy are worth elaborating.

Role of Hinduization and Sanskritization

The early historical circumstances which led to the initial introduction of Hinduism and the caste system into the Hills of Nepal have been mentioned above. The following centuries witnessed numerous attempts, on the part of the Hindu rulers, to reinforce the low status of the scheduled (impure or 'polluting') castes and to further assimilate the non-Hindu tribal populations into the caste system. This phenomenon is often described as the process of 'Sanskritization' by sociologists examining the Hindu religion and the caste system in India (Srinivas, 1962). Studies of Nepalese history document 'caste reforms' well before the Nepalese unification carried out by king Jayasthiti Malla (1382–95) of Kathmandu valley and king Ram Shah of Gorkha (1606–33), in which the former formalized an extensive caste system within the Newar peasants and artisans of Kathmandu, whilst the latter extended it into the tribal populations in the central Hills (Joshi and Rose, 1966: 11–13). But it was during the Jung Bahadur Rana's period of power (1846–76) that the caste system and caste-based social codes were legally enforced throughout the country (ibid). Many of these codes are still in existence. The intentions behind these measures were many and included ensuring supplies of cheap labour. For example, the Brahmins, who constituted the main landowning group, refused to plough themselves because of a religious taboo, so there was a high demand for people who would till their land. Labour was also needed on the fields of larger landholders for other agricultural activities (Höfer, 1978:180) and for domestic service. Similarly, labour was sought for porterage services in connection with the transportation of mail, military supplies, fodder and food grains to the royal palace and for the construction and repair of roads, bridges and other 'public facilities' (Regmi, 1978:93). In addition, certain groups of people were also needed to perform artisan services such as blacksmiths, masons, carpenters, leatherworkers and tailors. The extension and reinforcement of the caste system over a larger segment of the population in many respects precisely served the economic purposes of ensuring supplies of such labour.

The effects of these measures on the tribal and the lower caste people were that they were left very vulnerable to extreme poverty. Firstly, as the level of corvée labour sought by landlords as well as by the State grew, many households were unable to increase labour use on their own land. The corvée labour obligations forced many able-bodied males to remain away from home for a considerable length of time each year, even in areas where cultivable land existed, so that clearing and bringing this land under cultivation became difficult. Secondly, amongst those who were attached to artisan services, primarily blacksmiths (Kami), leatherworkers (Sarki) and tailors (Damain), many had extremely limited access to land. Also, the land around their dwellings tended to be an inferior type (i.e. on the slopes and in wasteland areas). Generally, in many parts of the Hills, a shortage of cultivable land was already reported by the end of the eighteenth century (Kirkpatrick, 1811:86, Caplan, 1970:56).

The integration of the Nepalese economy into the world market through British India undermined many cottage-industries, and steadily displaced the goods and services provided by various artisan groups. Consequently, most of the members of these groups were forced to work for landlords as 'bonded' labourers. As the caste system placed these people at a severe disadvantage with respect to education and training, any occupational change towards new professions and allowing upward social mobility became nearly impossible. It is interesting to note in this context that, before 1951, lower caste people were even prohibited from touching books. Lastly, the ideology of Hinduism, as noted by many writers on India (e.g. Weber, 1958; Basham, 1954) which stressed that only through doing one's duty as assigned by caste and by following proper ritual and behavioural practices could one be reincarnated into a higher social status created submissiveness and passivity amongst the lower caste people thus inhibiting the desire to struggle.

EROSION OF LAND-RIGHTS OF MONGOLOID POPULATION

The immigrants from India initially gained their sway over the local Mongoloid populations because of their superior warfare technologies. Hindu immigrants in large numbers then encroached upon the more fertile valley bottom land of the indigenous people in the central Hill-region (especially the Tamangs and the Rais) and pushed them up the slopes of the hillsides (Kansakar, 1973/4:59). As the immigrants entered both the eastern and the western Hills, not only the Tamangs and the Rais, but every Mongoloid community experienced some level of displacement. Evidence suggests that even after the unification of Nepal, encroachment into tribal areas and the subsequent alienation of land continued.[1] The policies of the unified State encouraged not only the internal migration of Hindus within the Hill areas but also provided them with the upper hand in land laws relating to individual ownership, inheritance and sale (Caplan, 1967:109). The following cases demonstrate this process.

The Magars were amongst the first who came in contact with Hindu immigrants from the Indian Plains (Morris, 1928:186). Accordingly, they became one of the first tribal groups to be subordinated by the Hindu immigrants and were subjected to forced military service, corvée labour and slavery. Historical studies indicate that the Magars had earlier cultivated spacious tracts of river banks and valley floors (ibid:187). But the steady penetration of Hindus into areas settled by the Magars and the rights given by the unified Nepalese State to a Hindu aristocracy to collect tribute and taxes plus an ability to lend money at high interest rates confirmed their overall economic supremacy over the Magars. As wet rice cultivation was the most preferred agricultural practice amongst the Hindu settlers and as this needed flat land with relatively easy irrigation facilities, the Magars were steadily dispossessed of their most fertile land. For example, an anthropological study of the Magars in the Tanahun district in west-central Nepal showed that, by the early 1960s, many Magar households in the area possessed no irrigated paddy land at all (Hitchcock, 1966:80). In fact, during the field survey of the 17 Hill-Panchayats of Nawalparasi district, I observed that the share of low and irrigated land by the Magars (despite their constituting the vast majority of the population in the area) was almost negligible; much of the low paddy land along the Kali Gandaki river was controlled by Brahmins and Chhetris, and Newars from the nearby trading centres, whilst the Magars cultivated predominantly rain-fed hill-slopes and practised a low-yield swidden cultivation.

A similar situation was seen amongst the Gurungs. Until the eighteenth century, pastoralism was one of the most important sources of livelihood amongst the Gurungs. But 'during the following century, population pressure forced them to establish villages lower down the slopes, where wet rice could be grown, but herds and flocks could no longer be grazed' (Macfarlane, 1976:293). At the same time, the Hindus continued to move into these areas and sought to maintain control over lower slopes and valleys suitable for wet-rice cultivation. This not only prevented the Gurungs from moving further southward, but their lands were also progressively encroached upon. As a result, many households were obliged to serve as porters and as farm workers (Messerschmidt, 1976:36), possibly to those who actually mortgaged or bought their land.

Caplan has carried out a comprehensive study of the process of land-alienation amongst the Limbus in east Nepal. He argued that the large-scale immigration of Hindus into the area left the Limbus 'with only a narrow margin to meet the demands of an expanding Limbu population' and eventually created 'growing land shortage' (1967:109). The Limbus maintained a 'communal form of landownership', known as *kipat*, under which the land was cultivated and inherited only by the member of a specific Limbu community and other Limbus and non-Limbus had no cultivation and ownership rights. Taxes collected from these lands were extremely low. Therefore, from the beginning of the nineteenth century, non-Limbus were encouraged to move into the area and cultivate the remaining arable land. These settlers were subsequently provided with formal titles to the land they cultivated, but in return they paid tax to the State. This led to a considerable reduction in the area under *kipat* landownership. Although for fear of political disturbances in the early twentieth century some measures were introduced to reverse this trend, the Hindu settlers continued to cultivate *kipat* lands under a 'possessory mortgage', and the Limbus continued to lose control over the land. Caplan noted that in 1964/5 in some areas nearly 70 per cent of *kipat*-lands were possessed by non-Limbus under mortgage (ibid:111). And, according to Regmi, the mortgaging of *kipat*-land by the Hindu settlers was 'the primary factor contributing to landlessness amongst the Limbus' (1976:96).

The consequences of land-alienation by the Hindus have been very severe on the Mongoloid populations. Despite the State's restrictions and the general public opposition to foreign powers, a large number of people belonging to various Mongoloid groups had already chosen, under the pressure of a diminished access to or income from land, to join the British army before the end of the eighteenth century; and the following century witnessed out-migration, especially from the eastern part of Nepal into Darjeeling, Sikkim and Bhutan (Kansakar, ibid:62) where many Nepalese migrants, primarily those of Mongoloid origin, also became small farmers and wage labourers in tea and orchard plantations. Seasonal or temporary migration into the northern Indian cities became equally common. But for many, portering for wealthy merchants and farm-labouring for large landowners in Nepal became the chief source of income and employment (Messerschmidt, ibid).

Land concentration in the hands of the few

The discussion so far dealt with the questions of caste and ethnicity. But this alone would not be sufficient for any complete analysis of the long term historical processes resulting in the landlessness and economic impoverishment of large sections of the peasantry. More specifically, economic factors have also affected Hindu upper-castes and people belonging to Indo-Aryan ethnic groups forcing some of them into the position of sukumbasis. Therefore, one also needs to examine more closely the economic aspects of production that developed over time. For this, what needs to be particularly looked at are the processes which led to the concentration of large landholdings within an aristocratic class whilst those who actually cultivated the land either possessed extremely small plots of land or were subjected to insecure and/or extractive tenureship regardless of caste or ethnicity.

Evidence suggests that after the 'unification' of Nepal, the monarchy began granting possession of and tax rights over large tracts of land to members of the royal family, the nobility, the senior civil and military personnel and priests and religious institutions (Regmi, ibid:22). These land grants were made both to consolidate the monarchy's own position and to increase land revenue. Land grants principally took the form of either *Birta, Guthi* and *Jagir*. The *Birta* system represented land grants to members of the royal family and nobility (and therefore primarily people belonging to the highest castes) as a symbol of patronage or as ritual gifts. Land donated for temples and monasteries and for religious and charitable purposes was known as *Guthi*. Lands that were given to soldiers and government officials for their services and loyalties were called *Jagir* land tenure. Lands granted under the *Birta* system were usually inheritable and transferable. A similar type of a relatively permanent ownership was also enjoyed by the beneficiaries of the *Guthi* land grants. But in the case of *Jagir* land grants, the recipient was allowed to benefit from land only during the period of his service (ibid:18, 75).

The lands granted under these three forms covered both cultivated and uncultivated areas. The grants involving cultivated areas often covered several villages from which the beneficiaries appropriated the agrarian surplus. Their main obligation to the State was to collect land taxes from these areas. In the case of uncultivated areas, they were expected to encourage peasants to clear land and bring it under cultivation;

again increased land revenue generation was the prime intention behind this measure. In return, the beneficiaries of land-grants were allowed to retain part of the land tax collected and were given substantial administrative and judiciary rights.

These extensive land grants and the emergence of intermediary groups had two major effects on the pre–existing peasant economy. First, peasants who initially possessed land, particularly when the *Birta* and *Guthi* systems were instituted, were reduced to tenants or even to sharecroppers and became economically subordinate to the beneficiaries of land grants. Even where land was available to bring under cultivation, peasants needed permission and taxes were imposed on them immediately after the first harvest was completed. Second, and closely related to the first, as greater amounts of agricultural surpluses were sought both by the State and the intermediary groups, peasants were subjected to increased levels of tax pressure, thus producing a severe disincentive to produce anything above their subsistence needs and resulting in an absence of investment. As mentioned before, besides paying land tax, they were compelled to provide free labour for agricultural works on fields of individuals and institutions benefiting from land grants, and porterage and artisan services demanded both at the local and the State level. The burden of corvée labour accompanied by heavy taxation made the economic conditions of the peasantry extremely oppressive. Evidence suggests that frequent occurrences of droughts and severe shortages of food caused many people to die of starvation (Regmi, 1978:154). At the same time the ruling classes, for their war efforts (during unification and war with British India), often raised taxes a year ahead (Bhandari, ibid: 217). In some areas, the condition of the peasantry was so serious that peasants left their holdings that they had cultivated and went en masse to other parts of the country as well as abroad (Regmi, 1971:99). Those who remained behind frequently responded with passive resistance and disregard to the demands made upon them by land title-holders. The situation was so grim that the State had to intervene on behalf of the landowners by issuing orders to the local officials to 'punish all tenants who disobey their landlords, do not reclaim waste fields, (and) keep lands uncultivated' (Regmi, ibid:78).

It may be mentioned that the first monarch after the 'unification' of Nepal (Prithivi Narayan) defined the peasantry as 'King's treasure' (Stiller, 1968:43). This attitude towards the peasantry was faithfully adhered to during the Rana period. The Rana rulers were concerned with the peasantry only when peasants responded with passive resistance which threatened the collection of land revenue. In the Hill areas, maize was introduced during the early eighteenth century and potatoes were introduced from 1866 on (cf. Seddon, 1984:5, 16), but there is no evidence of the State and the ruling classes playing any significant role in this and other agricultural extension activities. The agrarian technology remained basically what the Hindu immigrants from the plains of northern India had introduced during the eleventh and twelfth centuries. Apart from the introduction of maize and potatoes, agrarian changes during this period were primarily based on the extension of cultivated area.

The increasing importation of manufactured and luxury goods through British India, together with the financial burdens of maintaining a large army and bureaucracy necessitated increased extraction of agrarian surpluses. Efforts were made to bring marginal areas in the Hills under cultivation, but due to the steadily growing population pressure (Macfarlane, ibid: 204), in many parts of the Hills such possibilities were already diminishing by the beginning of the nineteenth century. Therefore, the Ranas attempted to open up new lands in the Tarai by encouraging people to migrate from across the border in India in an attempt to generate increased revenue. This measure proved to be very successful; in fact it ensured not only rising land-revenue but also increasing (internationally exchangeable) agricultural surpluses for the ruling classes, especially as by this time agricultural products from the Tarai had found a ready market in India (Feldman & Fournier, 1976:450). Because of these prospects, large tracts of productive lands in the Tarai were appropriated (usually under *Birta* land grants) by the members of the Rana family, to a lesser extent by other members of the nobility and by Brahmins close to the court and high level government officials and army generals. In view of timber extraction opportunities and the development of land settlements, these land grants often covered forested areas as well. As an outcome of this situation, by the first half of the twentieth century, the ruling classes in Nepal possessed almost half of the cultivated land (Regmi, 1973: 186), in which three leading Rana families alone owned as much as 227,000 acres (Pant and Jain, 1969: 9–10). The consequences of this concentration of possession of land and how the legacies of these economic inequalities and the lack of access to land on the part of the bulk of the population were perpetuated will be taken up later. In the following discussion the power structure that protected these inequalities will be examined.

Post-1951 Political Developments

By the 1940s, popular opposition to the Rana regime had steadily grown in urban areas, particularly in Kathmandu and in Biratnagar in the eastern Tarai. Events were also taking place in neighbouring countries which were to affect the country's future political developments. In this context, the independence of India from British colonial power in 1947 appears crucial. Because of their belief in 'socialist ideals' and because of the assistance received during the Indian independence movement from some of the members of their counterpart Party in Nepal, the Indian Congress Party which came to power in India after independence supported the Nepali Congress Party, which was leading the popular forces resisting the autocratic Rana rule. But simultaneously, owing to Nepal's strategic location and India's interest in having Nepal as a 'stable' buffer State, India was careful to see that popular movements in Nepal did not go so far as to induce radical changes which could undermine Indian national interests in Nepal.[2] Thus, the anti-Rana movement was restrained and in 1951 a 'power-sharing deal' was facilitated between the monarchy, the Ranas and the Nepalese Congress Party under direct Indian supervision.[3]

With Indian interest favouring a small degree of change and with the internal movements limited to a few urban centres, it was likely that the anti-Rana movement would fail to bring about any significant structural rural/agrarian transformation. According to the above 'power-sharing deal', the monarchy was restored, then with largely a constitutional role, and the Ranas and the members of Nepalese Congress Party (most of whom represented higher castes and large landowners) together formed the transitional cabinet, in which the former maintained the prime ministership and half the cabinet posts (Bhandari, ibid:339). This clearly indicated that the outcome of the 1951 movement was largely limited to internal adjustments within the existing ruling classes.

Although, after 1951, political parties and professional organizations emerged and the bureaucracy began to take the form of a 'modern institution', the political power structure and class relations did not undergo any radical changes. Both economic and political power continued to remain in the hands of the same classes consisting primarily of Brahmins, Chhetris and Newars. For example, one survey carried out in the early 1970s demonstrated that 80 per cent of the positions of power and profit were occupied by members of these castes (Beenhakker, 1973:25). Social mobility for other groups or castes other than these castes remained minimal.

A look at the Nepalese political economy shows that there are many old power relationships which are still intact and have been incorporated within the new forms of development. After the years 1951 and 1960 when Nepal experienced a short period of democracy and the role of the monarchy was relatively weakened, in 1960 the monarchy staged a coup d'état, dissolving the first ever elected parliament and cabinet, banning all political parties and independent organizations and suspending the right of opposition. The monarchy set in motion the Panchayat system, in which the elements of change and continuity became carefully integrated so as to ensure that the power structure remained the same, albeit under conditions of some economic growth. The Panchayat system (based on Hindu and caste philosophy) presented 'the king as God amongst the People' (Shah, 1982:23) and idealized the need for his 'absolute authority and leadership' (ibid:20) in all spheres. As a result, in Nepal in the 1980s, the monarchy controlled the State mechanism in all its aspects, from civil administration to the military and from the legislative to the judiciary with high-castes and landowning elements acting as its subordinates (see Figure 2). The limited

FIGURE 2 *Socio-economic and political stratification of Nepalese society in the 1980s*

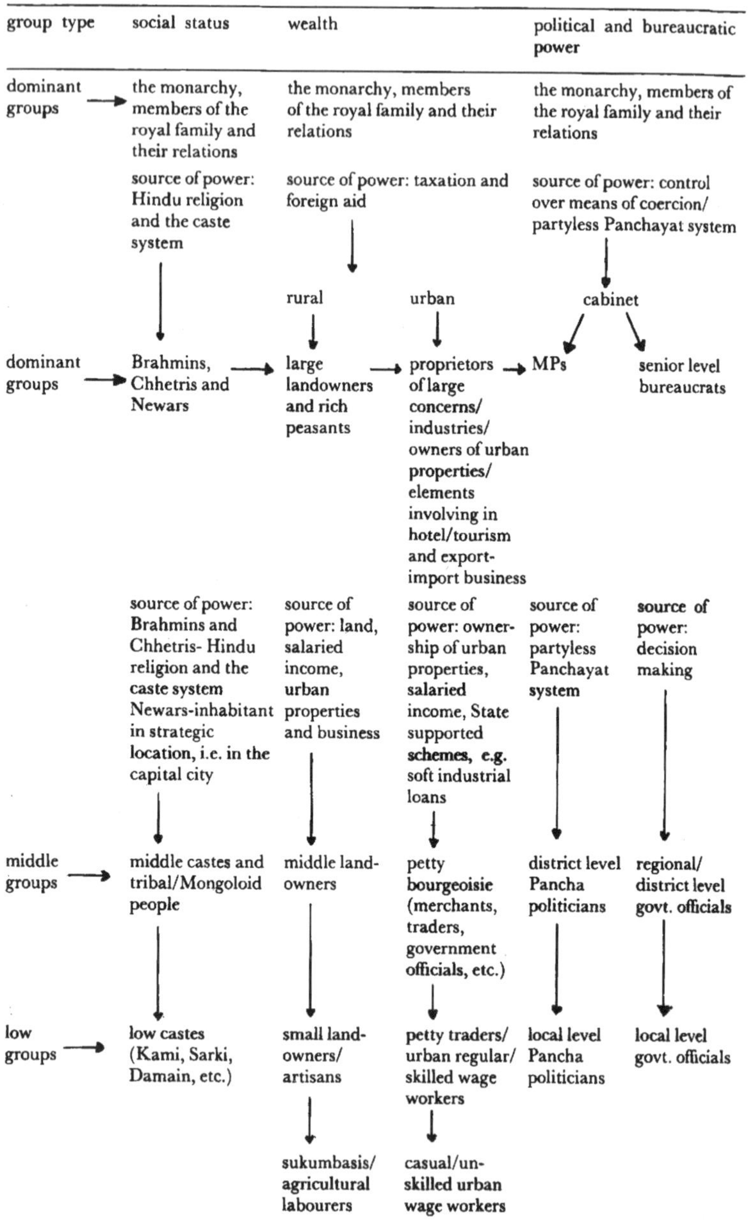

(For further reference see: Gaige, 1975, Ghimire, 1983, Seddon et al., 1981, Shah, 1982).

TABLE 3 *Foreign aid to Nepal (between 1976/7 to 1984/5)*
(in million Nepalese Rupees)

	bilateral	multilateral
1976–7	370.9	186.0
1977–8	456.7	391.7
1978–9	538.8	450.6
1979–80	846.4	494.1
1980–1	858.1	704.2
1981–2	909.5	813.7
1982–3	947.2	1128.7
1983–4	983.2	1564.3
1984–5	1156.3	1520.1
total	7067.1	7253.4

Source: CBS, *Statistical Year Book of Nepal* (Kathmandu: CBS, 1987, p. 421).

degree of challenges that did exist tended to come from within the elite groups themselves and took muted forms.

Also crucial to the survival of the political system in the 1980s has been the discovery of new economic resources, thus diminishing the need to excessively tax any socio-economic group. Evidence suggests that, during the late 1960s and throughout the 1970s, Nepal was already 'one of the highest recipients of aid per caput in the world' (Blaikie, 1983a:18) and the total amount received was still increasing in 1985 (see Table 3). The inflow of foreign aid in such large and increasing quantities through the central State apparatus into the country served the interests of the monarchy and its attendant socially dominant groups, specifically in the following ways:

(i) to limit dependence on the poorer peasantry (extraction of resources from which was becoming increasingly difficult with declining yields and growing population) as a source of surplus creation; this in turn helped the monarchy to avoid political opposition from the mass of the peasantry;

(ii) to ease any possible threat from middle groups, especially the youths, since foreign aid opened up new educational opportunities for these groups, and to some extent paid wages and incomes within the bureaucracy and in various development projects.

Having identified these historical and political processes, it is now possible to turn to the dynamics of agrarian development, particularly the nature of State intervention in agriculture and its impact in improving the economic conditions of the landpoor/ landless people.

The state, Agrarian Reforms and the Poor

Historically, the role of the Nepalese State has been limited to the collection of land revenue and to the maintenance of unequal property rights. However, in the post-1951 period, as some agrarian reforms were introduced, it might be thought that this extraction from the mass of the peasantry had ceased. So far, seven long-term economic plans have been implemented in the country. As part of these economic planning processes, in recent years, various regional and local integrated rural and agricultural projects have been launched and all the key phrases of recent development models such as 'social equity with growth', 'basic needs' and 'decentralisation and people's participation' are to be found in project documents (Blaikie, ibid:20). In some of these documents, rural dwellers and the poor are mentioned as 'target groups'. In light of these developments, the present State policies could appear as more caring and benign to the poor. In some cases in the past, the intervention measures undertaken on behalf of the State such as the introduction of land reform measures even seemed to have gone against the interests of the dominant groups. The Five-Year Plans and other development projects have given a high priority to agricultural development (Seddon, 1984:25–36) and any institutional and technological changes within this area could have some important indirect effects on the economic condition of the near-landless and landless people. Thus, in the following discussion the State intervention measures specifically related to land-reform legislation and the provision of extension services for small farmers are examined.

LAND-REFORM MEASURES

Although some limited land redistribution Acts were passed in the 1950s, extensive land-reform measures were not introduced until 1964. These were launched in three stages, covering 16 districts in 1964, 25 districts in 1965 and the rest of the 34 districts in 1966 (Pant and Jain, ibid:65). The main objectives of the 1964 land-reform programme were: the imposition of ceilings on land (applicable to both landowners and tenants), the compulsory State procurement of land above the ceilings and the redistribution of this land amongst tenants and landless people, the fixing of rents and the provision of a compulsory saving scheme in order to supply credit needed for investment in agriculture (K.C., 1980:55). But all evidence suggests that there has remained a great deal of discrepancy between these objectives and their actual implementation. In many respects the reform measures safeguarded the interests of the landowners instead of serving the interests of the tenants and the landless people.

First of all, it is worth recalling that the pressures for land reforms were actually brought by foreign aid donors, particularly by the US whose advocacy of land reform in Asia as a measure of deterrence against communism was at its height in the early 1960s (Ladejinsky, 1977:132; McCoy, 1971:15). The monarchy, after its 1960 coup d'état, was seeking international political and economic support and did not directly own any significant tracts of land. Also many of the larger landowners from the Tarai were lending support to political parties opposing the king's direct rule (Scholz, 1977:52–3). Thus it became advantageous for the monarchy to meet US wishes. However, as the monarchy was not prepared to take the risk of outright conflict with landed elements and as people within the bureaucracy maintained vested interests in land (many of whom owned large tracts of land themselves), the result was 'a product of expedience rather than a commitment to fundamental change' (Gaige, 1975:172).

One of the principal areas in which the land-reform measures favoured the landowners was in the field of land ceilings. Ceilings for landowners were set at 2.7 ha in the Kathmandu valley, 4.1 ha in the Hills and 17 ha in the Tarai whereas land ceilings were fixed for land rented/leased by tenants at 0.5 ha, 1.1 ha and 2.7

ha in the Kathmandu valley, the Hills and the Tarai respectively (APROSC, 1978a:8). This clearly indicates that the law favoured the landowners over the tenants. In fact, the landowners had a much greater advantage over tenants in terms of the size of land ceiling and production potential in all parts of the country. For, in addition to the land permitted under the ceilings, landowners were allowed to retain homesites, whereas no such provisions were made for tenants. Moreover, as sons above 16 years of age and unmarried daughters above 35 years of age were recognized as separate families for homesite purposes (even if they operated holdings together), it was possible for landowners to retain considerable portions of land as ostensible homesites.

It needs to be emphasized that, given the person-land ratios in the country, the overwhelmingly agrarian nature of the population and the land area needed for subsistence level cultivation, the ceilings on the landowners' land were fixed at relatively high levels, particularly in the Tarai where both large holdings and higher production potential existed. In some Asian countries which also underwent land-reform programmes, ceilings were determined at much lower levels than in Nepal's Tarai such as 3 ha in Japan, Taiwan and Korea; 4 to 6 ha in India and 7 ha in the Philippines (Poudyal, 1983:30). By fixing ceilings at these higher levels and by regionally favouring the Tarai, many large landowners were permitted to continue to hold all or most of their lands. Moreover, the inefficiency within the bureaucracy and the implementation of land reforms at three stages provided an opportunity to adjust the records by transferring the land not only to other family members, but also to their relatives and friends (Basnyat, 1981:58).

Not surprisingly, the outcome of the reform measures in terms of the appropriation and redistribution of excess land was unsuccessful. By 1978 about 50,580 ha were declared as excess land, out of which only 34,705 ha were actually confiscated; of this confiscated land only 21,050 ha were redistributed (APROSC, ibid:10). Moreover, it appears that a significant portion of this redistributed land was procured by government officials and their families, relatives and friends, rather than by tenants and the landless (Poudyal, ibid:31).

One other area where a great deal of inequality existed and nothing was done was in the rates of rent paid by the tenants.

The 1964 Land-Reform Act set land rents at 50 per cent of the gross product (later amended to 50 per cent of the main crop) and tenants were required to bear the costs of cultivation. This sharecropping arrangement was in fact the same as before the introduction of the land-reform programme (Zaman, 1973:15). The land rent for tenants appears to have been—and still is—far higher in Nepal than in India, Sri Lanka, Thailand and the Philippines, where maximum rents were set below 25 per cent of the agricultural produce (Dasgupta, 1977:38; Poudyal, ibid: 32). This situation confirmed the position and the interests of landowners as the law gave them the right to receive rents, but without any obligations towards production and tenants' welfare. As for the tenants, on top of the high level rents there remained neither any concrete security of their cultivation rights nor any resources to invest.

The land legislation measures resulted not only in the continuing economic and tenural insecurity of tenants, but in many cases they resulted in the complete termination of their access to land. As there was speculation regarding future stronger reform measures amongst the landowners and as the Act allowed them to reclaim land for personal cultivation, a large number of tenants were evicted by their landlords. For example, a sample-study concentrating on Parsa district in the Tarai showed that by the end of the 1960s about 30 per cent of the tenants were evicted by the landlords (Pant and Jain, ibid:75). Evidence suggests that between 1971 and 1981 the share of land cultivated under tenancy in Nepal as a whole was reduced from 18 to 5.6 per cent (CBS, 1976 and 1985a).

The absence of awareness about the reform measures amongst the tenants and the landless and the lack of real political will and determination on the part of the ruling elite involved in the reform measures meant that no structural changes within the existing agricultural relations were achieved; the poorest were increasingly rendered more vulnerable to loss of land rights.

Provision of agricultural support services

It is generally believed that, in addition to land reform, another area which is crucial for the rural poor is access to technological change based on the provision of agricultural inputs such as irrigation, fertilizer, improved seeds, and credit (Dasgupta, 1977:42–9; Mellor, 1976:76; Pinstrup-Andersen & Hazell, 1985:1–2). Consequent increases in agricultural production are crucial not only in terms of the availability of more food for the poor but also in terms of extending prospects for employment and income (Dandekar and Rath, 1971). But as such agricultural inputs are beyond the technical and economic reach of individual farmers, especially those with a lack of formal education and a weak economic base, the role of the State is seen as vital in extending access to agricultural inputs (Schultz, 1964). However, in the case of Nepal the role of the State has been quite limited in providing agricultural inputs and increasing agricultural productivity and has not created prospects for improved economic conditions amongst households dependent upon subsistence cropping and wage labouring.

As in much of the South Asian continent, new high-yielding varieties of seeds (HYVs) were introduced in Nepal during the 1960s. Government sources indicate that by the early 1980s, the area under HYVs constituted 13 per cent of the total cultivated land (NPC, 1984a:15). The use of HYVs is however mainly confined to wheat. An improved variety of rice seeds suitable for the local topography and altitude in various regions of the country remains to be developed; and improved varieties of maize have been introduced but are not as popular as local varieties because of their late maturity and higher fertilizer requirements (Maharjan, 1984:93). Between 1975 and 1985, the use of improved seeds of paddy and maize declined from 359 m.t. to 154 m.t. and 106 m.t. to 69 m.t. respectively; whilst wheat increased only slightly from 1810 m.t. to 2242 m.t. (CBS, 1987:195).

It is recognized that for the new HYVs to succeed the complementary provision of irrigation and chemical fertilizer is extremely crucial (Lipton, 1984:77). Evidence suggests that by the early 1980s, only 24,000 ha of land were provided with year-round irrigation through State-sponsored irrigation schemes (ADB/HMGN, 1982, VOL. II:75); and the level of Nepal's per hectare consumption of chemical fertilizers is one of the lowest in South Asia: only 1/5 of that in Bangladesh or Pakistan with the rate of consumption slowing even more in recent years (ibid:129).

A closely-linked crucial area where State intervention measures are needed but where very little has been done is in the provision of the necessary credit. It is estimated that by 1980, of the total estimated agricultural credit requirements, only 24 per cent were covered by institutional sources (World Bank, 1981:6–7) and the remaining credit needs were met by moneylenders, tenants' landlords and traders, who charged interest at rates as much as 150 per cent per annum (ABD/HMGN, vol. II, ibid:139).

In this context, what needs to be stressed is both the regional and class concentration of the services that are provided. The Kathmandu valley and the Tarai seemed to have consumed over 81 per cent of improved seeds and chemical fertilizers, and nearly 90 per cent of irrigation projects were in the Tarai (ibid:127 & 75). Similarly, in the last twenty-five years, increased yields remained the prime objective of agricultural policies, with the large landowners (the top 5 per cent who owned nearly 37 per cent of land; Table 1) becoming the chief beneficiaries of the agricultural support services. They not only procured much of the improved seeds distributed but also nearly 90 per cent of the highly subsidized chemical fertilizer (Agrawal et al., 1978). As these households owned large tracts of land and as the water distribution system tends to have returns to scale with the increasing size of one's plots, they have also been better able to take advantage of the State-financed irrigation projects. But it is in credit provisions that these households seemed to have benefited most. An agricultural credit survey indicates that by the late 1970s, this 5 per cent of households (i.e. the large landowners) had acquired over 89 per cent of all the credit supplied by the State institutions, and between 1969/70 and 1976/7 the proportion of households with State loans from this stratum increased by 19 per cent, whilst the number of small farmers taking loans over the same period declined by the same per cent (Nepal Rastra Bank, 1980). The relatively low rates of interest, their ability to influence the bureaucracy in delaying the repayment of loans (NPC, 1984a:14) and the possibility of using the credit for purposes other than agricultural production (e.g.

using tractors for transport, building houses for own use or rent) are some of the factors which attracted the large landowners to accumulate credits from institutional sources. This interest in acquiring cheap loans and the self-generated surpluses in non-agricultural sectors largely explain why the landed upper classes in Nepal, in spite of taking advantage of State agricultural extension services, have failed to transform agriculture on any significant scale.

The dilemma is that the top 5 per cent of large landowning households acquired much of the State support services yet brought no marked changes in agricultural production, whereas the bottom 66 per cent of the marginal and small farmers who cultivated just over 17 per cent of the total cultivated land (Table 1) received no significant level of State support services. Given their weak production base and the lack of economic resources to improve it, it could be argued that a greater degree of State assistance should have gone to them, rather than to those who had sufficient resources of their own.

Because of this situation and because of the pressure from the aid-agencies to target some resources towards the near-landless, a Small Farmer Development Programme (SFDP) was introduced in the mid-1970s. Since within this programme groups of small farmers were organized only on economic grounds and given no national political voice, the SFDP seemed politically safe for the government, and commercial banks were willing to fund the programme because of the group guarantee and the greater possibility of loan recovery. By 1983/4, 121 projects relating to SFDP were being carried out in 46 districts and the total number of farm households attached to these projects was 25,799 (ADBN, 1984:11). Despite a greater degree of institutional willingness and a rapid growth in the number of projects established in recent years, so far there has been no impact of the SFDP programme in altering the economic conditions of the vast majority of impoverished rural households.

The total of 25,799 households, out of an estimated 1,463,321 small farmers' households (see Table 1) meant that by 1983/4 the SFDP programmes covered less than two per cent of small farmers. Secondly, most of the SFDP programmes have been short-term and specific production-goal oriented, with minimal financial and technical support, whilst many of the problems of small farmers are structural and require long-term assistance. The extremely small average size of land held is well recognized, and even within this land-size, many small farmers tend to possess inferior types of land (e.g. stony uphill and sandy riverbank areas) where the provision of irrigation is both technically difficult and financially burdensome. Furthermore, many of these areas are prone to soil erosion (Blaikie, 1983b). This indicates that together with the introduction of agricultural technology, improvement in land quality and control of erosion would have to be undertaken. But within the SFDP projects, scarcely any attention is given to these factors. Thus, a vast majority of the small farmers have little chance of introducing double cropping or benefiting from the new HYVs which require more water.

Improvement in the production base and the creation of employment for the small farmers could have helped not only the farmers directly, but also landless labourers indirectly. Since small farmers are so numerous and derive part of their income from wage labouring, they compete directly with landless labourers for wage employment. This is specifically so during the dry season when fewer jobs are available and competition tends to drive down wage rates. Therefore, as is often asserted, the real need is to keep the small farmers on their own farms over the dry season by creating employment through double cropping (Mellor, ibid:77). But the lack of irrigation facilities amongst small farmers is such that this is hardly feasible without more effective land redistribution.

The interests of people who have become sukumbasis are even less represented within the SFDP. The SFDP does not provide loans where all the members of the group are formally landless and own no marketable assets. During the fieldwork in the Nawalparasi district, it was observed that even sharecroppers, unregistered tenants as well as the sukumbasis who operated land but maintained no formal titles, were unable to get loans from the local SFDP branches. In fact, what has still not been recognized within the ongoing rural and agricultural development programmes is that the problems of the landless and the people maintaining their livelihood primarily through wage labouring are in many respects entirely different from those of people who have title to land. In Nepal, even now, no legislative measures have been introduced to determine wage rates, working hours, security of employment and other working conditions of the rural and agricultural labourers. Furthermore, the lack of political consciousness and their low social position inhibit these people from developing a strong voice in order to bargain for 'their share' within the ongoing rural and agricultural development programmes.

The picture that emerges from the above discussion is that both the land-reform measures and the technological and financial support services of the State seem to have offered nothing of significant substance to the poor, especially from the point of view of altering the deep structural historical process of growing landlessness.

Given the nature of the State just described and given the introduction of institutional and technological measures without any change in the existing power structure, these outcomes are quite predictable. Indeed, it seems that no political group has emerged which is committed enough to implement the more radical aspects of these programmes; and secondly, the dominant groups are not at all restrained from taking advantage of these programmes and thus secure a large share for themselves leaving very little or nothing for the poor. This situation is further discussed in the following chapter, particularly through an examination of the planned resettlement programmes.

Notes

1. Around this period, a similar type of appropriation of tribal lands by Hindu settlers was commonly experienced in India as well (see e.g. Fürer-Haimendorf, 1967:184).
2. Some radical forces, such as the group led by Dr K.I. Singh in the western part of Nepal, which were not prepared to accept the Ranas in power were suppressed with the help of the Indian army (Bhandari, ibid:343).
3. It may be mentioned that India's decisive role in the political settlement of the anti-Rana movement and the accompanying Treaty of 1951 with Nepal strengthened not only its political domination over Nepal but also served its economic interests. This treaty permitted unrestricted sale of Indian goods in Nepal and allowed Indian citizens to engage in business and economic activities (Gaige, 1975:95). In the 1960s and the 1970s, further treaties were signed in the field of trade, but because of Nepal's absolute dependence for trade and transit on India, these treaties too have largely been in India's

favour, thus resulting in an increasing balance of trade deficit on Nepal's side (Rana, 1973:224–6). Furthermore, an open border and free movement of people have led to increasing immigration into Nepal and possession of land by Indian nationals. In view of this situation, some have located the Nepal and India relationship within the 'centre' and 'periphery' analysis (Seddon with Blaikie and Cameron, 1981).

3

The scale of illegal settlement in Nawalparasi district

General Background of Nawalparasi District

The Nawalparasi district, the area chosen for field study, is situated in west-central Tarai, with the Chitawan district to its east, the Rupendehi district to its west and the Palpa and Tanahun districts to its north. In the south and the south-east, this district is bordered by the Indian states of Uttar Pradesh and Bihar respectively (see Map I). Nawalparasi district comprises a total area of about 196,000 ha. By the mid-1980s, over 60 per cent of this land area was still under forest, of which about 44 per cent (i.e. 26.5 per cent of the district's total land surface) was located in the lowland areas and was potentially farmable (see Table 4).

The Nawalparasi district as a whole can be divided into two broad geographical zones: the Hills and the plains.

The Hills, parts of the Siwalik and Mahabharat ranges, lie in the northern and north-eastern part of the district. Although some small tracts of lowland areas are found close to the river basin of the Kali Gandaki river, this area is primarily a hilly terrain with elevation rising up to 1,932 metres above sea level. About 10 per cent of the Nawalparasi district's population live here and the Magars constitute over 96 per cent of this population. In this area, swidden cultivation is the dominant form of agricultural practice.

The plains are divided into two regions: outer-Tarai and inner-Tarai. The outer-Tarai is located in the western side of the district between the Rupendehi district in the west and Daunne Hills in the east. This area is the northernmost extension of the Gangetic plain, elevations being between 100 to 200 metres. The

TABLE 4 *Land-use in Nawalparasi district*

land category	early 1970s (a) (ha)	%	mid 1980s (b) (ha)	%
forest area:				
hill forests	65000	33.1	65000	33.1
plain forests	55000	28.1	53512	27.3
cultivated area:				
hill swidden cultivation	10000	5.1	10000	5.1
plain irrigated land	40000	20.4	40000	20.4
plain non-irrigated land	8000	4.1	9488	4.9
rivers etc.	18000	9.2	18000	9.2
total	196000	100	196000	100

Source: (a) Berry et al., 1974:42
(b) adjusted on the basis of information provided by resettlement agencies[1]

district headquarters (Parasi) is situated in this region; and because of this connection, 'Parasi' is the common geographical term usually applied to identify this region. About 65 per cent of the district's population inhabit this region, of whom people of recent Indian origin form the majority, followed by Hill-settlers and the earlier inhabitants such as the Tharus (generally referred to as the indigenous people of the plains). The inner-Tarai, known as Nawalpur, is a narrow strip of lowland stretching from Daunne Hills in the west to the Narayani river in the east. About 25 per cent of the district's population live in this region, of whom the Hill-settlers constitute over two-thirds and the indigenous people make up most of the remaining. Much of the Parasi and Nawalpur areas are flat; and soil, temperature and rainfall conditions are highly favourable for agricultural production. Partly because of this and partly for reasons that shall be explained later, illegal land settlements in the Nawalparasi district have essentially been a phenomenon of the plains.

Until the beginning of this century, much of the plain areas were under forest and were sparsely populated. Only the southern Parasi area, along the border with Uttar Pradesh (then United Provinces), was a major settlement area and a few scattered hamlets with small patches of cultivation had emerged in Nawalpur. The Tharus, who migrated from India around the fifteenth and sixteenth centuries and subsequently acquired some resistance to malaria, constituted the bulk of the inhabitants in Parasi and Nawalpur. From the end of the eighteenth century, some Tibeto-Nepalese ethnic groups such as Kumals, Darais, Botes and Danuwars also migrated from the Siwalik Hills on to the plains, primarily to escape from the repression of enforced slavery, military service, corvée duties and excessive taxation imposed by the Gorkha rulers after Nepal's 'unification' (Blaikie, Cameron, Feldman, Fournier, Seddon, 1976:5:139). The economy of the Tharus and the Darais in particular was based on livestock-raising and rice-growing. The Botes relied on fishing and on ferrycrossing payments; and the Kumals depended largely on 'pottery making'. But hunting and food-gathering from forests were common livelihood practices for all groups.

In Nawalparasi district, as in much of the Tarai, initial State-backed land-colonization efforts were made during the Rana period. As part of the government's strategy to promote land settlement, senior government officials stationed in the area were granted land under *Birta* arrangements and were offered tax-collecting rights. Such privileges were also given to landlords from Palpa and Tanahun, who were further encouraged to migrate by tax exemptions during the initial years of cultivation. These tax concessions were also extended to peasants. However, due to the existence of malaria, endemic diseases and other dangers (i.e. wild animals, bandits) in the plains, responses from both landlords and peasants from the Hills to land-colonization measures remained fairly limited. The peasants showed interest in clearing and cultivating lands only in the close adjacent plains so that they could get to higher ground to sleep, whilst the landlords came to the plains only during the winter when malaria was less prevalent and when harvests and rents were collected.

The unwillingness of the Hill people to migrate to the plains and the consequent lack of manpower remained the essential obstacle to land-clearance and agricultural settlement in Nawalparasi district. The Birtaholders and the zamindars initially relied on the indigenous people for cultivation, but as this population was very small and as most of these people must have preferred cultivating their own land rather than working for others, no substantial land colonization seemed feasible. As a result, from the second half of the nineteenth century, Birtaholders and zamindars began recruiting people from India. These people were brought in not only as tenant-cultivators and farm-labourers, but in some cases, as farm-managers as well. A much higher population density in the bordering Indian plains during this period (Gaige, 1975:66) and the intense exploitation of the peasantry by landlords as well as by the British colonial State (Burghart, 1978:209) seemed to have further facilitated the migration of Indian peasants and agricultural labourers into southern Parasi.

In the 1930s and 1940s, immigration from India grew at a remarkable rate. Severe harvest failures and widespread famine as a result of frequent and prolonged droughts during this period (Pradhan, 1979:22) resulted in the inability of both Nepalese landowners and tenants to meet the government's tax requirements. For fear of repression by the government, some landowners even left their holdings, whilst the tenants preferred to work as farm-labourers instead of undertake self-cultivation. The Rana government responded by confiscating and auctioning the land. Since only a few wealthy people from the Hills were prepared to invest, these lands were offered to Indian zamindars, who subsequently acquired permanent ownership rights (Yadav, 1984:43–4). This resulted in the immigration of a considerable number of zamindars (together with their farm-workers) to Parasi, especially from the dry areas of Uttar Pradesh.

In 1965, land-reform measures were introduced in the Nawalparasi district with the imposition of land ceilings for landlords of 17 ha. In order to avoid the excess land being appropriated by the government, the large landowners, amongst other things, sought to sell their land, and as such, a large area of land became available for purchase (Berry et al., ibid.:40). Many more affluent Indian landlords took advantage of this situation as well and moved permanently to the area; at the same time, many landless labourers accompanied them in order to maintain employment.

In the late 1960s and the early 1970s, the construction of the Gandak water-control project (1964–71) and the British funded Gaidakot-Butwal section of the East-West Highway (1968–75) brought many Indian labourers into Nawalparasi. The construction activities of the Gandak Project[2] relied entirely on Indian contractors and labourers. Similarly, in the case of the Gaidakot-Butwal section of the East-West highway, the initial construction work was carried out through Indian contractors who employed primarily Indian labourers. It is estimated that 6,000 labourers were brought from Bihar and Orissa on short-term contracts and were employed for earth-moving and stone-breaking (Fournier, 1976; Seddon with Blaikie and Cameron, 1981). Some of these labourers did not return home. In the case of the Gandak project, an even greater number of labourers were believed to have remained in and around the project area, mostly seeking employment in agriculture and settling down in vacant land where possible.

Because of the seasonal demand for agricultural labour (particularly during paddy-transplantation and harvest), each year a large number of Indian labourers entered into Nawalparasi district. Many of these migrant labourers returned home, but some especially those with poor economic backgrounds and with few prospects in India preferred to remain behind. In addition to this, one important factor which resulted in the permanent stay of these migrant labourers was the vested interest of large landowners, even of landlords with origins in the Hills, in employing Indian labourers as sharecroppers/tenants and as contract labourers as these people were not entitled to claim any tenancy rights.

These factors led to a substantial level of population increase in southern Parasi which has come to resemble the neighbouring areas of India in terms of population density. In recent years, population growth has also been witnessed in the northern parts of the Parasi plains and in Nawalpur. This latter development resulted mainly from the immigration of sukumbasi people from the Hills. Firstly, the expansion of the malaria eradication programme in the mid-1950s to Nawalpur under the Rapti Valley Project in neighbouring Chitawan and later its extension to the Nawalparasi district as a whole, encouraged migration and land settlement in previously malarial areas. After the control of malaria, many landlords of Hill origin, who previously stayed in the plains only on a seasonal basis, began living permanently in the area. Furthermore, they actively encouraged poor peasants and landless people in and around their Hill residences to move to the plains. Likewise, many people with large families and low economic status, predominantly Magars from the adjoining Hills, started clearing forests and cultivating land in the nearby plains along with rearing cattle and spending nights in the plains. The upper reaches of Binayakhola, Aarungkhola, Girbarikhola, Kirankhola and Jharahikhola rivers in Nawalpur and the areas connecting the plains south of Dhurkot (the northern parts of Sunwal, Ramnagar, Tilakpur and Panchanagar Panchayats) in Parasi were largely cleared during this time. Secondly, the positive impact in the Hills of the official land development policy in Chitawan and the setting up of another resettlement scheme in Nawalpur in 1965 (in close proximity to Chitawan) caused the Hill-people to become aware of the possibilities afforded by migration for acquiring land in Nawalparasi. Thirdly, the construction of roads, initiation of various projects relating to agriculture, new health-care and education services in the Tarai produced a high expectation of better life prospects. In this respect, an equally crucial interrelated pull factor has been the greater scope for wage employment in agriculture in the Tarai, especially as wages seemed to have been higher in the Tarai than in the Hills (some of these pull factors and the structure of labour relations are elaborated in the following chapter).

The high level of north-south migration of people from the Nepal Hills as well as south-north from the bordering areas of India into the plains has in recent years led to significant population growth in the Nawalparasi district. Table 5 demonstrates that, between 1961 and 1981, the population of the district rose nearly three-fold. One of the direct consequences of this situation has been the changing ethnic composition. Until 1950, Tharus, Darais, Kumals and Botes formed the majority of the population. But by the early 1960s, these groups seemed to have been outnumbered by the newcomers. In 1986, these earlier inhabitants constituted only 19 and 31 per cent of the population in Parasi and Nawalpur respectively (District Panchayat, Parasi, 1987). The continuous immigration into the area has furthermore resulted in an increasing competition for the remaining

TABLE 5 *Population growth in Nawalparasi district*

year	population size
1961	114,000 (a)
1971	146,548 (b)
1981	308,828 (c)
1986	393,672 (d)

Source: (a) Berry et al., ibid.: 39
(b) 1971 census; CBS, *Statistical Pocket Book Nepal* (Kathmandu: CBS, 1974:11)
(c) 1981 census; ibid., 1984:15
(d) District Panchayat, Parasi, 1987

land, forest and other natural resources; consequently the customary access of indigenous people to these resources has rapidly diminished.

The impact of this recent immigration could also be seen in the field of agrarian relations. Like the rest of the Tarai, in Nawalparasi district a few large and rich farmers owned substantial areas of land and the vast number of small farmers possessed very little. According to the 1981/2 agricultural census, in the Nawalparasi district the large and rich farmers, constituting 9.6 per cent of the households, owend 36 per cent of the total cultivated area, in which the largest (0.8 per cent) alone held nearly 9 per cent of the total land area; at the same time, the small farmers, representing nearly 52 per cent of the population, cultivated less than 16 per cent of the total agricultural land (see Table 6). Given their large farm size, the former were able to generate substantial levels of agricultural income, whilst amongst the latter (including therein also a large section of the middle farmers), the fulfilment of family subsistence needs remained the main agricultural activity and this was supplemented by income from wage employment.

Amongst the lower agrarian groups, the sukumbasis earned their livelihood mainly from wage labouring. The large-scale migration into the area affected the local agrarian structure and production relations in three specific ways: firstly, as the majority of the migrants tended to be poor and landless, the category of landless people in the area was continuously swelling. Secondly,

TABLE 6 *Land-holding pattern in Nawalparasi district*

group specification/ land size	% of households	% of land held
large (above 10 ha)	0.8	8.7
rich (3–10 ha)	8.8	27.3
middle (1–3 ha)	38.5	48.2
small (up to 1 ha)	51.9	15.8
landless	–	–
total	100.0	100.0

Source: CBS, *National Sample Census of Agriculture 1981/2 Nepal: District Nawalparasi* (Kathmandu: CBS, 1985b, p. 2).

as this (together with the seasonal migration of Indian labourers) resulted in a general competition for wage employment, the employers in the area (i.e. large and the rich farmers) were able to keep wages low and were able to generate substantial levels of agricultural surpluses without any significant investment in land. Thirdly, the development of the social and economic infrastructure and the high productivity of land encouraged many wealthier people from the Hill areas as well as from the nearby towns (e.g. Butwal-Bhairahawa, Narayanghat) to buy land in the area from the small farmers, particularly from the indigenous people, who thus joined the already expanded category of migrant landless people. Indeed, as shall be shown later, this high level in-flow of impoverished people, the low wages and the process of land loss amongst the small farmers and the indigenous people were some of the crucial factors which caused a large number of poor migrants and the landless people to be involved in 'illegal' land settlement in the Nawalparasi district.

GOVERNMENT RESETTLEMENT PROGRAMMES IN NAWALPARASI DISTRICT

Although land colonization in the Tarai as a whole was encouraged by the State throughout the nineteenth and early twentieth century, no organized land development projects were witnessed before 1951. After the downfall of the Rana regime, the new government launched the Rapti Valley Land Development Project in Chitawan district. The project initially began with the resettlement of people affected by devastating landslides and floods in 1954 in the central Hills. But in the following years the scope of the project was considerably expanded and the reduction of population pressure in the Hill areas and the provision of steady and cheap food-supplies to Kathmandu were regarded as its main objectives (Kansakar, vol. I, 1979:30–1). This project was largely initiated and funded by the U. S. within the context of its contemporary political interests i.e. Nepal's strategic location between China and India and the perceived threat of communist influence from China into Nepal (Mihaly, 1965). Nevertheless, as it was accompanied by a malaria-eradication programme and the development of some economic infrastructure (e.g. construction of roads), together with the government's wide publicity that all of those who migrated to the Tarai would secure land, this project succeeded in encouraging a large number of Hill-people to migrate to and settle permanently in Chitawan.[3] By the end of 1960, 5,233 migrant households had received land in the project. But since 40 per cent of the land, at the rate of 33.5 ha per head of household, was granted to government officials and large farmers (Paudel, 1979:5) and as the government turned a large section of arable land into 'protected forests' (primarily a royal hunting reserve and later designated Chitawan National Park), formally available land in the project area soon became scarce. Some of the later migrants became tenants and labourers of earlier beneficiaries, but many encroached upon surrounding forest areas where they established dwellings and fields. The migratory flow gained further momentum on the same informal basis as the malaria-eradication programme was subsequently extended to Nawalparasi and other parts of the Tarai;[4] and the absence of government agencies to organize resettlement programmes for the increasing number of migrants resulted in a significant level of spontaneous land clearance and settlement.

'Planned' resettlement schemes

Partly as a result of this situation and partly because of other political and economic considerations, in 1965 a government resettlement agency, Nepal Resettlement Company (NRC), was formed. Soon after its establishment, a resettlement project based on Israel's experience with the Kibbutz co-operative settlements was set up in Nawalpur. The project constituted 30 resettlement units covering five Panchayats. Some provision was made for initial food supplies, credit for bullocks and agricultural extension services. But the task of land clearance was the responsibility of the settlers themselves, and as many of them possessed only simple tools such as axes and knives, they initially had a difficult time both in clearing their plots and in growing food to support their families.

In the first year 1965/6, 713 households were settled in the project area; and by the end of 1973, this number had reached 1,550 households (see Table 7). Prior to 1970, a settler-household obtained 2.7 ha of land but after this date (as demand for land in the project area grew), the settlers were provided with only 2 ha for each household. It was observed that most of the settlers in the project came from the central Hills, although 299 of the households included were repatriated families from Burma (Paudel, 1979:27). The higher and more influential castes (Brahmin, Chhetri and Newar) constituted 43 per cent of the settlers, followed by Magars who formed 21 per cent. But the lower caste Hill migrants (Kami, Sarki and Damain) and the indigenous Tarai people (Tharu, Kumal, Bote) composed only

TABLE 7 *Planned resettlement schemes in Nawalparasi district (organized by NRC)*

name of project	during the period of	no. of households resettled	total land area distributed (ha)
Nawalpur project	1965–6	713	
	1966–73	837	3342
Parasi project	1976–86	3926	3615
total		5476	6957

Source: NRC Project Office, Dhanewa, Nawalparasi.

10 and 9 per cent of the households respectively (ibid.). It was also acknowledged that nearly one-quarter of Hill settlers probably owned properties elsewhere and acquired land in the project through personal, social and political contacts (Fournier, 1976).

After the implementation of the Nawalpur resettlement scheme, in 1976 the NRC established a new project in Parasi.[5] The project was divided into two main resettlement units; Maker-Daunnedevi and Shankarpur. Altogether it covered 19 villages. By 1985, 3,975 households were settled, in which the earlier settlers obtained plots of between 1 and 1.3 ha, whereas the later ones received only 0.3 ha (primarily because of the large number of people seeking land in the project). In this project, the higher and influential castes constituted 25 per cent of the settlers and Magars and lower caste people formed 24 and 16 per cent respectively. But the local indigenous people constituted only 10 per cent of the settlers (NRC, 1986). Some 100 households of Tibetan Khampa 'refugees' were also given land as a reward for their 'acquiescence' in agreeing not to use Nepalese territory for their 'armed resistance' against China. These households were also granted Rs 150,000 for purchasing tools, seeds and fertilizers and were given Rs 5 per person per day until their first harvest. Further, they were offered tractors to plough and pumpsets to irrigate their land (Paudel, ibid.:40–1).

Unlike in the Nawalpur project, in this project the settlers (except for the Khampa refugees) obtained no initial financial assistance, and the provision of other support services seemed to have considerably declined. For example, during my field-visits and stay in the project site, the settlers were observed complaining to resettlement officials about the lack of irrigation facilities and about difficulties in obtaining loans from the banks.[6] As a matter of fact, many of the settlers transferred from Nawalpur area (particularly from Dumkibas and Banimanipur Panchayats) who were provided with land in the Parasi project had left their plots and returned to Nawalpur. These settlers explained their return as being due to difficulties in clearing land, lack of irrigation facilities and most importantly the lack of availability of wage employment in the area.

In recent years, the NRC's capacity to resettle people as well as the quality of its schemes have rapidly deteriorated. In fact, the NRC was no longer involved in organizing resettlement schemes by the mid-1980s, and its recent activities were limited to the regularization of illegal settlers only. In order to illustrate this process, the NRC's most recent Rewa Rehta Settlement project may be cited here.

It is important to note that the government's policy to evict a large number of illegal settlers from their settlements in Nawalparasi and in the neighbouring Rupandehi district in the early 1980s caused a growing public opposition, and maintaining law and order in the area became difficult. At the same time, the 1981 general election was approaching and acquiring votes from illegal settlers was seen as crucial in order for the government candidate to win. Against this background, the local administration decided to accommodate 1,042 illegal settler households in the ongoing resettlement programmes and sought to organize these activities through the NRC. Most of the settlers chosen for resettlement in this project were from Nawalpur area (i.e. Kawasoti, Chormara, Lokaha, Belbas, Syaulibazaar), although some 182 households were from the Rupandehi district, primarily from Charparhatti settlement.

The Rewa Rehta settlement was spread over parts of Kudiya, Narsahi and Guthi Prasauni Panchayats near the Indian border (Map III). During the floods of 1953 and 1961, the fertile top-soil was washed away; therefore much of the land in the area was sandy and extremely infertile. Because of this poor quality of soil, not many people were interested in settling down and most of the area was used by the local people as cattle-strolling ground.

For the first 18 months, settlers received food rations (supported by the US World Food Program). But as no further arrangements were made to extend the food supplies and as the settlers were unable to grow any significant amount of food because of the poor quality of soil, many of them faced extreme economic hardship. In the case of the larger families, one or more members moved temporarily to urban centres such as Butwal, Bhairahawa and Narayanghat to become rickshaw-pullers, to work as dish-washers in restaurants and hotels or to be roadside luggage-bearers and porters. Alternatively, others moved to India in search of employment and income. But for smaller families with older persons and more female members (as most of

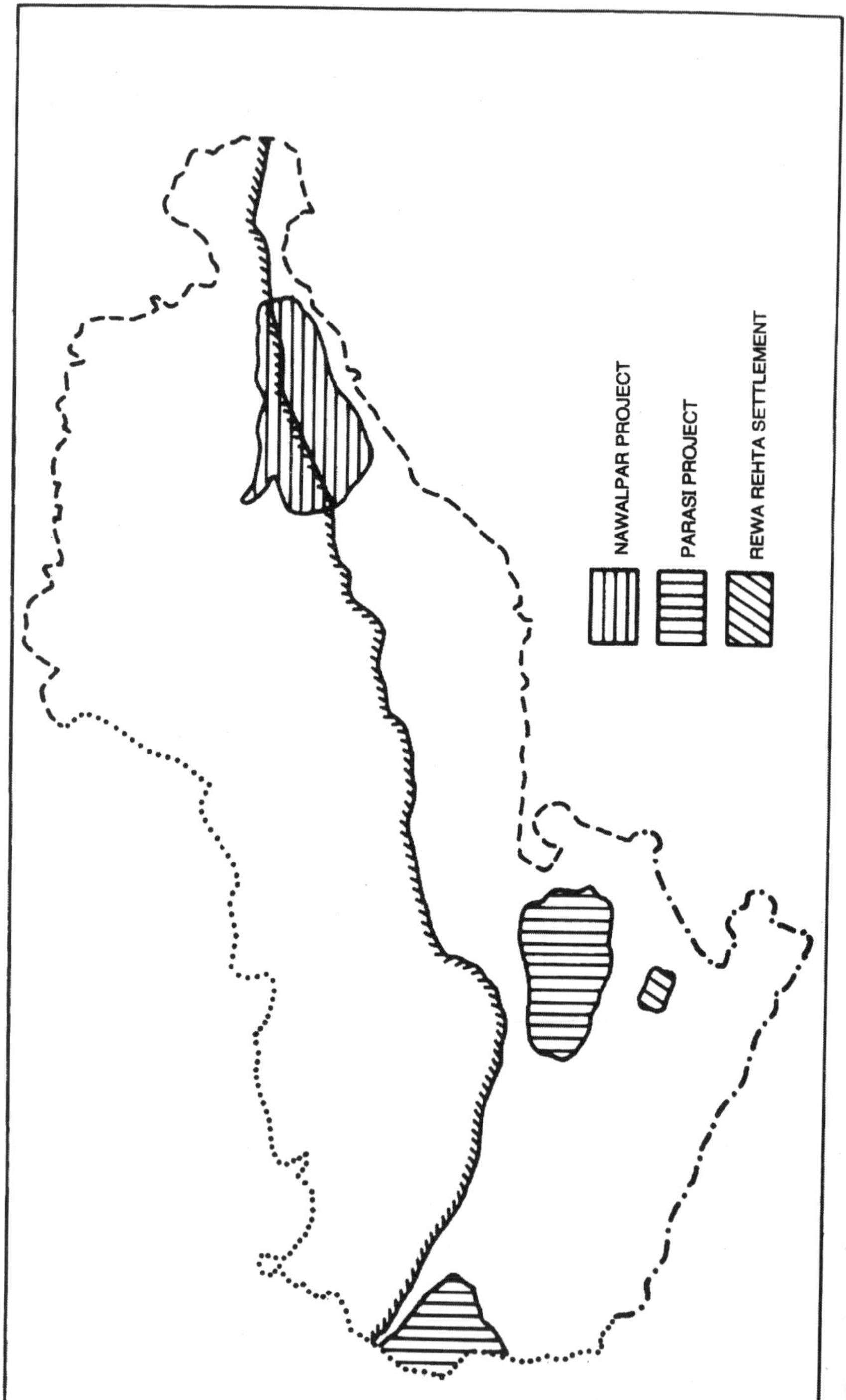
NAWALPAR PROJECT
PARASI PROJECT
REWA REHTA SETTLEMENT

the available work was for younger males), this opportunity barely existed. The prospect for wage-employment in agriculture in and around the project area was very limited. Moreover, after their arrival to the area, there were even more people added to the local labour force; hence getting wage-employment became more competitive and existing wage rates declined (from Rs 8 per day in 1981 to Rs 5 in 1988).

Due to the lack of wage-employment in agriculture in particular, many settlers were compelled to sell wood and timber to India illegally. Prices of firewood and timber were attractive but transport was not an easy task (primarily because of regular intimidation and the seeking of bribes by forest guards, police and customs officials). Consequently, the nearby 'public' forests were cleared. The government's eviction of settlers from their previous settlements on the ground of 'forest preservation' and their transfer to Rewa Rehta resulted in the depletion of forests in both areas. Indeed, if the settlers had been allowed to remain in their previous areas and had not been brought to Rewa Rehta, at least, forests in the Rewa Rehta area would have been saved, and most importantly, the settlers would have been able to grow crops in their previous settlements.

Regularization of illegal settlers

Parallel to the formal resettlement schemes, large-scale informal settlements were already witnessed in Nawalparasi district by the late 1960s. Owing to this situation, a number of short-term and specific-task oriented resettlement commissions were established, which worked on behalf of or under the policies established by the Resettlement Department (RD)[7] in Kathmandu or its regional office in Butwal. The fundamental task of these commissions was to legalize the status of some of the illegal settlers (viz. the politically important), primarily by providing them with a formal title. Most of the earlier households selected for regularization were allowed to remain in their original place of settlement, although no provisions for support services were made for them.

The first resettlement commission, headed by the Lumbini Zonal Commissioner, was set up in 1968. The main task of this commission was to regularize the status of the existing illegal

TABLE 8 *Regularization of illegal settlers by Resettlement Department or by various Commissions in Nawalparasi district*

year	no. of households regularized	total land distributed (ha)
1970	207	452
1976	505	503
1977	388	219
1978	647	405
1979	448	280
1980	72	39
1981	n/a	n/a
1982	412	42
1983–6	n/a	n/a
total	2679	1940

Source: Resettlement Department Regional Office (RDRO), Butwal

settlers and to prevent further forest encroachment. It regularized 207 settler-households and about 452 ha of land was distributed amongst these households.

In 1976, the Forest Area Determinance Commission was established, again chaired by the Zonal Commissioner. A commission of this nature was set up only in the Lumbini Zone (in which the Nawalparasi district is included), thus revealing the extent of illegal settlement in this zone. On the recommendations of this commission, between 1976–9 about 1,988 households were regularized in the Nawalparasi district (see Table 8). Out of these settlers, 115 households were 'political sufferers'[8] who obtained 2 ha of land per household; the other ordinary settlers obtained only between 0.3 to 1 ha per household. During the tenureship of this commission forest demarcations were drawn in many Panchayats. It also adopted a policy to clear up illegal settlements located north of the East-West Highway. This resulted in large-scale eviction of settlers during this period.

In 1979 another new commission named the Forest Area Resettlement Authorized Commission was established. It was a very powerful one-man operation. As this commission was established over the period of the 1979 Referendum (in which the monarchy and the Panchas were seeking to continue the Panchayat system) and continued until the general election of 1981, political interests overshadowed any straightforward regularization process. As shall be shown later, many settlers who pledged support for the Panchayat system in the Referendum and for the government candidate in the 1981 general election had their status legalized. During the fieldwork, it was learnt that the commission officials, acting on behalf of the politicians, even distributed false land-registration certificates to many settlers for this purpose.

After an interval of about a year, at the end of 1981, the Forest-Area Strengthening Commission (FASC) came into being. This time, an ex-Supreme Court judge was appointed for the job. This commission, unlike the previous ones, proclaimed that the preservation of forests, not the legalization of the settlers, was its main function. For this reason, settlers were evicted in large numbers. But it failed to maintain uniformity in its policy regarding which areas should be cleared and who should get formal titles to land and in what amounts. Nonetheless, during the period of this commission, some 412 households were legalized, primarily for political reasons similar to those mentioned above.

A new set of people were appointed in 1985 to carry out the task left by the earlier commission. The ex-Director of the Resettlement Department was appointed as the chief of this commission and two other national level Pancha-politicians were appointed as its members. These members were from the eastern part of Nepal and had no knowledge of the local situation in Nawalparasi district. It was widely believed that these appointments were closely related to the government's strategy to assist their candidate for the district to win in the following general election.

From the above, it should be clear that the role of the State in organizing resettlement activities in Nawalparasi district was very limited, a situation which was also common in other Tarai districts. Although initially some of the resettlement projects were of the 'planned' type (i.e. comprised of site selection and preparation and the provision for some support services), much of the State involvement seemed to have been limited to controlling voluntary population movements (i.e. primarily people migrating from the Hills to the Tarai). As large-scale immigration and the higher production potential in the Tarai created a high demand for land and settlers were eager to accept land plots under any conditions, the State did not need to provide any significant level of financial and other extension incentives for settlement.

Unlike in other Asian countries, e.g. Sri Lanka, Thailand, Malaysia, Indonesia (MacAndrews, 1978:1–9), the costs of resettlement schemes in Nepal have been very low. For example, a study of the Kanchanpur project showed that the total financial cost to the government per household was Rs 14,293. But since, out of this total, Rs 10,747 was for food rations covered by various aid programmes, the government bore only Rs 3,546. Much of this money went for project administration and overheads. As a result, the settlers received only Rs 585 per household in development loans and for agricultural implements (Ojha, 1982). The absence of support services for accommodation, medical facilities, irrigation, credit, tools and implements in most projects resulted in the settlers, particularly those with weak economic backgrounds, becoming heavily indebted to moneylenders and large landowners and being forced to sell their land soon after a permanent landownership certificate was obtained (APROSC, 1978b: 174). The last decade saw not only reductions in the level of infrastructural and support services provided to the settlers, but it also witnessed a sharp decline in the State-organized resettlement activities overall. By the mid-1980s, no major resettlement programmes were implemented in the Tarai and the existing resettlement agencies (including the NRC) were involved only in the regularization of some of the illegal settlers as described above.

In examining the experience of resettlement schemes in Nepal, the political context in which early resettlement schemes were initiated is important. After the coup d'état of 1960, much of the opposition to the king and the newly-introduced Panchayat system came from the Tarai where the majority of the population was of Indian origin and influenced by the Indian political culture (i.e. a multi-party system and direct franchise). In order to politically integrate the Tarai people into the monarchy-led Panchayat system, the migration of Hill people (who were believed to be more loyal to the monarchy and the Panchayat system) into the Tarai was seen as very crucial.[9] For this purpose, even the Nepalese of Hill-origin settled abroad (e.g. Burma, Assam) were encouraged to return home and were provided with land in the Tarai (*Matribhumi*, March 28, 1964). Similarly, in order to prevent the influence of opposition political groups (operating from across the border in India) amongst the Tarai people and to eliminate the possibility of their using the bordering Tarai-forests as sanctuary for arms raids and other political activities (Uprety, 1981:83), ex-servicemen retired from the British, Indian and Nepalese armed forces were encouraged to settle along the border. As a result of this policy and also because of their political significance,[10] the ex-servicemen became one of the largest beneficiary groups of the land development and resettlement schemes in the Tarai. The official figure shows that by the mid-1970s, 7,000 ex-servicemen households had obtained land in Jhapa, Sunsari, Rupandehi and Banke districts (Elder et al., 1975:19). But in actuality a much higher number of them probably secured land, as many of them were not registered as ex-servicemen as such in the resettlement/ regularization programmes and obtained land under a different status such as 'natural disaster victims' (sufferers of landslides and floods). The provision of land and the settlement of ex-servicemen enhanced the political consolidation of the regime in the Tarai and reduced the likelihood of these former military men being persuaded to join opposition political groups.

Similarly, the resettlement schemes were utilized as a means to co-opt opposition politicians and to receive continuing support from senior Panchas, who maintained their official status in the Panchayat system. In the 1970s, about 1,414 ha of land were distributed among 696 politicians in seven Tarai Zones, out of whom 115 were provided with land in the Nawalparasi district (NRC Project Office, Dhanewa, 1986).

Furthermore, the high economic profitability of the Tarai land was such that land became one of the most sought-after commodities; and therefore, many other influential groups and individuals sought to possess land in the Tarai. For example, in the eastern Tarai on various occasions, 31 families associated with the royal palace obtained 2,108 ha of land and other palace officials secured land ranging from 17 to 136 ha each—this being done at the expense of the earlier settlers who had initially cleared the land (Ojha, ibid.: 89–91). The provision of land of this kind was made directly through the royal palace or through the Ministry of Home Affairs, and was usually implemented by the Department of Resettlement. As discussed earlier, the other agencies through which a considerable number of local politicians, government officials and other influential individuals obtained land included the various commissions, which were led by Zonal Commissioners and other political appointees.

Consequently, most of the poorer and landless households, the most needy ones, were unable to secure land within the government's planned or unplanned (regularized) settlements. State policies were concerned with these households only when they were organized and threatened law and order. However, the past land development and resettlement policies, no matter how uneven and patchy, had succeeded in creating hopes for land and a 'better future' amongst these desperate people, thus leading to a large-scale concentration of poor and landless people in the frontier areas.

Major Causes of Illegal Settlement

The above discussion on government activities in resettlement revealed several issues which were closely connected to the development of 'illegal' settlements in the Nawalparasi district. Whilst these issues require further attention, a number of specific factors relating to the rise of 'illegal' settlements need to be elaborated upon.

As mentioned earlier, the population of Nawalparasi district in 1961 was only 114,000, rising in 1971 to 146,548 and in 1981 to 308,828. This upward trend continued and the district population by the end of 1986 reached 393,672 people. This rapid population growth was not only the outcome of immigration into the area, but also of the natural population growth in the district which was already building up by the late 1960s. For example, in 1971 over 43 per cent of the population was under the age of 16 years (Department of Information, 1974:897); with the control of malaria, cholera and other endemic diseases and with the limited impact of family-planning measures, there was a great likelihood of further non-immigration demographic expansion.

Over the last thirty years, whilst the population grew at an unprecedented scale—creating a corresponding higher demand for land, the formal government resettlement programmes remained extremely limited. As has been indicated above, between 1961 and 1971, the district saw an approximate net growth of 32,548 people (5,612 households), whereas only 1,757 households were resettled/regularized during this period. The decade from 1971 to 1981 witnessed a population growth of 162,280 people (27,979 households), but only 4,918 households were accommodated in the resettlement schemes. From 1981 to 1986, some 84,844 more people (14,628 households) were added to the total population, but during this time, only 1,480 households secured formal land titles. Examining the period 1961 to 1986 as a whole, the Nawalparasi district seemed to have seen a population increase of 279,672 (48,219 households), whilst concurrently a mere 8,155 households were included in resettlement or regularization programmes. The poor implementation of the government's resettlement programme, particularly given the high rate of net population growth, was the major factor contributing to 'illegal' settlements in the district.

Secondly, many of the illegal settlements in the district have arisen and expanded because of the government's lack of clarification about target-groups entitled to settle and the subsequent alienation of landless people from resettlement schemes. For example, until 1973, landless people were not even listed as a target settler-group and even after this date they have not been identified as the main beneficiary group. Conversely, the so-called 'victims of natural disaster' have long been considered a major priority group of settlers. But questions as to how much land was lost and how much remained, as well as questions as to what actually qualified them to acquire land, were not clarified. Besides, those who did not own land but were involved in other professions and obtaining a relatively high income from various sources (e.g. army pensions, trading and moneylending, paid employment) were considered as 'landless' and secured land in the resettlement projects. Similarly, due to political considerations, repatriated Nepalese, ex-servicemen, politicians and individuals having contacts with the royal palace and higher authorities benefited disproportionately from the recent land development and resettlement schemes in the Tarai.

In most cases, the government's existing resettlement policies only served to facilitate access to land for groups and individuals with access to income and productive resources, whilst failing to provide any priority to totally 'assetless' people.

Moreover, the settler-selection procedures were further complicated after 1973 due to a longer bureaucratic process[11] and increased demands on the applicants' time and finances. Consequently, many assetless people could not complete the selection procedure and hence acquired no land. In the late 1980s, since no major resettlement schemes had been set up, these selection procedures were redundant. During the fieldwork for this study these procedures were used only on a limited scale for the regularization of existing 'illegal' settlers, and the main selection method applied involved 'interviews' of the settlers by the resettlement and FASC officials. As these officials did not need to report to higher authorities about the selection of settlers and since the local Village Councils had no say in these matters, often considerable numbers of 'outsiders' and settlers favoured by the FASC (such as the ex-servicemen) were chosen for regularization. At the same time, lack of awareness about the selection time and the inability to pay bribes demanded by resettlement officials meant that many long-term landless 'illegal' settlers were not selected. In some cases, lands cleared and cultivated by the original settlers were forcibly given to people and settlers preferred by the government officials. Indeed, not only did many powerless and landless people not get land within planned resettlement programmes (primarily because of the government's failure to give preferential treatment) but also their further alienation by the selection procedure meant that regularization did not work to effectively reduce the numbers of people in 'illegal' settlements.

Another group of people whose depressed condition was not recognized and who as a result were involved in 'illegal' settlements were the earlier inhabitants of the area (i.e. Tharu, Darai, Kumal, Bote). Over the years, the migration of an increasing number of people into the area created a high level of competition for the remaining land resources. Many villages inhabited by these ethnic groups became encircled by new settlements established by new migrants and settlers on previously forested areas. This precluded the possibility of extending cultivation on to the adjacent forest land. At the same time, many such households were dispossessed of their land by wealthier and more powerful people; the latter acquired land not only through legal purchases, but in some cases they also captured land through lending money at exorbitant interest rates and through unscrupulous tricks.[12] As was pointed out earlier, during the two major resettlement schemes in the district, a significant number of these earlier inhabitants could not obtain land titles. As the notion of resettlement in the area was basically limited to the relocation of, and the distribution of land to, people of Hill origin, it was not surprising that out of the total number of settlers, these ethnic groups constituted only 9 and 10 per cent of the settlers in Nawalpur and Parasi resettlement projects respectively. As a result of this situation, one could see a very visible presence of these people, especially the younger generation, in many of the major 'illegal' settlements in the district.

The lack of long-term policy guidelines and haphazard coercion on the part of the government resettlement agencies in regularizing settlers were other factors responsible for the growth of new illegal settlements in the Nawalparasi district. As aforementioned, the recent commissions established in the district were concerned more with the 'preservation' of forests than with the legalization of the settlers. Consequently, these commissions adopted tougher measures towards households settled within forest boundaries. Between 1982 and 1984 in particular, the eviction of thousands of settlers was witnessed. This was carried out with a view to 'preserving' the forest north of the East-West Highway. But no clear socio-economic or environmental justification for such a policy was provided, nor was there any consistency in implementing it, for some settlements north of the road (such as Aarungkhola Bazaar) were legalized, whilst those at Chormara were evicted. Some of the settlement areas formally cleared were immediately fenced off; but where this was not done, a considerable number of settlers remained behind on their holdings. At the same time, others merely moved to new areas and developed fresh settlements. The result was that there was no diminution in the amount of 'illegal' settlement, but merely some shift in locations.

Furthermore, as the term-period of the commissioner and the members of the FASC was relatively short (between 1 to 3 years) and as their appointments were usually delayed, the process of regularization of settlers was never consistent and suffered from the lack of monitoring and evaluation of earlier activities. In many cases, the appointment of a new commissioner resulted in a completely different set of priorities. For example, many of the settlements regularized during 1979–81 were revoked by the succeeding commissioner and settlers were evicted from these settlements (*Yugdhara*, March 19, 1983). Piecemeal, incomplete eviction undoubtedly contributed towards the spread of locations of 'illegal' settlements across the district.

In this respect, some mention must also be made of the self-interested practice of local politicians and resettlement and forestry officials in actually encouraging 'illegal' settlements in various parts of the district. The 'illegal' settlers in the Nawalparaasi district constituted a large section of the local population. Because of the high potential for votes, during elections for the first tier of government, 'illegal' settlers became the focus of local politicians, especially aspiring MPs. In order to secure votes, promises were made to give political protection to settlers along with eventual registration of their land. Those already evicted were encouraged to settle in new areas. Although, after elections, the MPs lived in Kathmandu and could do little for the settlers, this nonetheless resulted in the expansion of previously established settlements as well as the emergence of some new settlements. These developments were particularly noted during the Referendum period and the general election which followed, as in this period new settlements appeared in Rupauliya, Panchanagar and Ramnagar Panchayats in Parasi and Kolhuwa, Narayani, Kawasoti, Pragatinagar, Shiva Mandir and Naya Belhani Panchayats in Nawalpur.

In addition to the local politicians, the commissioner and members and officials of the FASC encouraged 'illegal' settlements in the district. As the commissioner and the members in particular were 'political appointees' and were mostly from outside the district, they generally had little commitment either to the district development or to the predicament of the settlers. Instead they were frequently involved in seeking short-term or occasionally longer-term economic gains. During fieldwork, settlers often claimed they had been forced to pay bribes to the commissioner and the resettlement officials. Those who were not able to pay were frequently evicted, and in some cases, an entirely new set of people were given the land such as in Bhutaha in Panchanagar Panchayat and Kolhuwatar in Kolhuwa Panchahayat. In this instance, shopkeepers and road-construction contractors from Palpa and Butwal, along with local landlords, obtained legal title to the land, instead of the original settlers. In other cases, the settlers were either evicted or pressured to accept smaller land plots, whilst those associated with the commissioner (i.e. relatives and friends), members and staff of the FASC were granted the extra remaining land. A notable example was that of the commissioner between 1979–81, who registered in his wife's name some of the land earlier cleared and cultivated by settlers in ward number four Ghuseri village in Dumkibas Panchayat. And, with this connection to the district, he stood as an MP candidate in the 1986 election. Actions like these directly forced many of those genuinely in need on to new land.

Similarly, the forestry officials, primarily the forest guards and rangers, on occasion encouraged 'illegal' settlements. For example, when people began to settle inside the forest boundary, it was within the range of responsibilities of forestry officials to report illegal settlements to the higher authorities in the district headquarters or Butwal-Bhairahawa (Zonal headquarters). But local forestry officials instead raised money from the settlers (as well as sold wood and timber from the settlement area) and delayed reporting new settlements. As a result, an initial tentative settlement became transformed into a large permanent village on land still officially designated as forest.

Finally, the impact of declining land-holdings in formal resettlement schemes should be emphasized. Until the early 1970s, the settlers were offered land between 2 and 2.7 ha, but by the late 1970s, this land size decreased to under 1 ha. From 1980 on, this went down to 0.3 ha and in some cases the settlers were granted land only for housing. Such a decrease in land-plot size, along with an increasing family size, caused many settlers to experience steadily deteriorating economic conditions. As a consequence, many households were forced to use nearby forest areas for cultivation, to send some members of the family (often a young married couple) to another area to settle 'illegally', or to sell their present holding and move the entire family to a new location where 'illegal' land occupation as well as other economic opportunities were expected to be available (i.e. wage employment, selling of firewood, etc.).

The decrease in land size was witnessed not only in the 'planned' and 'regularized' sectors, but was also evident in the 'illegal' settlements. Rapid immigration as well as natural increases in the district's population outpaced the settlement of new land. As a result, more people were compelled to share increasingly smaller sizes of land plots. The vast majority of 'illegal' settlers, in fact, held under one-quarter of a hectare of land. Furthermore, constant evictions and the inability to realize harvests, along with the complete lack of external support services caused settlers to face economic hardships and chronic indebtedness. As a result, many households were pressured into putting up their land for sale, even though because of the illegal status of the land it fetched a low price. For example, a survey I conducted of 'illegal' settlers in the Tribeni-Susta Village Panchayat indicated that between 1976 and 1986, about 74 households of earlier settlers sold/lost their holdings. Out of these households, 50 per cent moved to new locations to settle 'illegally', whilst 43 per cent bought smaller or less productive plots with the remaining savings.

The picture that emerges from the above discussion is that in most parts the official resettlement and land use policies seemed to have been directly and indirectly responsible for prompting and spreading 'illegal' settlements in the Nawalparasi district. After having encouraged people through setting up resettlement projects and through publicizing the availability of land in these projects, the resettlement schemes in the district remained thoroughly inadequate since they could not keep pace with the flow of immigrants and the growing number of people seeking land. At the same time, since the landless and socially weaker sections of the population were not identified as the main target groups, powerful and politically significant groups were able to acquire much of the land that was being distributed. The lack of coherent policy guidelines amongst the government agencies involved in the resettlement/regularization of settlers and the vested political and economic interests actually encouraged the dispersal of 'illegal' settlements. Even within planned and legalized settlements, declining land units led to the re-creation of a considerable number of landless people who sought to regain land 'illegally'. Many of the 'illegal' settlers were forced to move around and settle in new places because of the constant evictions, meagre land size and the difficulties faced by them in maintaining subsistence. As a consequence of all these factors, the Nawalparasi district in recent years has been exposed to widespread illegal settlements by growing numbers of households.

Magnitude of Illegal Settlement in Nawalparasi District

During the fieldwork, a comprehensive settler-census was carried out in Nawalparasi district. The procedure followed for this census-undertaking was that every single 'illegal' settlement in the district was visited and settlers were interviewed and counted. Where settlements were too big to be counted in this fashion and the settlers were divided both geographically and ethnically (specifically the Shankarpur settlement), a group-interview of settlers was scheduled in the nearest market place when many settlers were present. To ensure that the figures obtained were accurate, another group of settlers was consulted and the results were further verified by the local people (the earlier inhabitants) and the forest guards.

The summary of the settler-census is presented in Table 9. The census revealed that by February 1987, 14,469 households were counted as 'illegally' settled in the Nawalparasi district. The census also showed that the Panchayats close to forest areas hosted most settlers; and nearly 99 per cent of the settlers were settled in the plains (i.e. Parasi and Nawalpur). Using the 6.1 person average family-size found amongst the sampled households, the total number of people involved in 'illegal' settlements seemed to have been approximately 88,260. As the population of Nawalparasi district during this time was 393,672, the population of 'illegal' settlers constituted over 22 per cent of the district's total population. But should this figure be compared with the population of Parasi and Nawalpur (where most of the 'illegal' settlements were located), the number of people involved in 'illegal' settlements formed nearly a quarter of the local population.[13]

The 'illegal' settlers in the Nawalparasi district were spread over numerous settlements. The size of settlements ranged from a few houses to over 1,000 households. In fact, in Tamaspur settlement (Naya Belhani Panchayat) as many as 1,800 households were settled and in Shankarpur settlement (Sunwal and Amrout Panchayats) about 1,764 migrant and landless households were identified. In general, most settlements contained between 100 to 500 households, but many of these settlements

TABLE 9 *Number of illegal settler households in Nawalparasi district*

region	Panchayats	number of households
Parasi:	Sunwal	1540
	Swathi	131
	Amrout	427
	Banjariya	21
	Harpur	17
	Sarawal	114
	Guthi Prasauni	309
	Pakalihawa	267
	Narsahi	436
	Kudiya	180
	Tribeni-Susta	277
	Rupauliya	467
	Daunnedevi	450
	Makar	754
	Panchanagar	251
	Tilakpur	173
	Ramnagar	176
subtotal:		5990
Nawalpur:	Dhurkot	299
	Banimanipur	334
	Dumkibas	561
	Prasauni	331
	Naya Belhani	2411
	Tamasariya	206
	Narayani	541
	Kolhuwa	262
	Kumarwarti	266
	Agyauli	147
	Deurali	193
	Shiva Mandir	730

region	Panchayats	number of households
	Kawasoti	164
	Pithauli	522
	Pragatinagar	214
	Deuchuli	300
	Dibyapuri	195
	Rajahar	205
	Amarapuri	134
	Mukundapur	214
	Gaidakot	76
subtotal:		8305
Hill-Panchayats		174
total		14,469

Source: settler-census undertaken by author

were expanding (see Table 10 for details). Some of these settlements, especially the older ones, were organized villages with a little road going through the village and houses being built on both sides of it in an orderly fashion. But to minimize the cost in the event of eviction, houses were poorly constructed. Newer settlements however looked badly organized with hut-like houses erected quite close to each other in a haphazard pattern (primarily because of the lack of land in and around the settlement).

'Illegal' settlements in the district were established on various types of land not formally designated for settlement. These included marginal areas (i.e. stream and riverbanks, reclaimed areas, canal and lakesides, steeps and rugged lands), public lands (i.e. village-commons and lands owned by public institutions such as schools and Panchayats), roadsides, town/market areas and forest lands. Table 11 shows that about 8 per cent of the settlers were settled in roadsides, town/market and public lands and a further 16 per cent were settled in agriculturally marginal areas. A slightly smaller percentage (i.e. 15 per cent of the settlers) were settled on land belonging to the NRC. This land, previously under forest, was formerly allocated by the

TABLE 10 *Selected illegal settlements in Nawalparasi district: some key features*

Name of settlement	location ward	location Panchayat	established in	number of households	settler category	ethnicity/caste	land type	other remarks
Shankarpur	3 4&9	Sunwal Amrout	1979–83	1,764	mostly landless	settlers of all ethnic groups	NRC land	largest settlement in the district (850 ha) and second biggest in terms of settler population
Settlement of repatriated Nepalese from Assam	1	Swathi	1979–80	62	Nepalese repatriated from Assam	mostly high castes of Hill-origin	marginal	many settlers believed to be possessing land and other properties elsewhere and came to the area to acquire land in resettlement projects; conflicts with local people over grazing issue
Susta	4	Tribeni-Susta	1973–7	113	mostly landless (both from Nepal and India)	mixed ethnicity	forest	disputed territory between Nepal and India
Singha-Bandevi	4	Rupauliya	1979	275	landless	Tharus	forest	———
Gangabasti	5	Daunnedevi	1979	210	landless	Hill-ethnic groups and some Tharus	roadside	these settlers were previously settled in NRC land but were evicted from there to allow officially selected households to settle
Barghat: Bazaar area	4	Makar	1970–1	180	mostly businessmen and landowners	Hill-ethnic groups, mostly Newars	town/ market	settlement with a rudimentary form of urban squatting which began initially with the construction of East-West Highway
Flood-victims corner	4	Makar	1981	415	households with weak economic background	Hill-migrants representing most castes	forest	as settlers were allocated only housing plots, they were obliged to encroach upon adjacent forests for crop production

Repatriated Nepalese unit	4	Makar	1964–71	49	Nepalese repatriated from Burma	mainly high castes of Hill-origin	forest	these settlers came to the area primarily to acquire free land in resettlement schemes; they were considerably better off than most settler households
Bhutaha	3	Panchanagar	1979	62	landless	Hill-ethnic groups	forest	worst example of corruption: FASC officials provided land titles to 'outsiders' by taking bribes, district court also approved this, but settlers continued to stay in with the help of nearby villagers
Bhadera-Thadaban	2	Ramnagar	1979	56	landless	Hill-ethnic groups	forest	previously 450 households settled, but harsh eviction measures and subsequent fencing of the area compelled most settlers to leave their holdings and move to new locations; some 56 households were left behind in areas where fencing was not completed
Jogikuti	1	Dumkibas	1970	129	landless	Hill-migrants representing most castes	forest	corruption and bribe-taking by government officials in the selection process reported in local newspapers
Aarungkhola Bazaar	8	Naya Belhani	1971	275	mainly shop-keepers, land-owners, but also some teachers and govt. officials	high caste people of Hill-origin	town/ market	settlement with a rudimentary form of urban squatting (expanded rapidly after the construction of East-West Highway)
Tamaspur	2	Naya Belhani	1979	1,800	ex-servicemen	mostly Gurungs and Magars	forest	politically volatile settlers; a favourable regularization-deal was believed to be forthcoming
Bagkhor	9	Narayani	1969	385	landless	road-construction labourers of Hill-origin and Tharus and Kumals	forest	settlers were evicted as many as 16 times over the last twenty years in this settlement

Table 10 *(Continued)*

Name of settlement	location		established in	number of households	settler category	ethnicity/caste	land type	other remarks
	ward	Panchayat						
Dhaja	4	Narayani	1984	71	landless	Botes, Tharus and Kumals	forest	settlement developed by people evicted previously in other locations
Kolhuwatar	4	Kolhuwa	1974	40	landless	mainly indigenous people	forest	land certificates provided by FASC officials to 'outsiders' instead of to the original settlers, but most households were still able to cultivate their holdings because of a strong internal solidarity
Hatikhor/ Koelapani-purba	8	Shiva Mandir	1979–83	435	landless	mainly Magars	forest	large-scale eviction and fencing of 'illegal' settlements in the area-requiring many households to settle on the school play-ground and on roadsides
Rudauligaire	2&6	Pithauli	1967	355	landless	Hill-migrants	forest	one of the oldest 'illegal' settlements in the district
Narayanitola	1	Pragatinagar	1973	69	landless	Hill-ethnic groups	forest	settlement developed by road-construction workers and the landless unable to acquire land in resettlement schemes
Sitabas	8	Deuchuli	1970	71	landless	mostly Magars	NRC land	settlement at the outskirts of Nawalpur Resettlement Project developed by people unable to obtain land within the Project
Rajahar Taikot	1	Rajahar	1983	35	landless	mostly Hill-migrants, but also some indigenous people	roadside	constant evictions by Road Department

TABLE 11 *Types of land and the number of illegal settler households in Nawalparasi district*

land type	no. of households	% of households
forest	8772	61
NRC land	2224	15
marginal	2305	16
roadsides	593	4
town/market	475	3
public land	100	1
total	14,469	100

Source: Settler-census undertaken by author

government to the NRC for resettlement purposes, but delays in both forest-clearance and resettlement of selected households provided the opportunity for fresh migrants and landless people to settle 'illegally'. The Shankarpur settlement was the typical case, although a similar situation was also seen in Maker and Daunnedevi Panchayats. The remaining 61 per cent of the settlers were settled on government forest land and they could be found in all the Panchayats with contiguous forest-frontiers. In the Parasi area, from Susta-Tribenighat in the east to Rupauliya, Daunnedevi, Makar, Tilakpur, Panchanagar, Ramnagar and Sunwal-Amrout in the north-west, numerous 'illegal' settlements evolved on the fringes of forests and on the outskirts of old villages. Such 'peripheral' forest-area settlements were equally common in Nawalpur as well, starting from Gaidakot in the east to Banimanipur-Dhurkot in the west. In both areas, most of these settlements were concentrated close to the East-West Highway (thus showing the impact of the construction of roads in the area), but some were far from the road and were located in fairly isolated locations such as Susta, Tamaspur, Kolhuwatar and Sitapur/Dhaja. Other settlements in the northern areas of Dhurkot-Banimanipur (i.e. Chukaha, Chidiya, Kusunde), Deurali (i.e. Jhayalbas/Chapaha), Shiva Mandir (i.e. Chilaha) and Devehuli (Rambas/Sitabas) were similarly away from the road, but were situated on the main migratory paths from the Hills.

The settlements in forest areas assumed even greater significance in that it was only on this category of land that further illegal settlements seemed feasible. There were no substantial prospects for settlement expansion in marginal areas, public lands, roadsides and market/town areas for the simple reason that the availability of land in these areas was limited and most of them were already occupied. In fact, except in some cases of marginal lands, most households settled in such areas only occupied land sufficient for housing and at best had only a kitchen garden. But in the case of forest areas, most settlers possessed at least some amount of cultivable land. Moreover, as has been discussed earlier, there existed very definite possibilities for extending cultivation and settlements in areas designated as forests (see Table 4).

It must be reemphasized that the 'illegal' settlers in the Nawalparasi district represented a sizeable proportion of the district's population and that their numbers also appeared to be increasing. Table 12 shows that by 1967 only 1,730 current settler households reported having settled 'illegally.' In the next ten years which followed, this figure reached 6,691 households. Between 1978 and 1982, there was a pronounced increase in the number of households settled, which was primarily due to the

TABLE 12 *Increase in the number of illegally settled households in Nawalparasi district*

year of settlement	number of households reporting having first settled
1958–62	90
1963–7	1,640
1968–72	3,013
1973–7	1,622
1978–82	5,129
1983–7	2,975
total	14,469

Source: Settler-census undertaken by author

political liberalization experienced during the period between the 1979 Referendum and the 1981 general election.[14] What was surprising was that by 1982 the number of 'illegally' settled households was 11,494, despite the fact that, as indicated earlier, 3,721 households had been legalized and given land titles during this period. Over the period of the last four years (1983–7), some 2,975 additional households were settled. Although compared to the 1978–82 figure, the growth rate in the number of settlers settled during this period seemed to have slightly declined, overall there was still a strong upward trend (i.e. rising from 11,494 households in 1982 to 14,469 households in 1987).

'Illegal' settlement in the Nawalparasi district certainly seemed to be a widespread phenomenon, involving numerous and growing numbers of people. And it was the poorer and assetless households who formed the vast majority of people involved in 'illegal' settlements. There is little doubt that for many poorer migrant households, having left their original place of residence, it was of utmost importance that they at least secured land to build their houses. The lack of economic alternatives, especially as wage-employment in the area remained seasonal and wages paid were low, also created a pressure to cultivate subsistence crops. A slight lessening of repression (as seen during the period between 1979–81), or a little encouragement by the local politicians, was often sufficient for propertyless migrants and the local landless households to venture into 'illegal' settlements and attempt cultivation. In the following chapter, the economic conditions and the actual structure of the poor and assetless households involved in 'illegal' settlements in Nawalparasi district will be examined.

Notes

1. As lands for planned resettlement projects in the district were already allocated by the early 1970s, and as during 1976–85 only 1,488 ha of forest-land was used in regularizing 'illegal' settlers (details in next section), much of the land area under plain-forests remained as in the early 1970s: shown in Berry et al.'s study.
2. This project which was funded and executed by the Indian government involved construction of a dam in the Narayani river, an electrical plant in

Surajpura and two enormous canals, mainly to provide irrigation in Uttar Pradesh and Bihar

3. Between 1954 and 1961, as a result of this high level of immigration, the population in Chitawan district grew by 6.8 per cent per annum (Kansakar, vol. I, 1979: 65)
4. It is estimated that between 1961 and 1971 the population of the Tarai as a whole grew by 137 per cent (NPC/Task Force on Population, 1983:16).
5. During this time, the NRC also launched resettlement projects in Jhapa, Bardia, Kailali, Banke and Kanchanpur districts, in which (including Nawalparasi district) 15,689 households were provided with land (Singh, 1984:18).
6. The main reason for this was the lack of landownership certificates (provided only after 10 years of registration of title) which were sought by banks (including the Small Farmer Development Programme: SFDP) as collateral before extending credits.
7. This government agency was established in 1969 primarily in view of the political need for the government to regularize some of the 'illegal' settlers. Over the years, it has also implemented various royal decrees and government orders relating to land assignment to individuals and specific groups.
8. This terminology is used to identify politicians who participated (and subsequently were supposed to have suffered politically and economically) in the anti-Rana movement during the late 1940s and the early 1950s.
9. Some of the other measures applied in this field included the introduction of the Nepali language and a New Education System to the Tarai, the control of the mass media and other existing communication systems and the appointment of senior zonal and district administrators: i.e. Zonal Commissioner, Chief District Officer (CDO) from people of Hill origins (Gaige, 1975).
10. It is estimated that in the early 1970s, as many as 150,000 Nepalese ex-servicemen from the British and Indian armed forces were pensioners in Nepal (Elder et al., 1975:18). Given this high number and their experience in armed struggles, their political support to the monarchy was undoubtedly crucial.
11. Until 1973, the selection of settlers rested on the concerned project manager. But from 1973 onward, households seeking land in resettlement projects were required to apply firstly to the CDO with a letter of reference from their Village Panchayat. The CDO after 'verifying' the applicant's family and economic background forwarded it to the Zonal Commissioner. The Zonal Commissioner after his approval sent the Application to the RD in Kathmandu. In most cases, the RD did not actually resettle the selected household but needed to contact the NRC. The NRC then, depending upon the availability of land in its ongoing projects, finally decided whether or not and in what area the settler would be given land.

12. For example, on one occasion, it was observed that 'an entire village in Nawalpur was expropriated of their land by a hill-family which threatened to go to the authorities and accuse them of a feigned murder if they did not give their land' (Blaikie et al.,1976:5.143).
13. In this, if the Hill-swidden cultivators are included (who comprised 4,531 households and approximately 25,373 persons), the people involved in unauthorized cultivation of government forest areas constituted about 29 per cent of the district's total population.
14. This development was widely noted throughout the Tarai (see Kaplan and Shretha, 1982).

4

Groups and people involved in illegal settlement

When land becomes scarce[1], competition between all groups and types of households is bound to grow, especially in a predominantly agrarian society like Nepal. Even those with substantial landholdings must have a concern for future generations in a system which divides property equally between male children. In recent years, the rising demand for land has also pushed land prices up enormously. Furthermore, the high production potential of land and the greater economic prospects in the Tarai in general have resulted in an increasing desire for possession of land. As a consequence, there has been an intense competition for the remaining land resources between individuals and between social groups. In Nawalparasi, these contending individuals and groups can be broadly divided into two main categories: (a) people with profit-motives and (b) people seeking land for subsistence purposes (see Table 13).

Profit-Seeking Settlers

In frontier areas, the households which held assets other than the 'illegally' occupied land were known as *hukumbasis*. These households (and their family members, often living elsewhere) possessed other wealth, primarily land, but some also operated shops/businesses and had regular sources of income (e.g. army pensions, employment within the bureaucracy). In the political field, they maintained personal and other forms of contacts with government officials and senior politicians (especially MPs), and sometimes even with the royal palace. These connections were crucial in terms of securing registration of their land plots; or at least in avoiding frequent evictions by the Department of Forest

TABLE 13 *Major categories of illegal settlers in Nawalparasi district*

settler category	number of households	per cent of households
profit-seeking settlers	3,360	23
peasant settlers	11,109	77
total	14,469	100

Source: settler-census undertaken by author

(FD) or FASC, or by the Department of Roads. These privileged settlers formed about 23 per cent of total settler-households in the Nawalparasi district and consisted of four major groups: landowners, ex-servicemen, shop-keepers/businessmen and repatriated Nepalese.

Landowners. During the fieldsurvey, some 797 local landowner-households were found to be engaged in the cultivation of unauthorized areas, particularly where forest land existed near their settlement. This was a common phenomenon both in Parasi and Nawalpur. Firstly, since forest boundaries were not marked in many parts of the district, the landowners in those areas were able to claim land beyond the border of their legitimate plots. Secondly, even in areas where forest demarcations existed, since the forest boundaries were marked only by small wooden pillars, the landowners shifted them and brought the additional forest area under cultivation. Lastly, as houses were constructed on their 'registered land', any possible destruction of houses by forest guards was also avoided. Crops (i.e. those grown within the unauthorized forest areas) were most commonly protected by bribing the forest guards. In areas where the landowners could not avoid conflict with the forest guards, they often used the added forest areas as private pasture land growing fodder and grass used for thatching; therefore, the area looked unclaimed. This strategy remained viable especially for households who owned registered land beyond their subsistence requirements and did not need to use forest land for staple food-crop production.

Ex-servicemen. In view of the government's policy of encouraging ex-servicemen to settle along the Indo-Nepalese border, in Nawalparasi district, the ex-servicemen were originally granted land in the eastern part of Parasi, mainly in Pakalihawa and Narsahi Panchayats. But the continuous influx of ex-servicemen into the area led to the emergence of ex-servicemen settlements in unauthorized forest areas. Many of these households were either legalized in their original place of settlement or encouraged to settle in Susta, and later secured registered land in Tribeni area. However, 165 cases of such households settled in Narsahi Panchayat were not resolved.

The major 'illegal' settlement of ex-servicemen in the district was at Tamaspur (Nawalpur), where as many as 1,800 households were settled. Since their arrival in the area in 1979, these households had launched a relentless campaign to legalize their status (e.g. by directly approaching the royal palace and exerting influence over the FASC). As most of the settler households received pensions and other forms of outside income they did not experience day-to-day economic pressures and were thus able to engage in these pursuits. They also became highly powerful politically. In fact, they were able to influence not only the local politicians, but also succeeded in electing an ex-serviceman as *Pradhanpancha* (the chairman of Village Panchayat) of Naya Belhani Panchayat. This political weight combined with their high level of organization was such that they at least did not need to fear government evictions.

Shopkeepers/businessmen. As mentioned in the foregoing chapter, the development of 'illegal' settlements in market and town areas (formally designated as forests) in Nawalparasi district began with the construction of the East-West Highway. The earlier settlers came into the area to run shops for road contractors and labourers, but once the road was completed ensuring continuing commercial prospects, many new shopkeeper and business households moved in. The bulk of these migrants were from Hill-towns such as Tansen, Pokhara and Bandipur, but bigger grain-merchants and retailers of Indian consumer goods came from larger commercial centres like Narayanghat and Butwal-Bhairahawa. Because of the predominance of the Newar community in trade and business in the country in general, a majority of these settlers were from this community. Other large settler groups were high caste Brahmins and Chhetris who settled in the area for business purposes and because of the better living conditions. During fieldwork, some 457 households of shop-keepers/businessmen were counted as having settled 'illegally' in the district, primarily in Barghat and Aarungkhola Bazaars. Over the last twenty years or so, a large number of these settlers made fortunes both as a result of their business activity and/or because of the enormous increase in the price of the land they held. Many of the earlier thatched-roofed houses have been replaced by large concrete buildings, and many households have invested their savings in buying registered land and in educating their children.

Repatriated Nepalese. These were primarily the Nepalese returning from Burma and Assam. The households settled in Burma were repatriated mainly because of their unwillingness to submit to more stringent legislation on cultural-religious matters, property relations and most importantly, their reluctance to take up Burmese citizenship. But around this time, the Nepalese government was also involved in encouraging them to return to Nepal, making use of the public media to do this (*Gorkhapatra*, May 20, 1964) and accommodating the early returnees in resettlement projects. In the process of resettling these households, the government failed to investigate their economic position; therefore, even the households who returned to Nepal with a considerable amount of wealth managed to obtain land. This easy access to land encouraged a large number of households then still settled in Burma to return to Nepal. As land became steadily scarce within resettlement projects, many of them started to settle in unauthorized areas in the expectation that the government would eventually legalize them. In fact, many of these households were later included in the NRC projects or regularized in their original settlements. But during fieldwork some 55 households of Burmese returnees, most of whom were settled in Makar Panchayat (particularly in Barghat area), had not yet been legalized.

Similar factors seemed to have governed the repatriation of Nepalese settled in Assam. In some cases, even those economically better-off in Assam sold their properties and business to acquire free land in the Tarai. However, since the late 1970s, as a result of a heightening of the nationalist movement in Assam, many also fled into Nepal to escape violence. Aware that the government was involved in formally resettling people in Nawalparasi district, many came to the area in anticipation of acquiring land. But delays in the government's decision to provide land led them to settle spontaneously in unauthorized locations. During the field survey, 88 of such households of Nepalese repatriated from Assam were identified, principally in Sunwal and Swathi Panchayats (see Table 10). It may be added that the Nepalese repatriated both from Burma and Assam consisted entirely of high caste people, and all were originally from the Hill areas. As none of these households were found engaged in wage employment within agriculture during the fieldwork, it was likely that they had other reliable sources of income.

As discussed in the introductory chapter, the control and the use of unauthorized forest areas by wealthier and more powerful groups (together with the poorer ones) is a common phenomenon in many Third World countries. This is particularly typical in Latin American countries such as Brazil, Peru and Bolivia, where large landowners and cattle ranchers have sought to bring a large part of forest land for their direct use, and where, frequently, the original migrant peasants are evicted from their holdings so that the former can have control over these areas as well—often through legal and political manipulations (Foweraker, 1981:14; Gill, 1987:388–9). To a lesser extent, the control of forest land by relatively better-off elements has also been noted in Africa and Asia. For example, in Thailand, it was observed that the landless migrants were pushed further into the forest and their lands were 'taken over by a wave of follow-on agriculturalists who established themselves on the deforested territories with various forms of large-scale commercial crops such as sugarcane' (Myers, ibid: 147). Similarly, in the Philippines, the 'speculator cultivators' undertook 'forest farming on a substantial scale as a commercial proposition' (ibid: 152).

Although the occupation of forest and other types of public lands by wealthier and powerful people has not occurred on the same scale in Nepal's Tarai, profit-maximization rather than a desperate need for subsistence has been the main motive of the groups of settlers described above. These groups continued to have access to wealth and various forms of regular incomes. Furthermore, because of their higher social status (i.e. they belonged to higher and more influential castes) and their general political importance, they were able to maintain useful contacts with the government officials and politicians. As a result, their interests were largely protected even when not regularized with formal land titles. For example, the occupation of forest areas by landed elements, mainly large and powerful landowners, was largely tolerated. The ex-servicemen were able to get political support not only from the local administration and politicians, but their case was also heard at the level of the central government and the royal palace. The settlements of wealthy shopkeepers/businessmen in town/market areas within the forest boundary were also ignored and they were provided with drinking water, electricity, schooling, banking and other facilities. Likewise, the State, particularly the monarchy, attempted to prove itself as benign and caring amongst the repatriated population by providing them with land within resettlement projects, even if most of them seemed economically well-off. In fact, it is these connections with the administration, the politicians and the monarchy which made these settlers significantly different from the assetless and powerless sukumbasis who are the central subject of this study.

PEASANT SETTLERS

Of the 'illegal' settlers in Nawalparasi district, the sukumbasis constituted nearly 77 per cent (see Table 13). These settlers originated primarily from landless or nearlandless backgrounds having neither wealth nor political influence. Many of them also came from socially deprived groups (i.e. low castes). In terms of their original place of residence, these settlers can be classified into three sub-categories.

HILL-MIGRANT PEASANT SETTLERS

Amongst the sukumbasis, the households from this group represented nearly two-thirds of the population (Table 14). On the basis of place of origin of the sampled households, most of these people came from the Hill-areas adjoining the Nawalparasi district. This can partly be explained by the geographical proximity of the Nawalparasi district to their previous place of

TABLE 14 *Classification of peasant settlers on the basis of their origin*

place of origin/category	number of households	per cent of households
Hill-migrant peasant settlers	7,265	65.4
Tarai-origin peasant settlers:		
indigenous inhabitants	2,321	20.9
'plains' people of distant India-origin	1,169	10.5
India-migrant peasant settlers	354	3.2
total	11,109	100.0

Source: settler-census undertaken by author

residence. More importantly, however, this movement was the result of the general economic and agrarian decline. For example, Table 15 shows that prior to their migration, 45 per cent of the households held no land and a further 25 per cent cultivated land below the minimum subsistence requirement. Indebtedness and difficulties in finding wage-employment in agriculture together with low wages remained the main causes of migration for 20 per cent of the households.[2] According to the caste/ethnicity composition (Table 16), Magars constituted the largest category. Apart from the physical proximity to the Nawalparasi plains, their lack of access to irrigated land and subsequent heavy reliance on low-producing swidden cultivation on erosion-prone slopes together with the absence of wage employment in the area were the main factors associated with their out-migration. The second largest group were the *Viswakarmas* (Kamis and Sunars) who constituted about 18 per cent of the total number of households. All the low caste people together constituted 30 per cent of the Hill-migrant peasant settlers. This was, to a large extent, the direct result of the loss of their customary occupations, their previous weak land-base and their alienation in 'planned' resettlement schemes. As for the higher castes, there were fewer of them within the 'illegal' settlement sector, especially when compared to those who had been 'legally' resettled. Amongst the high-caste sukumbasis, however, a

TABLE 15 *Primary 'push' and 'pull' factors with respect to the out-migration of peasant settlers from their previous place of residence*

Push factors	*settler groups and households in %*		
	Hill-migrant peasant settlers	Tarai origin peasant settlers	India-migrant peasant settlers
no land	45	56	67
insufficient and unproductive land/ declining yield/big family	25	–	13
indebtedness	10.5	13	10
difficulties in finding wage employment/low wage/repression by employers	9	11	7
eviction in earlier place/land included in National Park/government projects	–	13	–
other	10.5	7	3
total	100	100	100
Pull factors			
availability of land	46	73	7
availability of wage employment	39	20	90
other (better facilities in the plain–easier terrain/family reunion etc.)	15	7	3
total	100	100	100

Source: personal interviews
sample size: Hill-migrant peasant settlers: 85 households
Tarai-origin peasant settlers: 45 households
India-migrant peasant settlers: 30 households

substantial number of them were equally marginalized economically in their previous place of residence; so most of their savings were spent on what was required for migration and for initial settlement in their present destination. It was also observed that there was a great tendency amongst these households to invest their remaining savings in buying 'illegally' occupied unregistered

TABLE 16 *Caste/ethnicity composition of peasant settler households*

Caste/ethnicity	*settler group and households in %*		
	Hill-migrant peasant settlers	Tarai-origin peasant settlers	India-migrant peasant settlers
high castes			
Brahmin	14	2	–
Chhetri	11	7	7
other	2	2	–
middle castes			
(tribal and indigenous people)			
Magar	28	–	–
Gurung	7	–	–
Tamang	6	–	–
Tharu	–	40	–
Darai	–	4	–
Kumal	–	9	–
Bote/Bin/Mallaha	–	12	17
Mushere	–	11	43
others	2	2	–
low castes			
Kami	18	7	–
Harijan	–	–	20
Sarki/Chamar	7	4	13
Damain	5	–	–
total	100	100	100

Source: personal interviews;
sample size: Hill-migrant peasant settlers: 85 households
Tarai-origin peasant settlers: 45 households
India-migrant peasant settlers: 30 households

land so that any eviction from such settlements was likely to render them totally without assets.

Tarai-origin peasant settlers

These households comprised over 31 per cent of the sukumbasis (see Table 14). These settlers were drawn from (a) the indigenous inhabitants such as Tharu, Darai, Kumal and Bote and (b) the 'plains' people of India-origin such as Mushere, Bin/Mallaha, Harijan and Chamar. In terms of their proportion within the sub-group, the former constituted approximately two-thirds and the latter formed the remaining one-third. About 80 per cent of the settlers from this category were from the Nawalparasi district itself and most of the remaining households came from the neighbouring Chitawan and Rupandehi districts. The migration of these and of the local sukumbasis in and around frontier areas was initially prompted by the establishment of a second resettlement scheme in Parasi and the possibility of spontaneous settlements, particularly in Shankarpur and in Daunnedevi Panchayat. As many as 56 per cent of the households from among these settlers held no land previously (see Table 15). This was partly a result of the government's inclusion of some of their previous customary settlement areas within Chitawan National Park and their eviction from these areas; but it was mainly because of the large-scale immigration of people from the Hills which restricted them from exclusive land use and livestock-raising and the legal and illegal appropriation of their land by more powerful and wealthier people. Their ignorance concerning land laws and the registration of holdings often put them technically in a position of 'illegal settlers', whilst others filed claims and secured the legal title to land. At the same time, fear of repression by the government, the high level of bonded labour arrangements with the local landlords (for whom they worked) and the difficulties in sparing free time from wage-labouring inhibited them from settling in the area when some possibility for land settlement and for acquiring a legal title existed.

India-migrant peasant settlers

The third group of sukumbasis identified were Indian landless settlers. This was a relatively small group, constituting just over 3 per cent of all sukumbasi households (see Table 14). These settlers were essentially settled in Parasi area, especially in Pakalihawa, Narsahi, Kudiya, Tribeni-Susta and Rupauliya Panchayats. But a considerable number of them were also settled at Shankarpur in Sunwal and Amrout Panchayats. These households had migrated mainly from the adjoining areas of Uttar Pradesh and Bihar, and most of them had initially come as seasonal agricultural labourers. Once they acquired knowledge about the availability of vacant land during their stay in the area, they established their huts and subsequently brought the rest of the family to the new location. Often with a view to securing a constant labour-supply, their employers assisted them in finding a vacant place to reside.

In recent years, as the competition for the remaining vacant land grew from all sides, finding land suitable for settlement in Parasi even with assistance was becoming extremely difficult. Furthermore, the requirement of Nepalese citizenship for acquiring a legal title to land, the necessity of paying a considerable sum of money, and the need to have family or political contacts with district politicians in order to secure citizenship was such that many of these households had a very uncertain future. Nonetheless, the local people knowing that vacant land for settlement was not readily available across the border in India believed that it was easier for the poor Indian settlers to find empty land on the Nepalese part of the Tarai. Moreover, the demand for Indian labour on the part of the larger landowners in the Nepalese Tarai meant that at least a certain level of wage employment was guaranteed to them. This made even the smallest possibility of access to land a quite attractive alternative for households who lived in appalling poverty and had little economic prospects in India. Overall, the small size of this group does indicate the limited role played by poorer Indian migrants in the growing land shortage in Nepal.

Peasant Settlers as a Social Group

The above discussion identified three major sukumbasi groups. What needs to be recognized is that there was a certain degree of differentiation in the socio-economic status of the sukumbasi groups involved. For example, the majority of the sukumbasis came from the middle (Mongoloid and the indigenous people of the plains) and the low castes (untouchables) who lacked social prestige and were subjected to differing degrees of social subordination by higher and dominant castes. In terms of their economic position, only half of the sukumbasi households seemed to have been always completely landless in their previous place of residence though all were landless at the time of migration.

Such variations in the socio-economic origins of the sukumbasis prior to their migration need to be related to their current social and production roles and their actions with respect to access to the means of production and to see if such variations have implications for their experiences as sukumbasis. In the analysis that follows the socio-economic condition of the sukumbasis will be examined, particularly by looking into their landholding pattern, crop production, livestock and other sources of income, and by examining the extent to which they were involved in wage-employment. Moreover, the extent to which the sukumbasis have come to regard themselves as a distinct category for social identification and action and separated from other groups will be discussed.

Peasant settlers and their present access to means of production

(a) *Pattern of land-holding*. As settlers, all sukumbasi households occupied some land but did not have title to it. Those settled on roadsides, public lands (especially on school play-grounds) and in market/town areas held land barely sufficient for housing, and at best, they maintained only a kitchen-garden. Table 17a reveals that even amongst those who cultivated some agricultural land, the vast majority of them, (about 71 per cent) cultivated less then 0.3 ha per average household of 6.1 persons. Another 19 per cent of the settler-households possessed land between 0.3 to 0.6 ha. This suggests that in terms of the size of the land held, only 10 per cent of the sukumbasis retained viable subsistent plots of land (0.6 ha or more) during the time of fieldwork. But for various reasons, very few from among this 10 per cent were actually able to derive subsistence from their land.

(b) *Crop Production*. Where possible, the sukumbasis always grew crops. Given the acute food shortage that characterized most of the households, their main priority was to produce staple food-crops, although a few of them in east Parasi also cultivated cash crops, chiefly sugarcane. Amongst the food-crops, wetland-rice, maize and wheat were the principal ones, along with beans

TABLE 17 *Land-holding pattern and production of food-grain amongst peasant settlers*

a. land-holding pattern

land size	no. of households	% of households
less than 0.1 ha	42	26
0.1–0.9 ha	30	19
0.2–0.29 ha	42	26
0.3–0.59 ha	30	19
0.6–0.99 ha	13	8
1 ha and above	3	2
total	160	100

b. production of food-grain

food-grain enough for the period of	quantity (M.T.)	% of households
no food-crops grown	nil	6.2
less than 1 month	0.1 to 0.3	23.5
1–3 months	0.4 to 0.5	41.2
4–5 months	0.6 to 1.0	12.6
6 months	1.0 to 1.5	10.0
7–8 months	1.5 to 2.0	4.4
12 months	2.0 and over	2.1
total		100

Source: personal interviews;
sample size: 160 households

and lentils. But as rice, and wheat to a lesser extent, needed regular water supply and most of the sukumbasis were settled on dry and upland areas, many of them were able to grow only maize, beans and lentils.

Table 17b indicates that over 6 per cent of the households did not realize any food-grain because these households held no agricultural land. For another 23.5 per cent, although they grew some food-grain (0.1 to 0.3 M.T.), their annual production was enough for the equivalent of only one month's household food requirement. The information on production of food-grains suggests that over 70 per cent of the households produced less than 0.5 M.T. of food, which covered their family food needs for less than three months a year. Only 10 per cent of the settlers produced between 1 to 1.5 M.T. which fulfilled their food demands for half the year. It appears that only 2 per cent of the households were able to satisfy food requirements throughout the year. Besides the small plots of land which the vast majority of households held, the complete absence of support services, frequent evictions and destruction of their crops by the forest guards resulted in most of them realizing smaller amounts of food-grains than their land plots' actual physical potential.

(c) *Livestock.* Raising animals is an integral part of the farming system in Nepal–an activity in which the sukumbasis themselves were engaged. But livestock ownership amongst sukumbasis was extremely limited. According to Table 18, among the 160 sampled households there were only 269 cattle, and 69 per cent of the households owned no cows, 76 per cent no oxen and 90 per cent no buffaloes. Furthermore, only 3 per cent of the households possessed more than 5 cattle. These latter households were mostly Tharus who, with their herding tradition, kept large herds of cows at pasture in the forest. The most sought-after cattle amongst sukumbasis were draught oxen, as these were necessary for ploughing their own fields, as well as for undertaking any sharecropping. But as many as 76 per cent of the households owned no oxen. With regard to other livestock, there were only 14 pigs, these being raised mostly by 'lower caste' people and Magars. About 75 per cent of the households possessed some poultry. But with only 526 poultry among 160 households, there clearly was no great possibility of generating significant cash income through sales. Most poultry was consumed within the households for religious festivals and hosting guests. Goats were the only stock which had some marketing prospects, since over 5 per cent of the households owned more than 5 goats. But none of the households owned more than 8 goats, and therefore the income potential from the sales of goats was also limited.

TABLE 18 *Peasant settlers and livestock raising*

a. cattle:	cows	oxen	buffaloes
total number	145	107	17
% of households owning no stock	69.0	76.0	90.0
% of households owning 1 stock	14.0	0.0	6.0
% of households owning 2–4 stock	14.0	24.0	4.0
% of households owning 5 or more	3.0	0.0	0.0
total	100	100	100
b. others:	pigs	goats	poultry
total number	14	126	526
% of households owning no stock	86.0	82.0	25.0
% of households owning 1 stock	12.0	4.0	5.0
% of households owning 2–4 stock	2.0	9.0	4.0
% of households owning 5–7	0.0	5.0	66.0
% of households owning 8 or more	0.0	0.0	0.0
total	100	100	100

Source: personal interviews;
sample size: 160 households

(d) *Other Sources of Income.* In addition to cultivating land and raising livestock, sukumbasis participated in wage-labouring which constituted the major source of their earnings. Some households were also involved in other economic activities. These involved petty trading, artisan services, firewood selling, etc. The seasonal operation of tea-shops and *Bhattis* (eating and liquor houses), and the sale of small amounts of self-produced and purchased fruit and vegetables in the local market were the main forms of petty trading. The setting-up of local workshops for the repair of agricultural tools and kitchen utensils by the settlers from the blacksmith (*kami*) caste was the main artisan activity. Similarly, some sukumbasis specialized in thatching, carpentry and masonry works, undertaking these activities especially over the winter period when wage employment in agriculture was limited. As for outside employment, a few households had family member/s engaged as part-time labourers in road and canal repair work. Finally, during the agricultural slack season many settlers collected firewood from the nearby forest and sold it in the local market or to passing truck/bus drivers on the East-West Highway who transported it to the bigger urban centres. In the case of households settled near the Indian border in Parasi, the sukumbasis themselves carried firewood to the adjoining Indian towns and sold it there.

Table 19 reflects the sources of income and the degree to which the sukumbasis were involved. It can be seen that only 24 per cent of the total sampled households were involved in self-employed, non-agricultural income-generating activities. It should be noted that even amongst those who received outside income, most of this income was of a seasonal or temporary type. Moreover, these activities tended to have such low returns that they were undertaken largely as 'substitute measures' when other employment opportunities did not exist.

TABLE 19 *Major source of outside income besides cultivation, livestock-raising and wage-employment*

sources	no. of households	% of households
petty trading	14	9
artisan service	5	3
personal specialization and skills	4	3
involvement of family member/s in wage-employment outside labour market	7	4
fire-wood selling	5	3
other	3	2
no other income than farming, livestock rearing and wage-employment in local wage market	122	76
total	160	100

Source: personal interviews;
sample size: 160 households

Peasant settlers and their participation in wage-employment

Most sukumbasis therefore were required to sell their labour in order to maintain their livelihood. According to the responses from the sampled households, 95 per cent of the sukumbasis were involved in local labour market wage-employment (Table 20). It must be emphasized that the households who did not participate in wage-labour were not necessarily better-off economically. Disabilities such as physical and mental handicaps, sickness and old age were the main reasons for their not being able to 'hire themselves out'. Table 20 shows that almost 42 per cent of the households had members involved in wage labour throughout the year; another 23 per cent had members participating in this activity for between 6 and 11 months; and 30 per cent of the households relied on wage-employment for up to 6 months a year. The lack of employment opportunities in the area was the main reason given for many of the households not working throughout the year.

Although a few sukumbasis and their household members generated some income through self-employment, for most of the households, agricultural wage-labouring was the biggest and the

TABLE 20 *Participation of peasant settlers in wage labouring*

duration of participation	*before migration*		*after migration*	
	no. of households	% of households	no. of households	% of households
not involved in wage labouring	40	25	8	5
upto 6 months in a year	37	23	48	30
between 7 to 11 months in a year	32	20	37	23
throughout the year	51	32	67	42
total	160	100	160	100

Source: personal interviews;
sample size: 160 households

most reliable employment. Rice-cultivation was the main form of employment, but in certain parts of the district some households were able to secure jobs in wheat and sugarcane production as well. The sukumbasis and their families were involved in all agricultural activities including ploughing, digging, sowing and planting, weeding and harvesting. In many cases, men and women specialized in particular tasks; for example, ploughing and digging were mostly done by men and sowing and planting was carried out by women.

Wages earned by sukumbasis differed from area to area and between men and women. Near the East-West Highway, where settlers could alternatively seek employment in the town centres (where wage rates were higher) and where agricultural labourers were relatively scarce, the employers paid as much as Rs 10 a day without food and 7 to 8 with a snack in the afternoon and a meal in the evening. But in the hinterland wages were very low. For example, in east Parasi (at Pakalihawa, Narsahi, Guthi Surya Pura and Kudiya Panchyats) only Rs 5 a day was paid with no accompanying snacks or meals. This was due chiefly to the intense competition between the local long-term resident agricultural labourers and the sukumbasis for the limited number of jobs that were available. Moreover, the seasonal migration of Indian labourers into the area allowed the employers to keep the wages generally low even at labour-demand peaks.

It can be seen from Table 21 that the most common form of wage-employment amongst sukumbasis was casual labouring in which a sukumbasi-labourer was not bound to the employer. This kind of labour-relationship was practised by 91 per cent of the households. The remaining 9 per cent were engaged in one or another form of 'attached' labour-relationships. The households involved in 'attached' labour-relationships worked on a regular basis for the employer, normally for the entire year, but often they had worked for the same employer for several years. On the basis of the continuous nature of this work and the extension of a work-contract, this form of labour-relationship could clearly be seen as 'attached' or 'permanent' even if not formally 'bonded'. Most of the sukumbasis who were involved in 'attached' labour arrangements were employed as ploughmen and herders and almost all of them were male members of the household,

TABLE 21 *Peasant settlers and types of labour arrangement*

types of labour arrangement	no. of households	% of households
attached/'bonded'	14	9
free	146	91
total	160	100

Source: personal interviews;
sample size: 160 households

although occasionally women and children were also employed as herders or shepherds. However their wages were substantially lower than those of men. In most parts of the district, a ploughman was paid 12 *muris* of paddy (i.e. about 585 kg), and herders were paid somewhat less. Furthermore, wages differed between men, women and children, and also depended upon locations. In this context, the interesting aspect was that generally no cash wages were involved in 'attached' labour arrangements so that sukumbasis had to sell the earned food-grains in order to purchase needed consumer items.

The involvement of the vast majority of sukumbasis in casual labouring demonstrates that the 'unattached' or 'free' type of labour-relationship was the dominant form of wage-employment, despite the fact that the daily wage employment was not secure. In this respect, a few points are worth stressing. Firstly, wages received in casual labouring seemed to be considerably higher than those earned through 'attached' labour arrangements. For example, an 'attached' labourer in a month received paddy worth about Rs 130, whilst an 'unattached' day labourer could make Rs 150 to 300 per month if working most or all days. Secondly, by undertaking 'day labouring', settlers were able to utilize the morning and evening 'free' time in cultivating their own land, because casual labouring usually started from 9 in the morning and ended at 6 in the evening. But 'attached' labourers were required to work for employers throughout the day and they often lived with them functioning also as nightwatchmen. Lastly, as an 'unattached' labourer, a sukumbasi, to some extent, had the freedom to move from one employer to another.

It should be noted that amongst sukumbasis there was not only a high degree of participation in wage employment, but there was also a high level of development of selling labour power as a commodity (since receiving a bare subsistence wage for a long working day in an unattached and free wage-labouring relationship seemed to be the dominant form of labour relations). The most important aspect was the significant increase in the percentage of households involved in wage-employment after migration. For example, before migration, 25 per cent of the households were not engaged in wage-employment whereas after migration and in their present location only 5 per cent of the households were not involved in wage-employment. Similarly, the percentage of households dependent on wage-employment throughout the year increased from 32 to 42 per cent (see Table 20). This suggests a possible qualitative shift in the economic position of the sukumbasis towards being a more homogeneous group after migration.

Sukumbasis and the level of 'group identification'

A few days' stay in sukumbasi settlements was sufficient to observe that sukumbasis had in fact a significant level of group cohesion. Despite some degree of internal social and economic differentiation, the sukumbasis in general identified themselves as 'us' and the people from outside of their settlement as 'others'. The word 'us' and the various contexts in which it was applied however were extremely broad. The sukumbasis mainly identified the word 'us' with 'neglected', 'poor' persons as well as with people who had 'insecure economic resources and future'. Thus, even if the sukumbasis' identification and commitment were first and always with their particular settlement, as 'neglected' and 'poor', they felt some degree of closeness to other 'poor' persons in the area. These involved, first of all, the agricultural labourers. In some cases, it was noticed that the sukumbasis not only assisted the local agricultural labourers with information about available vacant land in their settlement where the latter could come and settle, but they were also often prepared to share some of their occupied land with the newcomers. The best example in this respect was the Bhagra settlement (the outskirts of Aarungkhola bazaar) where, in accommodating fellow-migrants and the local landless agricultural labourers, some of the original sukumbasi households who had initially cultivated over 1 ha, by the time of fieldwork, possessed as little as 0.1 ha. Secondly, sukumbasis kept themselves well informed about fellow-sukumbasis settled in the neighbouring Panchayats and occasionally about the sukumbasis settled in another region of the district. Sukumbasis maintained kinship and marriage ties with sukumbasis from other settlements and they often, especially during the festivals and religious ceremonies, met and exchanged personal news as well as information related to their settlement even if these meetings remained fairly apolitical and, in general, offered nothing more than moral support to each other.

Similarly, the word 'others' embraced a wider context. But basically it was employed to identify, first of all, the landed elements, who were regarded as 'rich' and 'fortunate' and who showed little or no concern for their economic condition and their aspirations for land. Many sukumbasis thought these households would contact them only 'when they were needed'. Secondly, the word 'others' was often used to designate the hukumbasi settlers. There existed a great deal of hostility towards the profit-seeking settlers. The sukumbasis generally did not appreciate these households settling in their settlements. They were considered 'liars' and 'dishonest' about their economic background, and the sukumbasis recognized that these households, with their connections with government officials, would eventually manage to get land title. For that reason, they also considered government employees as 'uncaring' and as 'collaborators' with the profit-seeking settlers. It is in this and other contexts that the sukumbasis included the government employees within the word 'others' and regarded them as 'corrupt' and 'suppressing elements'.

These differences perceived between themselves and the 'others' encouraged the sukumbasis to develop close bonds with the fellow-settlers in their settlement. Many sukumbasis who did not know each other before migration developed a real intimacy within a short period of time. They lived, and often worked, together. In each sukumbasi settlement, I often came across scenes of a group of men smoking together, women gossiping at the water-source and children playing together. People in the settlement were faithful to their settlement, kept secrets among themselves and if any disputes arose they tried to sort them out amongst themselves. The sukumbasis co-operated a great deal with each other in sickness and in family disputes; they also came together to celebrate festivals, marriages and other religious ceremonies. Every settler knew that only through total co-operation and solidarity could he protect his home, crops and possibly acquire the legal title to his land. For this reason the sukumbasis acted together in matters relating to defending their settlement and to the registration of land-title, even though this collectivism was limited to only their particular settlement.

It should be noted that the development of a strong sense of belonging to each other in their capacity as settlers was motivated primarily by the possibility of sharing the resultant gains.

The intention of the foregoing discussion has been to indicate the complex economic and agrarian position as well as the 'group consciousness' of the sukumbasis. A common economic poverty and insecurity is clearly evident as the vast majority of them cultivated extremely small land plots. Furthermore, they lacked not only legal ownership of land, but also effective control and use of it (because of frequent evictions and destruction of their crops). This indicates that the sukumbasis were one of the least independent and lowest agrarian groupings with respect to control of land. Their dependent, non-marginalized position could be seen in their overwhelming dependence on wage-employment and their growing participation in it. This complex experience produced a level of 'group identification' amongst the sukumbasis at the settlement level which showed that they were in general highly conscious of their place in society and their attitudes and actions were marked by a clear realization of their interests. One of the crucial issues in understanding these interests is to determine whether questions of land and labour have been the bases of antagonism between the sukumbasis and other social groups in the area, particularly the landed classes—an analysis which will be undertaken in the following chapter.

Notes

1. It will be indicated later in the discussion that much of this scarcity is artificial, resulting primarily from the State's present forest protection measures and its unwillingness to release the remaining arable land for agriculture.
2. The general economic deprivation leading to the out-migration of Hill people is highlighted in numerous studies (see e.g. Blaikie et al., 1976, Conway and Shrestha, 1981, NPC, 1983, Seddon, 1984).

5

Agrarian relations at the local level

Relations between Settler-Enclaves and Established Villages

A typical settlement-landscape in the Nawalparasi district consists of established villages separated from each other and from the smaller settlement units of sukumbasis often surrounding these villages. It is also common to find the villages and the sukumbasi-settlements separated from each other by a stretch of village agricultural land, a stream, or by a village grazing area. However, this physical separation did not mean that the settlements of sukumbasis were isolated from the social relations that prevailed in the nearby villages, or from the wider socio-economic systems which influenced these villages. As Table 22 shows, some 687 sukumbasi households were settled in public lands, roadsides and the market/town areas. These households maintained close and constant social contacts with larger areas near to their settlements. Another 313 households which were settled within the NRC project area in Amarapuri, Pragatinagar, Deuchuli and Makar Panchayats were equally integrated within the socio-economic sphere of the older formal settlements, as many of them were settled on the remaining vacant land within the boundary of these settlements. Of the 1,854 households settled in marginal areas, many were located near long-established villages and they too formed an integral part of the village social and economic system. Similarly, a considerable number of sukumbasis settled on the fringe of forests were also involved in a great deal of social and economic interaction with nearby villages.

In this respect, it should be pointed out that even those settlements which were relatively far from main villages such as Shankarpur, Susta, Kolhuwatar, Chukaha-Chidiya-Kusunde,

TABLE 22 *Types of land and number of peasant settler households settled in Nawalparasi district*

land type	no. of households	% of households
forest	6350	57.1
NRC land	2218	20.0
marginal	1854	16.7
roadsides	569	5.1
town/market	18	0.2
public	100	0.9
total	11,109	100

Source: settler-census undertaken by author

Jhayalbas/Chapaha, Chilaha settlements were by no means completely isolated from the outside world. They maintained close contact with nearby villages for exchanging commodities and for many of the necessary elements of their day-to-day living. Similarly, during the fieldwork, many sukumbasis were observed travelling to the East-West Highway market-centres to buy necessary goods. They frequently visited weekly and bi-weekly markets where they exchanged their produce (generally a little fruit or vegetables) for other items, or bought new articles with their limited cash. During the slack season of employment, at least one member of most households always went to these markets. Indeed, many of the sukumbasi settlements, although they were physically separated from the main villages and looked like independent subsistence units, operated essentially as integrated parts of larger social and economic systems. In this context, it is relevant to examine a typical sukumbasi household's involvement in exchange relations as distinct from production relations.

Since the sukumbasis held mainly small plots of land and raised only a few livestock, their cultivation and livestock-raising activities were geared primarily towards subsistence. But this is not to say that their entire production was for their own consumption and that they were not involved in any exchange relations. The data on the sources of income amongst sukumbasis suggested that, despite the overall inability to meet food requirements, about 12 per cent of the households were involved in the sale of staple food-crops which they had produced in the past year; similarly, 6 per cent of the households were also involved in selling livestock, mostly goats. In general, the sukumbasis sold crops and livestock in order to obtain immediate cash for non-food items.

Within a sukumbasi household, cash was needed for a variety of purposes. It was required for purchasing basic consumption goods such as clothes, food, dishes and pots, kerosene, cigarettes, matches, soap, umbrellas, lamps and for buying items related to productive activity such as spades, sickles, axes, ploughs and seeds. Similarly, cash was essential for purchasing goods for gift-giving and for social and religious ceremonies (e.g. items given in marriages as presents or articles needed for funeral services and for other religious rituals). Many of these items were available from peddlers and merchants who often visited their settlements and from the markets used by the sukumbasis. Markets, ranging from village-level weekly markets to those in permanent towns such as Barghat, Aarungkhola and Tribenighat were located within walking distance of their settlements. Even though the goods purchased by the sukumbasis remained modest in quantity, a certain amount of cash was always necessary for them to satisfy these needs.

Cash was also needed for emergency purposes such as medical treatment, for paying bribes to forest guards or to cover repayments of loans. Most sukumbasi households relied entirely, or almost entirely, on the earnings from wage-employment for the satisfaction of their cash needs. Wages for casual labouring were commonly received in cash, especially in areas near the East-West Highway where a strong cash economy prevailed. The fact that wages were obtained in cash meant that many households also needed to buy food in the open market. During the agricultural season when work could be easily and readily found, the wages earned covered much of their food requirements, but as the agricultural season lasted only for a few months and employment during the rest of the year was scarce, sukumbasis were frequently pressured into borrowing money in order to meet food and other essential needs during slack labour-demand periods.

Money was borrowed chiefly from their regular employers from the nearby village, to be repaid in the form of labour in the following agricultural season. This situation increased the sukumbasis' dependence on the large landowners. Another important source of credit was the local shopkeepers. These shopkeepers were often employing large landowners themselves or had close social and economic contact with the larger landowners. Once a local shopkeeper knew a sukumbasi through an employing landowner then short-term credit for goods would be given provided the sukumbasi became a regular customer. However, the main disadvantage of buying goods on credit in the nearby shops was that they tended to be more expensive and had a more limited selection of goods than in the larger town centres. The shopkeepers benefited from the fact that the sukumbasis would sell their produce to the shopkeeper immediately after harvest when prices would normally be low. Furthermore, shopkeepers could demand that the sukumbasis work for them (to pay off debts) when other employers also were looking to hire (i.e. over the peak season). Often pressure was put on sukumbasis' children to wash dishes or babysit for the shopkeepers. It was because of these disadvantages that most sukumbasis preferred not to take loans or buy goods on credit. It was understood that any loans or credit would greatly restrict their freedom of choice of work and of employer as well as the marketing of their limited produce. As a matter of fact, 'never trust a shopkeeper' was a common saying amongst the sukumbasis. However, they very often had no alternative when cash had run out but to buy things from local shopkeepers on credit. Thus, the physical proximity and the need for non-self produced items led sukumbasis into a complex pattern of visible exchange relations, with various accompanying levels of co-operation and distrust, with people outside their settlements.

Production Relations

The sukumbasis' overall relations with the local social groupings were primarily in production activities associated with land and labour.

Land issue: The sukumbasis were settled on different types of vacant land, involving village commons, marginal areas, forest land, etc. Most of these lands were situated either within the formal boundary of a long established village or on its outskirts and were previously utilized by local people for a variety of purposes. Given this situation, the sukumbasis needed to interrelate with the local inhabitants in and around their settlement from the very first day of their arrival. This remained vital until they consolidated themselves in the settlement. In chapter three, the major agrarian classes in the Nawalparasi district have been identified, the lowest amongst them being the agricultural labourers and the sukumbasis themselves. As most agricultural labourers did not own any land, the development of an illegal settlement in the area was often viewed as highly favourable to their interest since they then had the opportunity to join these settlements. As for the sukumbasi households already established, the arrival of more people and the expansion in the size of the settlement was considered as a positive occurrence; first, there would be 'strength in numbers' and second, more voices would be joined in making their case heard. Consequently, as far as the land issue was concerned, there existed no apparent conflict between the agricultural labouring households and the sukumbasis.

The remaining agrarian classes in the area consisted basically of small, middle and large farmers. Although there existed a considerable differentiation between these groups in terms of the size of land held, all of them nonetheless owned land. The small farmers' production activities revolved primarily around ensuring family-subsistence whilst many of the middle, and all of the large farmers, concentrated on surplus and profit-generating activities. Laying claim to the vacant land in and around the village to supplement their land-holdings was in the interest of all the farmers. Consequently, there was the potential for all these landed elements to come into conflict with the sukumbasis. A number of such conflicts between the sukumbasis and the landed classes were observed during the fieldwork.

Areas of conflict: The most common cause of conflict between the sukumbasis and the local farmers was the question of access to grazing. Prior to the settlement of the sukumbasis, most vacant lands within the village and in its periphery were used for grazing by the landed groups. When spontaneous settlements of sukumbasis developed in those areas, these groups found their grazing facilities being restricted and steadily diminishing. This seemed to have become acute particularly in old parts of Parasi where no forest area existed in the close vicinity and the remaining vacant land (i.e. village commons, marginal areas), previously used by the local farmers for grazing, was being occupied by the sukumbasis. At Sarawal and Hathiban in Sarawal Panchayat and at Rewa Rehta in Kudiya Panchayat in particular, sukumbasis had experienced constant opposition from the landed groups over the grazing issue. In a personal conversation, the sukumbasis claimed that the local landowners deliberately brought cattle to graze on their crops; and the sukumbasis were frequently accused of stealing grain, fruit and vegetables in the village. Allowing cattle to eat sukumbasis' crops (although it was usually claimed to be unintentional by the cattle-owners) was a very common form of harassment used by the landed groups. Even in the case of settlements within forest areas such as at Bhumahi in Ramnagar Panchayat, at Magarmudha in Tilakpur Panchayat, at Baraulitar in Kumarwarti Panchayat, at Gauripur in Rajahar Panchayat, at Harkapur in Mukundapur Panchayat and at Jhapardi in Gaidakot Panchayat, the sukumbasis said that they were regularly faced with hostility from the landed elements for limiting grazing access.

The second cause of conflict was the land where the sukumbasis were settled. In many parts of the Nawalparasi district, the settlement of sukumbasis in areas adjoining the land of a farmer or in nearby vacant areas had resulted in the effective ending of the possibility of the landed groups cultivating such land. Given the contacts of landed elements, especially large landowners, with government officials and given the ability to obtain ownership rights on the basis of cultivation, taking individual ownership rights of *aelani*[1] land in the past was very much the practice of existing large landowners. For example, during the fieldwork it was learnt that, on one occasion, the local landlord in Ramnagar (who was also the *pradhanpancha* of the time) registered over 8 ha of *aelani* land under his wife's name, despite strong opposition from other groups of farmers. In recent years, it was becoming apparent that unless the landed elements protected these opportunities in one way or the other, the sukumbasis were likely to settle in and cultivate the remaining land in the area. Thus, it was in the interests of the landed elements not to allow sukumbasis to settle in areas potentially useful for themselves and to make their life difficult in cases where the sukumbasis were already settled. In many parts of the district, sukumbasis expressed the view that the landowning elements were in favour of their eviction by the government primarily because they could then claim this land themselves.

Thirdly, the landed elements were also opposed to the development of a sukumbasi settlement in the area because they wanted to monopolize the water sources for their own irrigation. The fact that sukumbasis were settled on the outskirts of a village occasionally meant that they were closer to the existing water sources, and thereby had access to water before the landed elements in the main village. This problem seemed to have emerged particularly in areas where the volume of water from the existing water sources was limited. For example, the settlement of sukumbasis on the outskirts of the Karamghari village in Naya Belhani Panchayat was constantly opposed by the local landed elements because the sukumbasis would have first access to the limited water flowing in a nearby stream. But, as the number of sukumbasi households in the village grew, rapidly outnumbering the larger landed elements, the latter had no alternative but to agree to share the available water with the former. Furthermore, the settlement of sukumbasis on the outskirts of a village or on the fringe of the forest meant that the rain water flowing from the forest must pass their land first. This was particularly important in areas where little or no permanent water sources existed and where the landed elements had largely relied on rain water for irrigation. It was crucial especially for paddy transplantation, since this needed a great deal of water and the transplantation season was short. As a result, this problem was found to be quite prevalent in much of the dryland areas in the district.

Lastly, the opposition to the settlement of sukumbasis from landed elements came over the issue of the future use of forest resources, viz. forest grass and fodder, firewood and timber. This was because, in certain areas of the district, the settlement of swelling numbers of landless and migrant people had resulted in the depletion of many of these resources. For example, some of the local landowners in Nawalpur claimed that much of the available tree-fodder near to the village, which was previously secured for feeding their livestock, was being appropriated by the sukumbasis because of their close proximity to the forest. Similarly, the firewood and timber available near to the village were also used by the sukumbasis for heating and cooking, as well as for constructing houses. In some areas, moreover, the heavy reliance of most of the sukumbasi households on firewood-selling during the slack season of employment had led to a growing scarcity of firewood and timber. This meant that the landed elements had had difficulty in meeting their own requirements, or they needed to undertake longer journeys and use more labour for the collection of firewood and timber. Although the opposition of landed elements to the settlement of sukumbasis during the time of the fieldwork was not observed in any explicit manner, in the long run, (given the process of increasing in-migration and settlement of sukumbasis and their growing use of these resources) a stronger opposition is likely. The landed are even likely to support the official forest protection measures provided these policies result in only the nominal protection of forests and in the determined eviction of sukumbasis settled in and around their areas.

Areas of tolerance: It should be noted that the method and extent to which the landed elements opposed the settlement of sukumbasis in each area depended upon a number of circumstances, primarily the location of the sukumbasis' settlements and the type of land on which they were settled. Regarding the settlement of sukumbasis on NRC's land, in town/market areas and on roadsides, there was no apparent antagonism from the landed elements for the simple reason that the area and size of land utilized by the sukumbasis was small and was not significant in terms of competing uses. Additionally, in the case of settlements adjacent to the forest, as long as the sukumbasis did not take the area alongside the immediate plot-boundary of a landowner and as long as usable forests for grazing, fodder, wood and timber, remained at a reasonable distance from the established village, the sukumbasis were not usually objected to by the landed elements.

As a matter of fact, even in the case of settlements on village commons or on marginal areas, an open and direct opposition to sukumbasis from the landed elements was rare. This was because, firstly, as such lands were deteriorating common property resources, the sukumbasi households were not conflicting with individual access-rights to those areas. This was particularly so when the sukumbasi households were from the local area itself or had been settled in the area for a considerable length of time. Secondly, the small farmers, the majority of the inhabitants in the area, often took the side of the sukumbasis against the large landowners who, through their economic and political influence, were involved in registering much of these areas under their own names. Many of the small farmer households seemed to have preferred that the sukumbasis settle in those areas as against the large landowners' attempts to establish individual claims. This was because they knew the sukumbasis were resourceless and politically powerless and that much of those areas were likely to be monopolized by the large landowners anyway. Since the large landowners had very little or no support and were possibly opposed by other groups of farmers, they were unable to physically evict the sukumbasis from those areas. As a result, the sukumbasis were very often able to settle in village commons and marginal areas and were able to avoid direct opposition.

Besides these factors, in some cases the existence of kinship/ ethnicity links between the landed elements and the sukumbasis had led the former to tolerate the settlement of the latter in the area. This was particularly the case amongst the Tharus and other indigenous communities in the district, and to a lesser extent, amongst the India-origin local people in Parasi.

The protection from *dacoits* (armed robbers) afforded by the new settlements established around their village was another positive feature associated with the development of sukumbasis' settlements in the area. In the southern and western parts of Parasi in particular (i.e. Pakalihawa, Narsahi and Guthi Suryapura in the south and Banjariya, Amrout and parts of Sunwal Panchayat in the west) armed robberies from across the border in India had been a constant problem; obviously the large landowners possessing considerable amounts of wealth were the main targets of such armed robberies. Therefore, it was seen as desirable for sukumbasi settlements to exist as a first line of defence around their village.

Lastly, in villages located near the forest, protecting crops from wild animals was an extremely difficult task. This was particularly so in villages adjacent to the Chitawan National

Park in the eastern part of the district, although to a limited extent this was also the case in settlements close to forests in the northern and the western parts of the district. In the eastern part, the rhinoceros was the main enemy of the villagers, whilst monkeys, deer and wild pigs were a constant problem in the western and northern parts of the district. Again, it was the large landowners who lost the most from wild animals. The absence of strong fences and the high sentences imposed by the government for killing and shooting of wild animals had further worsened this situation. Therefore, allowing the sukumbasis to settle in the areas surrounding their village had become an alternative method of protecting their crops.

Labour issue: As with land, there were complex relationships on the labour front. Most sukumbasi households had to sell their labour to maintain their livelihood. They worked for the middle and large farmers. Most small farmers sold labour themselves and, when the need arose for a small amount of labour such as over the peak season of cultivation, these households usually entered into relations of reciprocal exchange of labour. Therefore, in terms of labour relations, sukumbasis had no direct relationship with small farmers except to a limited extent when they both competed for opportunities in the wage-labour market. Concerning the local agricultural labourers, since these households were attached to individual employers, sukumbasis working predominantly as casual, daily labourers were also not required to relate with them directly. Again, only to a limited extent did sukumbasis and these labouring households clash over the availability of employment. In other words, in a situation where employment was in short supply, some conflict could be expected. However, the existence of a continuing pattern of attached and unattached agricultural wage-employment in the area was such that no serious divisions were actually observed.

It may be noted that over much of the Tarai, the peak period of wage-employment in agriculture is specifically during the paddy transplantation (June–August) and harvest (November–December) seasons. During these periods, the demand for labour is high enough to provide wage-employment to every labouring household. In fact, during these periods, many

Indian labourers migrate to work in the area. But over the winter and spring, very few agricultural jobs exist; as a result, most labouring households are forced to remain out of employment. Hence competition is limited since either virtually everyone or no-one is employed depending upon the season. In the course of fieldwork, it was only in the Rewa Rehta areas that some level of competition amongst the agricultural labourers and the sukumbasis was observed. As discussed in chapter three, this situation developed primarily because the government had transferred from other parts of the district (as well as from Rupandehi district) a large number of settlers who were (due to the poor quality of soil) required to look for wage-employment. This had served the interests of the large landowners who were then able to reduce the wage rates. But despite intense competition for wage-employment and the decline in wages, no open animosity was noticed amongst the labouring households. It appeared that each household knew that their 'neighbours' were there and were competing for employment for the same reasons as themselves and that the large landowners were taking advantage of their difficult situation by paying lower wages.

Areas of conflict between employers and peasant settlers: With respect to the labour issue, it was the middle and the large farmers with whom the sukumbasis were specifically required to relate. These farmers not only owned large areas of agricultural land where wage labour was needed for cultivation, but they also possessed larger herds and flocks of livestock and were also occasionally involved in agro-business and trading. This meant that sukumbasis and their family members (besides working in the field) were able to get employment as herders, cart-drivers, porters, etc. The nature of agricultural wage-employment which existed in the Nawalparasi district was such that the most common form of wage-employment was essentially the 'unattached' or casual type. But this notion of 'casualness' did not mean that the sukumbasis did not want better working conditions. Higher wages, shorter working hours, pauses every few hours, supply of cigarettes, snacks and drinks at work, respect for their working rhythm and their personal dignity were some of the most common wishes of the sukumbasis. In terms of security, the sukumbasis desired that employers provide them with food-loans or financial credit when their crops failed or were destroyed by the forest guards, or when sickness and other 'misfortunes' occurred in the family.

Under these circumstances, various kinds of conflicts arose between the sukumbasis and their employers who were unwilling to meet such demands and desired to obtain more from the labour power they were purchasing. On the part of the sukumbasis, the most common form of opposition was that of 'passive resistance'. This usually involved coming late to work, working slowly and encouraging fellow-workers to do the same, deliberate carelessness with crops and tools and blocking any unpaid supply of family labour to the employer. Landowners claimed that 'illness' was the main excuse given by the sukumbasis for not coming to work or for working slowly. For instance, one employer in Pragatinagar talked of a sukumbasi who informed him that he had fallen ill but who in fact had gone to work for another landowner in the area. Other employers said that they were forced to repeatedly ask the sukumbasis to come to work (especially in cases where wages were given in advance). As to the employers' responses to the sukumbasis, they usually sought to dismiss 'trouble-makers' and undermine all forms of social, economic and political support. According to some of the employers, the sukumbasis would have usually received more money than they earned (often in the form of credit) and, given the sukumbasis' lack of possessions, labour was the only viable form of loan-recovery. Thus, open conflict did not serve the interests of the employers, especially when critical agricultural operations required prompt action. The 'passive resistance' of the sukumbasis in many respects was indeed effective in asserting an element of worker control over the labour process.

Areas of non-confrontation: However, both the sukumbasis and the employing landowners were careful that these conflicts did not lead to an open confrontation. For the sukumbasis, it was paramount that wage employment remained available, primarily as other means of earning a livelihood were limited. Furthermore, what was equally important for them was that the large landowners at least tolerated their settlement in the area. They were conscious that a full-fledged confrontation with the large landowners could jeopardize not only their present access to land, but also their critical base for wage-employment. On the other hand, the shortage of labour over the peak season of cultivation caused the employing landowners to be cautious not to alienate the sukumbasis altogether. It should be emphasized here that in the Nawalparasi district, as in much of the Tarai, the higher demands for labour were created particularly because of:

a) cultivation being based on a short period monsoon rainfall which required a greater labour supply during the peak season of cultivation; some argue that it was primarily because of this need of an assured labour supply for the peak season that the landlords preferred to employ labourers on 'attached' arrangements (Katwal, 1986:12); and

b) the interests of the large landowners in hiring wage labourers for cultivation of their land, rather than in utilizing labour on a sharecropping or tenancy basis, primarily because of their fear of the claim of permanent land-owning rights by tenants.

It is estimated that in Parasi in the mid–1970s, 50 per cent of the labour requirement was satisfied by recruiting seasonally migrating labourers from India (Feldman and Fournier, 1976:459). But in Nawalpur, possibly because of ethnic differences as well as because of the relatively longer distance from the border, the seasonal migration of Indian labourers did not seem as common as in Parasi. There the large landowners largely relied on labourers from the Hills and from among the indigenous population. Moreover, amongst the Tharu landowners, there was a tendency to recruit labourers from within the Tharu community. To an extent, these factors also contributed to seasonal labour market tightness in the area. It must be pointed out that even though the demand for labour was critical only over the peak season of cultivation, it was obviously in the interest of the individual landowners to maintain committed labourers, who could then be utilized in the peak season as well as at other times.

The sukumbasis too were well aware that it was the labour-associated vested interests of the employers which largely restrained the latter from directly opposing their settlement. An attitudinal question (i.e. Table 23) revealed that 82 per cent of the sukumbasis viewed the provision of labour as the major factor in guaranteeing the support of the landed elements. Another 2.5 per cent of the households thought that the need for

TABLE 23 *Main reason why local farmers did not oppose settlement in their area*

Peasant settlers' response	no. of house-holds	% of house-holds
because of their need for our labour	131	82.0
because of their need for our artisan services	4	2.5
other reasons (e.g. same ethnicity, 'we have done nothing to them')	20	12.5
no response	5	3.0
total	160	100

Source: personal interviews;
sample size: 160 households

certain artisan services (e.g. metal work, tailoring) was the main reason for the 'harmonious' attitudes of the landed classes. Since many of these artisan services were part of wider labour relations, about 84.5 per cent of the households clearly saw the labour factor as being the main determinant for the 'soft' attitudes of the larger landowners towards the development of sukumbasis' settlements in the area.

Patron-client Relationship Reinforced

To sum up, it may be noted that although differences of interests between the sukumbasis and the landed classes existed over the issues of land and labour, these differences seldom led to open and direct conflict. As a matter of fact, when asked whether or to what extent they experienced direct opposition from the landed elements during their initial settlement or over the course of their stay in the area, only 2 per cent of the sukumbasi households said that they experienced this opposition (see Table 24). It could well be that some households did not want to openly criticize their employers and 'neighbours'. But the fact that none of the sampled households were involved in any serious physical or legal confrontations with the landed elements meant that, in general, their relations with the landed elements were characterized by non-negative and some actually positive links.

TABLE 24 *Attitudes of local farmers towards the development of settlement in the area*

sukumbasis' views	no. of house-holds	% of house-holds
opposing	3	2.0
non-opposing	157	98.0
total	160	100.0

Source: personal interviews;
sample size: 160 households

Outright opposition to sukumbasis' settlement from the landed elements depended upon their specific locations and the types of land on which they were settled. In general, landowners could see a number of direct benefits from the development of sukumbasi settlements. One additional area in which individual large landowners benefited was on the question of electoral support as many of them held political positions (ranging from local, district to national level) and as a large number of votes were sought during elections, the peaceful settlement of sukumbasis in the area under their patronage often served their interests.

However, the provision of labour was the main advantage derived from the settlement of sukumbasis in the area. It should be noted though that the sukumbasi settlements did not only function as a 'reservoir of labour' for landed elements requiring outside labour. These settlements also provided land for labourers' dwellings (as well as a limited amount of subsistence crop production). So the sukumbasis were tied to the area, and the employers did not need to allocate their own land for labourers' homesteads and could thus pay lower wages than required for full subsistence.

On the other hand, as far as the sukumbasis were concerned, the landed elements ensured them their very survival. Without the income from agricultural labouring, the sukumbasis would have been unable to press for eventual access to the land and the registration of their holdings, and they and their household members would have faced severe starvation. At financially critical periods, many sukumbasi households were able to borrow food and cash from their employers. Also, as many of their employers held important political positions and maintained contacts with the district administration, the sukumbasis, to a limited extent, were able to receive political protection as well. In some cases, the local landlords mediated between the sukumbasis and the forest guards, particularly when bribes were sought by the latter and a degree of negotiation was required. Occasionally, these large landowners also provided information to the sukumbasis about the FD or FASC's eviction dates, so that they could take their belongings out of their houses and fields and flee from the settlement before destruction of their homes and crops took place. Additionally, they sometimes received help from large landowners, mainly those functioning as *Pradhanpanchas*, in writing appeals to the district administration or in obtaining important names of people to whom they could formally appeal for the registration of their settlement.

It is thus evident that the social relations which existed between the sukumbasis and the landowners had elements of a symbolic patron-client type as well as of class conflict. Both social groups had their own specific interests and this generated a continuing level of tension. At the same time, socio-economic and political 'dependence' on each other meant that these tensions did not crystallize to the extent that their relationships were altogether threatened. It has been noted that, in peasant societies, the increasing market penetration and accompanying processes of commercialization of agriculture lead to a decline in the existing level of patron-client relationships (Scott, 1972:7; Dasgupta, 1977:321). The processes of change in the present production relations and the future prospects for capitalist development in agriculture in Nepal's Tarai are disputable, but this is not within the scope of this study. However, the continuous in-migration of the poor and landless and the rapid population growth in the Tarai are such that the labour supply is steadily expanding. Under these circumstances, it is difficult to see how the patron-client aspect of sukumbasi-landowner relationships observed above can last. But during the late 1980s the major area of social conflict did not appear to be between sukumbasis and local landowners. The relationship between the sukumbasis and the Nepalese State, possibly more critical, is the subject of the next chapter.

Notes

1. Any land mentioned in the land survey but no owner identified. Customarily, much of this land was used as village commons.

6

Peasant settlers and the State: land and underlying relationships of conflict

Even though most sukumbasis were settled in relatively remote locations, paid no land-tax and were excluded from the government's ongoing rural and agricultural development programmes, on the question of land no other group in the rural population was drawn into such direct contact with the State than the sukumbasis. In order to understand the manner in which the sukumbasis came into direct contact with the State, it is essential to examine how their actions were in large part determined by their pressing survival needs.

Survival Imperatives and Peasant Settlers' Contacts with the State

It should be stressed that the land which all sukumbasis held first of all provided them with the necessary ground for setting up their shelters. Obtaining land for dwelling was of utmost importance for the bulk of the households, as they had nowhere else to live. About 75 per cent of the sukumbasis who had settled in Nawalparasi district were relatively long-distance migrants. Having left their original place of residence and having secured no other place to live, these households had no other shelter-alternative than to squat on unoccupied land. Similarly, even the local sukumbasis (i.e. originating from Nawalparasi district itself) who entered into casual labour relationships and did not live with their employers needed to find a shelter of their own; and, over 90 per cent of sukumbasis involved in wage-employment consisted of casual or 'free' wage labourers and employers acknowledged no responsibility for providing house plots.

Secondly, for the majority of sukumbasis, the cultivation of land for producing staple food-crops was extremely crucial. Although some households occupied no agricultural land and hence cultivated no crops, large numbers of sukumbasis (about 94 per cent) nonetheless produced some food-crops. It was also true that even amongst those who produced food-crops, only a very insignificant percentage met all their subsistence needs. However, whatever limited amount of food-grains they realized could not have been produced if they had not had access to land.

Thirdly, the establishment of settlements in certain places provided sukumbasis with the possibilities for livestock-raising. For example, the location of settlements in frontier areas was favourable not only in terms of providing easier access to forest for fodder and grazing, but it also enabled many sukumbasi households to find the necessary unoccupied land for building animal-shades.

Lastly, since most households occupied small land plots, produced only small amounts of food-grains and owned few livestock, they had to look for outside employment to sustain their livelihood. Since there existed no wage-employment opportunities within sukumbasi-settlements, most households worked in nearby villages as agricultural labourers. As a result, most of the 'illegal' sukumbasi settlements were located near or within a reasonable distance from the old villages to which they could travel and work. Any alteration in the location and the distance of the settlement was likely to seriously restrict employment prospects for the sukumbasis. Moreover, wage-employment was not available in all parts of the district. For example, in the sukumbasi-colonies near the old settlements of indigenous people and in recently resettled/regularized areas, there existed very little opportunity for wage-employment, as these areas were characterized by smaller land plots with a higher population density. Thus, in order to secure agricultural wage-employment, the proper location of settlements was very important for the sukumbasis.

However, most sukumbasi-households lived in extremely uncertain situations. As most of their settlements were based in unauthorized forest areas, the sukumbasis could be evicted by the government at any time. They could thus lose their shelter, provisions for crop production and livestock raising as well as opportunities for wage-employment. It must be recognized that there was no legal right of cultivation if the land was not formally registered, and in most cases occupation of land was prima facie illegal. Because of this situation, their strongest desire was to acquire a legal title to their holdings.

Although individual sukumbasis wished to obtain legal title to land immediately after their settlement, concrete efforts to gain such a title were usually made after settlements were well established, i.e. after houses were built and a couple of harvests were realized. But most households would have had contact with the State long before this stage. In fact, sukumbasis very often came into direct contact with the forestry officials and the State bureaucracy from the very early days of their settlement and this relationship of conflict continued until they secured a legal entitlement. To understand the degree of sukumbasis' contact with the State and the extent to which they were influenced by State policies, the following aspects must be appreciated:

a) all the forest land on which the sukumbasis were settled remained under the jurisdiction of the central State;

b) all decisions relating to the use of such land (i.e. how it should be used and who should utilize it) were the prerogative of the central State and

c) any legalization of land illegally occupied by sukumbasis was carried out solely by the central State, or agencies established by it.

Figure 3 illustrates, in a simplified fashion, the structure of the bureaucracy which was responsible for designing and implementing the State's forest protection policies. Technically speaking, the remaining forest areas as well as most of the areas currently cleared and settled by the sukumbasis remained under the domain of the Ministry of Forest. It was this administrative arm of the State which was directly involved in formulating decisions as to how much forest land should be released for resettlement purposes or to what extent and under what criteria the 'illegal' settlers should be evicted, ignored or regularized.[1] Some of the responsibilities relating to forestry management and to resettlement schemes were delegated to the Department of Forest (FD), but the FD's functions were by and large limited to

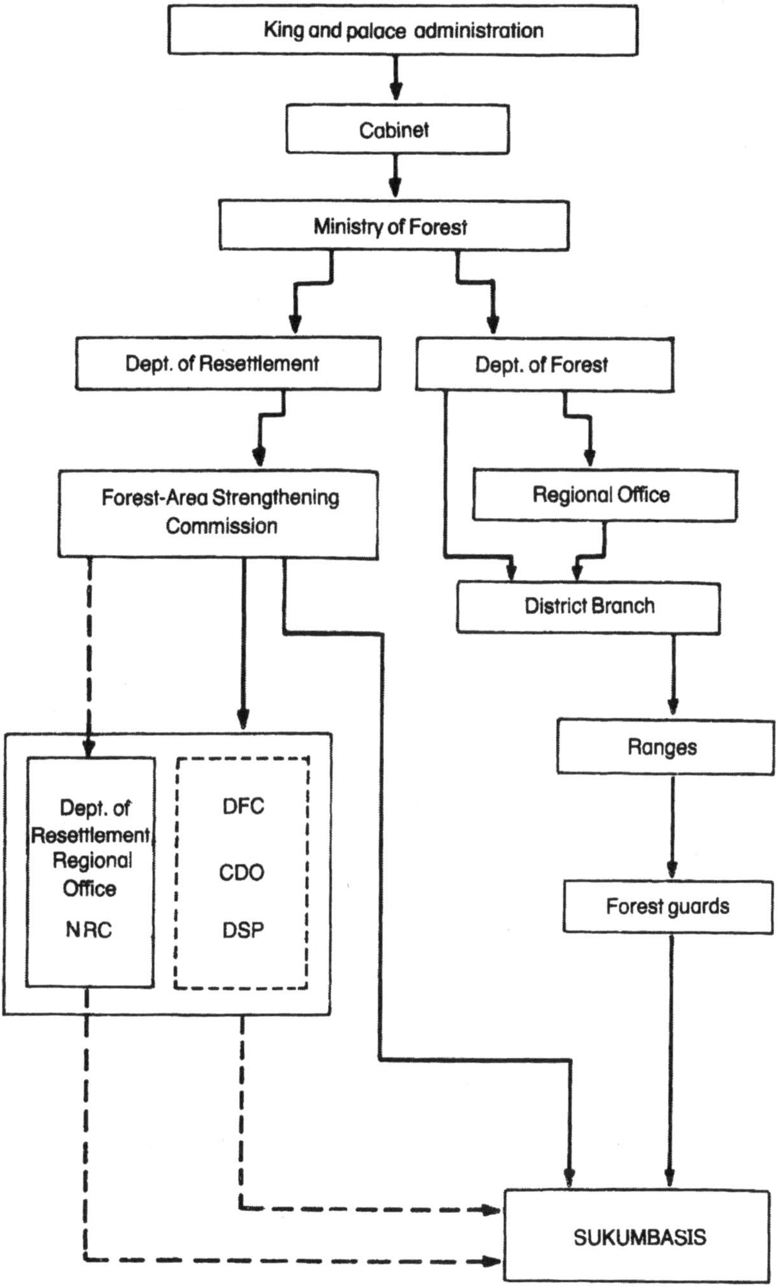

Figure 3. THE BUREAUCRATIC STRUCTURE AND THE SUKUMBASIS' CONTACTS WITH THE STATE

implementation. To facilitate the implementation of forestry policies, there were regional branches and district level offices which were responsible to the FD central office in Kathmandu for their day-to-day activities. In Nawalparasi, the headquarters of the FD district office was located in Parasi and operated through three forest ranges based in Sunwal, Dumkibas and Kawasoti. In the late 1980s, in each range there were provisions for 12 regular unarmed forest guards (thus totalling 36 in the district as a whole). Besides these unarmed forest guards, there were also 19 armed forest guards, who were directly connected to the FD district office.

With a view to controlling encroachment in a co-ordinated manner, alongside the above administrative hierarchy, the Forest-Area Strengthening Commission (FASC) was formed under the Department of Resettlement (RD). As has been noted earlier, the FASC was composed of a Commissioner and two members who were appointed by the government at the national level. In addition to the Commissioner and these two members, the Chief District Officer (CDO), District Police Superintendent (DSP), District Forest Controller (DFC), Director of the Department of Resettlement Regional Office (RDRO) and Project Manager of Nepal Resettlement Company (NRC) were included as members of the FASC. As a result, the local administration, police and forest officials all played a role in the FASC's operations.

In addition to this, what made the FASC more powerful was the fact that it was the sole authority in matters relating to the registration of land occupied by the settlers. The FASC had the power not only to decide which of the settlements within the forest boundary should be registered, but since the early 1980s, it had also gained the ultimate right to register marginal and wasteland areas.[2] Thus, without the approval of the FASC, no land in the district could be registered in the private or public sector. In this context, it should also be noted that even the forest land which had already been released by the Ministry of Forest to the NRC for resettling people was expected to be used according to the recommendations of the FASC. Similarly, the RDRO, which was previously involved in regularizing the settlers, was required to seek prior approval from the FASC and had no independent authority to legalize settlers' claims. Thus it was virtually impossible to challenge the position of the FASC in the district from within the State and para-State apparatus; and with regard to the 'fate' of the sukumbasis, in particular, this agency remained extremely powerful.

As far as direct contact with the State at the local level was concerned, the sukumbasis came in conflict with the unarmed forest guards, who frequently intimidated them and asked for bribes. As these guards were an integral part of the wider bureaucratic structure they were able to request the higher authorities in the district headquarters to evict the sukumbasis and to arrange for the fining and imprisonment of sukumbasis by the Rangers and the DFCs. Moreover, the forest guards held wide discretionary powers to seize the implements of the sukumbasis and arrest them.

Apart from the regular unarmed forest guards, the sukumbasis also confronted the armed forest guards, principally when evictions took place. The police as well as the *gaida gasti* (National Park Guards) came to the aid of the armed forest guards during evictions. Additionally, to discourage the sukumbasis from settling and consolidating their position, occasional arrests were made through the local administration, allegedly for disturbing 'law and order'. The local administration became especially sensitive when sukumbasis were suspected to have come in contact with underground political parties or began to make their demands collectively.

In many of these circumstances, the sukumbasis were drawn into direct contact with the State. Given the State's fundamentally negative attitude towards the registration of land, the official forest policies were regarded by the sukumbasis as 'unsympathetic' to and 'uncaring' of the poor, and the men executing these policies were regarded as 'arrogant', 'dishonest' and 'corrupt'. On the official side, the sukumbasis were blamed for deforestation, and their claim to land was considered as 'hunger for property'. This situation led the sukumbasi-State relationship to a virtual break-down in many locations. What seemed more important was that these conflicts were not taking place in isolated clashes, but were structurally escalating.

Official Responses Towards Peasant Settlers' Demand for Land

There was no doubt that the establishment of a high-powered agency like the FASC was a clear manifestation of the State's growing concern over forest protection measures. In fact, the FASC's policies not only included the protection of forests from further illegal settlements, but also the bringing back of settled areas under forest by removing the settlers. For example, in one of the government's publications the main functions of the FASC were stated as follows:

> a) to evict people from areas where they have settled encroaching forests and
> b) to strengthen forest and to safeguard it from further encroachment[3] (Ministry of Forest and Soil Conservation, 1980: 12).

Against the background of these objectives, the official response towards the sukumbasis can easily be envisaged. The sukumbasis were constantly intimidated and evicted from settlements or threatened with eviction without any regard for their subsistence needs. And government policies were also marked by increasingly harsher measures.

First of all, a look at the exercise of violence that appeared legitimate within the prevailing legal and political system is useful. As discussed in chapter two, in 1960–after having abandoned a universal-franchise, multi-party democratic political system–the monarchy with a view to re-affirming its central political position introduced a partyless Panchayat political system. But the final consolidation of its new position and of the Panchayat system were far from easy due to the political activities of the opposition parties and the growth of popular social movements involving students, intellectuals, urban workers and peasants. To curb these political and social movements, the 1960s saw the introduction of various special legislation. Legal (and extra-legal) measures were taken involving control of political organizations, meetings, publications, restrictions on possession of arms, unrestricted police searches and detention without trial (Amnesty International, 1986). As far as the sukumbasis were concerned, this body of legislation meant increasing difficulties in organizing themselves and in maintaining contacts with the wider political and social movements in order to press the government on the issue of legal title to land. Furthermore, the isolation from the wider political and social movements made them extremely vulnerable to intimidation at the local level by government officials.

As the illegal settlements grew rapidly, the effective expulsion of sukumbasis from their settlements became a formidable task for the government. In Nawalparasi district, this seemed to have become critical especially after 1981 when the government decided that there should be no new settlements north of the East-West Highway and sought to evict a large number of sukumbasis settled in those areas. In order to co-ordinate these eviction activities, the CDO and the DSP were made members of the FASC and the eviction of sukumbasis was regarded as part of their overall responsibility. This allowed the FASC to mobilize all of the coercive forces of the State under centralized administrative and operational control, and assured two important pre-conditions.

Firstly, a sufficient number of police officers became available (in addition to regular and armed forest guards) to combat the growing encroachment into the forest and to assist in evicting the sukumbasis. In this respect, it is interesting to note that between 1977/8 and 1986/7, the police force in Nepal grew twofold, from 12,000 to 25,000 (The Military Balance, 1977/8:62 & 1986/7:164). Such an increase in the police force can be attributed to the government's mounting concern for law and order. As far as the question of rural law and order was concerned, the sukumbasis became one of the focal points for the local administration, primarily because (a) it was thought that there was a great tendency amongst the sukumbasis towards lawlessness i.e. open defiance of the State's forest protection policies and hatred of officials; (b) there was a continuous expansion in the number of sukumbasis settling in the area and (c) there was a fear of the involvement of the sukumbasis with opposition political parties (personal conversation with a senior government official at CDO office, Parasi). Furthermore, any failure to maintain law and order in the area over people who flagrantly breached the law would have put the credibility and careers of the local administrators at stake. Because of these reasons, the local administration wished to ensure the presence of a strong police force. This also suited the FASC, as it guaranteed a strong police force in reserve and on call when required.

Secondly, the local administration had wide discretionary powers such as the right of the police to search, arrest, shoot on sight and establish independent tribunals to impose fines and imprisonment in matters relating particularly to law and order. Since the sukumbasis' attempts to settle down in unauthorized areas could be interpreted as threatening to law and order, the FASC was also able to notify the local administration or utilize its power when such measures became necessary.

Ever since the early stage of development of 'illegal' settlements in Nawalparasi district (i.e. from the early 1970s onwards) there has been a continuous stress on the use of more repressive measures to handle the problem, even where scope for land settlement existed. For example, during this period, the government had been setting up relatively large-scale resettlement projects in the western Tarai (i.e. Banke, Bardia, Kailai and Kanchanpur districts), but instead of accommodating sukumbasis in these planned resettlement schemes, or providing them with legal entitlements, evidence suggests that the government took a predominantly negative attitude towards the sukumbasis. By the mid-1970s, the RDRO based in Butwal, which was then also responsible for the regularization of settlers in the Nawalparasi district, maintained an armed police squad of 14 persons to control illegal settlement (Department of Resettlement, 1974:217). Similarly, recommendations were made to enable the Director of the RDRO to use the Public Security Act (ibid: 218) to arrest and imprison any illegal settler without the authorities having to provide any proof of forest destruction; moreover, the settler would have no right of appeal.

Parallel to the provision of an armed police squad for the RDRO, the FD Regional Division in Butwal was separately provided with more than twenty armed forest guards for similar purposes (ibid: 196). In times of need these armed forest guards could be deployed by the FD district office and the FASC. Also, the armed police squad previously placed under the RDRO was transferred to the FASC. Besides these armed police and forest guards, the government likewise increased the number of regular forest guards in the area. For instance, by the late 1970s, there was already a provision of one forest guard for every five square miles both in Nawalparasi and Rupandehi districts (personal communication with a senior forest official in Bhairahawa).

The 1980s witnessed not only an increase in the numbers of regular forest guards in the area, but also an increase in their powers as well. The Forestry Act gave the forest guards very wide powers of arrest with regard to the settlers as well as the power to seize their implements. Similarly, the Rangers–the immediate superiors of the forest guards–were empowered to fine settlers up to Rs 50, and recommendations were made to give them the right to impose fines up to Rs 180 (FASC, 1984:4).

Similar recommendations were made for increasing fines for the unauthorized cultivation of forest area. Previously, sukumbasis could have been fined Rs 200 for each *bigha* in the plains and Rs 50 per *ropani* in the Hills. But since 1984, the government sought to increase this amount to Rs 2,000 per *bigha* in the plains and Rs 500 per *ropani* in the Hills, a fourfold increase (ibid). As a matter of fact, on the basis of the existing incomes in the area, sukumbasis would have surrendered more than half their annual income to pay one fine on a *bigha*.

In addition to the above fines, there was a provision for punishment depending on the quantity of timber and wood destroyed through clearing the land for agriculture. The Act stated that this could be as much as Rs 2,000, along with imprisonment for a maximum period of one year (Ministry of Law and Justice, vol. VII Kha, 1986a: 172). This clearly showed the severity of the punitive measures intended to be applied against the sukumbasis. Although fines and imprisonment were applicable to any person involved in the theft of wood and the 'destruction of forest', it must be emphasized that sukumbasis were the group most liable to these forms of punishment as they resided on the 'forest land' itself; thus they could be arrested at any time. Other groups of people living outside the 'forest land' had an advantage in that tracing them and establishing their offence was more difficult; therefore, many of them were able to avoid persecution. In the course of this research, it was found that in some cases the Forest Act clearly favoured richer elements. For example, the Forest Act explicitly stated that the bigger means of transport such as tractors, lorry and trucks would not be seized (ibid:164). As noted above, this was not the case with the hand implements used by the sukumbasis and other groups of small farmers. Secondly, by not making any distinction between the clearing of forests for subsistence and for profit, the government allowed the people involved in large-scale timber-smuggling to escape with relatively insignificant punishment.

I shall now examine the level of persecution that the sukumbasis actually suffered in Nawalparasi district, even though it was extremely difficult to determine the exact degree because the coercive measures applied to sukumbasis varied greatly between the type and location of settlements; furthermore, the circumstances were often not a matter of public record. Therefore, this discussion is primarily based on the responses obtained from the sukumbasis, combined with the knowledge gained through direct observation.

Intimidation. The sukumbasis were intimidated in various ways. Given the lack of political representation and the situation of complete defencelessness, they lived under constant fear of being suppressed by the government. The primary form of intimidation was necessarily associated with regular threats of eviction; and the local forest guards were the main elements of intimidation. According to the sukumbasis, the forest guards often came to their settlement and alarmed them by saying 'you have not got long to stay here'. Besides this, rumours spread in frontier areas that plans had been prepared in Butwal or Parasi to evict all the sukumbasis in the district, which caused consternation amongst them. If someone saw armed forest guards and forestry officials passing by on the East-West Highway during the day, that became the main subject of conversation in the evening. They feared that the government had actually started evicting in another area and soon it would be their turn. 'Are they not going to let us stay under a shelter until the *barsat* (monsoon) goes? Are they not going to let us have even the standing crops? Where shall we go if they evict us?' Questions like these constantly haunted the sukumbasis.

Demand for bribes. In frontier areas, corruption was an established feature of life. The most common story was that the forest guards would start asking for bribes once the sukumbasis began to settle in an area. The forest guards mostly demanded cash, but along with it, they regularly took chickens, vegetables and fruit; they also occasionally demanded free alcoholic drinks and food. These bribes were so frequently demanded that if the sukumbasis' chickens died of disease or their vegetables and fruit suffered insect damage, they made jokes saying that 'they must have been exposed to the greedy eyes of the forest guards'. Similarly, when sukumbasis were arrested, an illegal payment was almost always required, especially to escape from further heavy fines and imprisonment. Furthermore, if a selection or land registration procedure started, the sukumbasis were required to pay cash to resettlement and FASC officials (the most common going rate in the early 1980s was Rs 500).[4] It is interesting to note that as corruption was an integral part of the land settlement and regularization process and as the government employees were directly or indirectly (through intermediaries) involved in such activities, most sukumbasis viewed this as a part of the existing repression formally instigated by the government itself.

Physical harm to people and their cattle. Although, unlike in other Tarai districts, no incidents of actual killings of sukumbasis[5] were noted in the Nawalparasi district, their relationship with the State was by no means non-violent. Incidents of shooting, stabbing and beating of sukumbasis by the armed forest guards and the police were reported in the area. Many of the sampled sukumbasi-households said that they had been assaulted by government officials (mainly forest guards). In order to escape from beatings, arrests and other persecutions, most male sukumbasis would attempt to flee into adjoining forests during visits by forest guards. But they were very often chased into the forest and were beaten up and arrested. While the men ran away, it was the women and children who remained behind to face the officials in the hope that the forest guards and the police would not be too hard on them. Consequently, women became vulnerable to abuse and children to assaults.

During evictions, livestock were also harmed. Some sukumbasis, especially in Nawalpur area, told stories of how the forest guards and the police set their cattle-shades on fire whilst animals were tied inside; and how, as a result, the whole area smelled of burnt flesh. Most households had seen their cattle being stabbed by bayonets attached to the muzzle of the gun used by the forest guards, or being beaten by riot-sticks. Many of them thought that these bayonets were poisoned since their cattle often died of horrible wounds; others claimed that their cattle were attacked so violently that pregnant cows and buffaloes had premature and defective births.

Destruction of houses, belongings and crops. The destruction of houses was the most common and widespread form of repression; an overwhelming percentage of the interviewed households had experienced destruction of their houses. For example, over the last twenty years, houses of sukumbasis in Bagkhor settlement in Nawalpur had been demolished as many as 16 times (see Table 10). In the course of eviction, houses were not only wrecked but very often they were burnt down as well. The rationale was that if houses were not burnt down, the sukumbasis would utilize the same material to build new ones and would not leave their settlement. Because of this experience, many households had moved not only within the local areas but also to another locality of the district (e.g. fromNawalpur to Parasi) in search of safer and more congenial places. But many of them had suffered destruction of their houses in almost every place of residence. Some of those who were unwilling to carry on settling in forest areas built their huts on the roadsides. Such was the case in Bhaisakhori, Rajahar and Lokaha-Purba. However, these huts were regularly demolished by the Road Department.[6]

During their evictions, many of the households also experienced destruction of their belongings. As eviction agents often struck without prior warning, the sukumbasis had no time to remove belongings from their houses before they were set on fire or destroyed. Some of the commonly destroyed belongings were kitchen utensils, agricultural tools, clothes and, in some cases, the food-grains stored both inside and outside of the house.

Apart from the destruction of their houses and belongings, most of the households experienced loss of their crops as well. During evictions, the forest guards and the police not only smashed the vegetables and fruit grown in the kitchen gardens, but they also destroyed cereal crops grown in the field. In the 1970s, especially in Nawalpur, the local administration used elephants to destroy crops grown by the sukumbasis—primarily maize–as it was difficult for the forest guards to destroy this crop swiftly. But, government officials commonly used grazing cattle to destroy crops. In some cases, the sukumbasis' own cattle were used to trample the crops.

Arrests, fining and imprisonment. Given the government's general unwillingness to provide relevant data, it was difficult to assess the actual scale of arrests, imposition of fines and imprisonment that the sukumbasis suffered over time. One source however revealed that between July to December 1986 alone as many as 33 'forest destruction' and 'illegal' settlement related cases were dealt with in the district headquarters in Parasi (personal communication with the FD district judge). This official declined to give further details concerning the identification of individuals, the location of their settlements and the charges that were made against them. The above figure nonetheless gave an idea of the degree to which the settlers were subjected to arrests, fines and imprisonment. It must be added that the sukumbasis were also arrested and fined by the local forest Rangers as well as by the district administration (i.e. CDO). It was not possible to obtain these records.

Amongst the sampled households, a few had also experienced arrests. Many of these individuals had also been subjected to fines and imprisonment as well. Those who were not fined and imprisoned were released after a few days of detention. Here bribery played an important role. By giving bribes, some sukumbasis avoided heavy fines and prison sentences; and with lesser offences, some were acquitted. But where they failed to pay bribes, fines and prison sentences became punitive. For example, some of the sukumbasis from Bhutaha settlement who were arrested and imprisoned for over six months claimed that they were kept in jail primarily because they were unable to meet the amount of bribes demanded by the government officials. As a matter of fact, in all cases where arrests were followed by fines and imprisonments such as in Baruwa-Bankattiya (Singaha-Bandevi), Jogikuti and Bagkhor, the sukumbasis claimed that they were fined and imprisoned primarily because they did not satisfy the bribe demands made by the government officials.

The above empirical evidence suggests that the nature of government response, both formal and informal, to the sukumbasis' aspirations to land, was fundamentally coercive. It will now be explored how the government's failure to understand the sukumbasis' basic needs and its reliance on more repressive measures generated an increasing degree of resistance amongst the sukumbasis.

Popular Discontent of Peasant Settlers

Rural social movements are poorly documented in Nepal. Rural clashes have not entered the public domain unless they involved large-scale participation or significant casualties. The lack of literacy, an urban-oriented press and the government's censorship regulations have resulted in very little documentary evidence of events involving the sukumbasis. Even those events that have been reported, the background and causes of these incidents have been presented in a distorted fashion so as not to appear critical of the government. Moreover, as is characteristic of agrarian movements which tend to be limited in time and space (Paige, 1975:90), many of the incidents involving the sukumbasis' open conflict with the State lasted for a short period and were limited to a particular settlement or to one Panchayat, thus creating further difficulties in the documentation of individual incidents which might in the aggregate have signified a powerful social movement. Nonetheless, the recollections of the sukumbasis and a few accounts by non-sukumbasi contemporary observers (e.g. the nearby villagers) as well as some newspaper reports gave important clues as to the forms, if not to the full extent, of the sukumbasis' resistance to repression.

Indirect Resistance: As the vast majority of sukumbasis were fully occupied with the daily struggle for survival and as any direct confrontation with the State was likely to prompt further repression–what one writer calls 'the expected repression' (Scott, 1985: 246) opposition to government eviction and other coercive measures was generally expressed in an indirect manner, often subtly and principally at the individual level.

An indirect rejection of circumstances was expressed in various forms. The psychological fear of eviction and future insecurity made many sukumbasis exhibit strong negative emotions and self-destructive tendencies. One of the local newspapers carried a report that some sukumbasis attempted to commit suicide by taking poison because of extreme hardships created by the government's frequent evictions (*Tarka*, 10 July

1978). One of the common sayings of the sukumbasis was that 'the government has no eyes' and therefore it could not see the extent of their pain and fear. It was because of this and other perceptions that the sukumbasis, particularly men (from alcohol-imbibing castes as well as those not observing their rituals properly) after some drinks, used abusive language aimed at government employees and institutions, whilst women (from all castes) frequently cursed them behind their backs.

The sukumbasis also had open contempt for the government. Government officials were not only distrusted and disrespected by the sukumbasis, but they were also the main cultural target of their hatred. Within sukumbasi-settlements, there were numerous jokes and songs about the corrupt behaviour of the forest guards and government officials. Officials, especially the forest guards in the area, were individually known by insulting nicknames and rumours were often spread about their sexual habits. When a forest guard or senior forestry/resettlement official sought to visit the area, children often encouraged dogs to bark in order to discourage them from entering the settlement. Women mocked them in their faces with indirect insults, for example, by saying that 'if one has eaten too much one will have diarrhoea', meaning that too much asking for bribes would do them harm. As major bribes were demanded from male sukumbasis only, the men, for their part, usually kept away from the forest guards and government officials. If confronted, at first they ignored them, kept quiet, or simply said 'don't know' or 'don't have' and secondly, if possible, they refused to give money and food on various other grounds. For example, in one extreme case in Banimanipur village in Nawalpur, the local forest guard told me that he did not drink water or eat food in one of the 'illegal' settlements in the area as he had heard of sukumbasis there giving previous forest guards water mixed with a certain type of indigenous slow-poison, known as *kukhat*, and food affected by witchcraft. Of course, it is possible that such rumours were passed around by the sukumbasis themselves in order to discourage the forest guards from visiting the settlement.

Direct Resistance: In addition to these indirect expressions of discontent, the sukumbasis were also involved in more direct forms of resistance.

In *Struggle for Basic Needs in Nepal*, the authors refer to an example of some thirty sukumbasi households in the area applying jointly to the CDO, albeit unsuccessfully, for the formal title to their land (Blaikie, Cameron, Seddon, 1979:66). This type of action was also identified in this current research. As there were no standard government forms that the sukumbasis could obtain and complete for the registration of land, such applications to the authorities were sent merely in a letter form. In these letters they listed names of heads of household, mentioned the date of their settlement and the small size of the land they cultivated, together with the marginal location of their settlement in order to indicate that their settlement had no damaging effect on the forest. In their desperate attempt to gain the consideration of the authorities, in these letters (often prepared with the help of a local landlord or teacher, as most sukumbasis could not read and write) they also described the appalling poverty and misery they suffered and the extreme importance of the piece of land they cultivated. These letters were addressed primarily to the CDO or to the Commissioner of the FASC, but a few of them were also written to the king.[7] But the sukumbasis rarely received replies from the authorities. In short, even though these letters had no perceptible impact upon the securing of formal title, they were written and sent collectively by the sukumbasis of a settlement as a whole, so the direct and co-operative nature of their action must be recognized.

In pursuing their applications and in order to press the authorities for registration of land, sukumbasis also occasionally sent 'delegations' and paid informal visits to government offices in Parasi. Such 'delegations' and informal visits were combined with their annual shopping, and were undertaken mostly during the agricultural slack season. During these visits, they would seek to see the authorities concerned to request some action in their favour but they were frequently ignored by government officials. For example, during a fieldwork visit to the FASC office in Parasi, I observed a group of seven sukumbasis from Nawalpur hesitantly entering the office building and asking if they could appeal their case to the Commissioner. The clerk at the desk responded that the Commissioner was occupied with some other important matters. The sukumbasis waited uneasily for some time and finally left the place reluctantly leaving behind an application. The clerk did not even bother to look at it; he threw it in one of the files, with a typical remark that 'they think by just coming here they will get the land'. Similarly, on another occasion at the NRC project office at Dhanewa, it was noted that some sukumbasis were standing outside the Manager's office for almost the entire afternoon to request him to recommend their case to the FASC. The response of the Manager was to ignore their presence, and he later dismissed them by saying, 'they just bother me too much, come in a group, sit here the whole day and give me no peace' (personal communication).

However, not all these 'delegations' and informal visits were unassertive. The sukumbasis sometimes made their demands more effectively by surrounding the government officials and refusing to leave the office unless some immediate actions were taken. Such actions were particularly common during the Referendum period when, according to the Manager of the NRC, 'the settlers frequently raided the office in large numbers and threatened even our lives' (ibid). For example, it was during this time that a similar case was reported in Dhangadi (the headquarters of Kailali district), where about 500 previously evicted sukumbasis invaded the office of the Zonal Commissioner and insisted that they 'will not leave the land, will rather leave lives'[8] (*Samaj*, 24 May 1980). The response of the Dhangadi authorities was punitive; the sukumbasis were ruthlessly beaten up and as they still refused to disperse, the police opened fire on them. Although nobody was reported to have been killed by the shooting, there were serious injuries reported, and according to the above newspaper, 'Dhangadi was completely terrorized and the town was closed until the late afternoon'[9] (ibid).

Besides sending applications for the registration of land and following through with delegations and informal visits and other more assertive means (e.g. surrounding of the government officials), in some cases, the sukumbasis in Nawalparasi district were also involved in a legal battle with the State. The first case in which the sukumbasis were involved in a legal dispute with the State was related to the legal status of the land which they had cleared and cultivated in areas of the old zamindari jurisdiction. Prior to the mid-1970s some areas in Nawalpur had been administered under the zamindari system. Under this system, the zamindars took advantage of the growing demand for land and encouraged migrants and landless people to settle down on land within their jurisdiction, which was then mostly under forest. The sukumbasis paid some modest price for the land, together with the land tax to the State through the zamindar. It was on the basis of their possession of land and the payment of land tax to the State that the sukumbasis claimed ownership of the land. But the FD and the FASC refused to recognize the sukumbasis' demands and maintained that those areas should remain within the forest boundary. As a result, the sukumbasis were frequently evicted. But the sukumbasis (along with the former zamindars) on their part became involved in a continuing legal battle with the State. For example, in Dumkibas area, at the beginning of 1987 a legal dispute between the sukumbasis and the State reached the Supreme Court. Similar kinds of legal cases were also being conducted by sukumbasis in Tamasariya and Shiva Mandir areas. It must be noted that, where sukumbasis' interests coincided with those of the former zamindars, these legal battles were more effective, since a large part of the financial and other essential resources were provided by the former zamindars themselves.

Another example in which the sukumbasis entered into a legal dispute with the State was in the case of the Bhutaha settlement. In this settlement, the original sukumbasis were evicted (some of them even being imprisoned) and the land cleared and cultivated by them was allocated to merchants, road-contractors and to local powerful elements by the FASC. This led not only to physical confrontations between the sukumbasis and the land beneficiaries but it also evolved into a legal dispute, as the latter took the case before the District Court in Parasi, claiming that since they were the legal owners of the land they should be allowed to cultivate without any interference. The Court's decision was to support the interest of the 'outsiders'. However, the sukumbasis insisted that they were the most deserving and maintained that the registration of land to the 'outsiders' was against the principle of natural justice and therefore the government should reverse its decision and grant them the legal title. They hence defied the District Court's order and during the time of fieldwork they had appealed the case to the Zonal Court.

In addition to these collective actions within the framework of existing laws, the sukumbasis also responded to repression with physical attacks on forest guards and other forestry and resettlement officials. During some casual visits, selection or eviction, the sukumbasis physically confronted government officials. The forest guards were the prime target of such physical attacks. On numerous occasions such as during the local fairs, if sukumbasis found them in isolated areas (e.g. in the forest), or caught them assaulting women at night in the sukumbasi-settlement, forest guards were attacked and beaten up. Rangers, DFCs and the resettlement officials were also attacked. Physical attacks upon the forest guards and the forestry/resettlement officials were especially common during the 1979–80 Referendum period, but this also continued in the early 1980s. For example, in 1983 and 1984, resettlement officials were frequently attacked by sukumbasis expelled from the NRC's land in Daunnedevi and Makar Panchayats (personal communication with the resettlement officials, Dhanewa).

In many settlements, the sukumbasis actively resisted eviction, sometimes through violent confrontation with the forest guards and other government officials. Such violent resistance was notable particularly in Nawalpur where some sukumbasis gave many accounts of how they had fought pitched battles with the eviction forces. For example, in one such confrontation in the neighbouring Rupandehi district, some of the government officials (who were also involved in evicting the sukumbasis in Nawalparasi district) were seriously injured; one was even admitted to the Zonal Hospital in Bhairahawa for treatment (*Tarka*, ibid). Similarly, a government daily newspaper reported that during this time two forest guards and a policeman were seriously injured in an open conflict with the sukumbasis at Jhora area in Morang district and had to be hospitalized (*Gorkhapatra*, 18 September 1977). Indeed, incidents of sukumbasis' active resistance during evictions were reported in many other Tarai districts (Gaige, 1975).

The sukumbasis were also involved in open mass protests such as rallies, meetings and road blockades. As has been mentioned earlier, the popular movements of students, opposition political parties, and dissident professional organizations during the Referendum and the political 'tolerance' associated with this period encouraged sukumbasis to openly resist evictions and other suppressive measures. In common with other Tarai districts, a wave of resistance could be seen in the Nawalparasi district during this time. In Chitawan district, for example, Kaplan and Shrestha noted the process of 'illegal' settlement by the sukumbasis occurring on an unprecedented scale, and they argued that the sukumbasis 'were acting in their own interests and only in response to the prevailing political climate, in which they felt relatively secure. They were keenly aware of what moves other Sukumbasi groups in their locality and elsewhere had made and what government response had been' (Kaplan and Shrestha, 1982:78). To explain the nature and the scale of open protests that were taking place during this time in the Nawalparasi district, the Barghat incident will serve as an example.

According to local observers, in early May 1979, the forest guards in the Barghat area seized tools and firewood collected by the sukumbasis and also arrested a number of them. These settlers were put in custody in the local police station in Barghat. In opposition to the seizure of tools and firewood and the detention of their fellow-settlers, some five hundred sukumbasis assembled in Barghat and surrounded the local Police Station on May 20th. The incident occurred at a time when the Assistant Education Minister, accompanied by a number of senior Pancha politicians and the local CDO, was on a political tour (campaigning for the Panchayat system in the Referendum) in the area. When the sukumbasis heard that the Minister along with other Panchas and the CDO were going to pass through Barghat, they constructed barricades on the East-West Highway. When the Minister arrived, his car was stopped and the sukumbasis demanded that the intimidation by the forest guards and the police be stopped and they be provided with legal title to land. The official response to the sukumbasis' demonstration and their demands was immediate repression. The official report claimed that the sukumbasis 'damaged the Minister's car, ripped the national flag off the car and attacked the CDO with weapons' and 'for protection' the police fired on the sukumbasi demonstration[10] (*Gorkhapatra*, 21 May 1979). But, according to local observers consulted during the fieldwork, the police opened fire indiscriminately without any prior warning. In the incident, the official report claimed that four people were injured (ibid), but according to the local people and the sukumbasis interviewed in the area, many more were seriously hurt.

This incident can be better understood if one examines the following two factors. Firstly, as has been noted earlier, it was during this time that the forest guards and the police had been given a wide range of powers, authorizing them to seize the tools used by the sukumbasis as well as to arrest them. This had caused a great deal of resentment amongst the sukumbasis. Secondly, the Minister who was stopped and asked to end the intimidation by the forest guards and police and to institute the legalization of land was in fact the MP from the Nawalparasi district. During his election campaign (for vote-getting purposes) he had not only made promises that the sukumbasis would get formal title to their holdings, but he had actually distributed false land registration certificates to a large number of households, particularly in Nawalpur. After the election, those certificates were declared invalid by the FASC and the sukumbasis were evicted from their land. As a result of this, the sukumbasis in the district were bitter towards the MP and these feelings seemed to have found some expression in the Barghat incident.

Another issue which led to tremendous discontent amongst the sukumbasis in Nawalparasi district was the indiscriminate eviction of a large number of households in Nawalpur in the early 1980s primarily because of the government's policy to include the areas settled by sukumbasis north of the East-West Highway within the forest boundary. The years 1981 to 1983 were marked by an increase in the sukumbasis' open demonstrations, simultaneous with the government's evictions. In the early days of the evictions, for example, according to the local people in Kawasoti Bazaar, a large demonstration of sukumbasis took place against the government eviction measures. Amongst the people supporting the sukumbasis' demands was the newly elected District Chairman (who was believed to have been a supporter of the banned Nepal Congress Party), who addressed the rally and criticized the government's repressive measures. According to the local people, the police fired on the demonstration and the Chairman was arrested and detained in the district headquarters.

A similar demonstration was later reported in a local newspaper. According to the report, on 14 March 1983, a protest march started from Bishnunagar area of Shiva Mandir Panchayat ending up in a mass meeting in Kawasoti Bazaar

(*Yugdhara*, 19 March 1983). According to some participants in the demonstration, both the protest march and the gathering in Kawasoti Bazaar were peaceful. The demonstrators listened to speakers and clapped excitedly. Although one after another the speakers condemned the government's repressive policy and expressed their determination to 'defend their homes and land until their last drop of blood', the march and the gathering were peaceful. However, after a number of speakers had spoken, the police moved in and sought to disperse the gathering by force. Unresisting demonstrators were beaten up and many women and children were hurt while trying to escape. According to the above newspaper, two demonstrators were arrested and imprisoned in Bhairahawa jail; shortly thereafter, warrants were executed for over fifty sukumbasis and the area was 'terrorized by threatening to set houses on fire and to shoot the sukumbasis'[11] (ibid).

These examples provide a picture of the nature and forms of sukumbasis' resistance against official repressive measures, both at the individual and the collective level. What is noticeable is that, due to their socio-economic and political weakness and their geographical separation, the sukumbasis in their social behaviour and actions seemed to have pursued similar ends using similar means but in a relatively isolated manner and without any measurable success.

Present Landuse and Resettlement Policies

In the preceding discussion, the relationship that existed between the sukumbasis and the State was found to be totally antagonistic. It should also be clear that this situation was due primarily to the official emphasis on forest protection and the subsequent opposition to further resettlement and the legalization of sukumbasis' holdings. With regard to the abandonment of resettlement schemes and to the legalization of the status of the sukumbasis, the Nepalese government seemed to have justified its policies on two specific grounds:

(a) there existed no more land for further resettlement programmes and
(b) the present resettlement programme and the pattern of illegal settlement based on the clearing of forests

threatened the ecological balance in the country (ADB/HMGN, vol. I, 1982:51; NPC/Task Force on Resettlement, 1984b:5).

On the issue of the availability of land for resettlement, as far as the field-area of this research was concerned, there existed considerable prospects for resettlement. For example, a study undertaken in the area in 1974 indicated that about 42,000 ha of forest area were potentially cultivable, leaving aside as much as 22,000 ha of (arable) forest area for wildlife protection and commercial exploitation (Berry et al., 1974:91). Out of this 42,000 ha, by the late 1980s, about 1,488 ha had been brought under agriculture as a result of the regularization of the settlers. This meant that there remained as much as 40,512 ha of potentially farmable area in the Nawalparasi district. Furthermore, according to the local resettlement officials, out of the forest land allocated by the Ministry of Forest for resettlement purposes, about 1,203 ha were still vacant.[12] Similarly, one report during this time suggested that there was a possibility of using 546 ha of land in Susta area (apart from the area claimed by the Indian government) for resettling landless people (Baral, 1987). These figures seem to suggest that there was as much as 42,261 ha of land available for further resettlement and extension of cultivation in the district. Against this background, it is evident that with the present land-size per household offered by the resettlement agencies (i.e. 1/3 ha per household), over 126,783 landless households could have been accommodated. This shows that the potential land supply in the district was much higher than the area sought by the sukumbasis who totalled 11,109 households during the period of fieldwork.

It must be noted that such possibilities for initiating resettlement programmes existed in many Tarai districts. For example, in Kailali district, a study suggested that as much as 60,330 ha could be brought into production without any serious degradation consequences (Shah and Schreier, 1985:146). As a matter of fact, a thorough study on the landuse situation of the country as a whole has demonstrated that, in 1986 as much as 43 per cent of Nepal's land surface was still under forest (LRMP, 1986:46). It established that a total of 4,964,000 ha was suitable for agriculture, as compared to 2,968,000 ha currently under cultivation (ibid). This suggested that the agricultural area could be extended by over two-thirds. Some even claimed that there existed the 'possibility for doubling cultivated area' (Devkota/ APROSC, 1986:2.1). It is possible that much of this area could be used for resettling the landless without causing any serious adverse effects on the local environment.

The State's negative attitude towards the sukumbasis was also related to the ongoing problem of haphazard deforestation. It was claimed that much of the current deforestation was caused by the development of illegal settlements. The claim that the sukumbasis destroyed forests was in fact evident in many government publications (e.g. Nepal Australia Forestry Project, 1976:3, ADB/HMGN, ibid: 51, NPC/Task Force on Population, 1983: 65–6 and NPC/Task Force on Resettlement, 1984b:5). For example, the government newspaper in its editorial wrote, 'without discouraging illegal settlements, the forests of Tarai and inner-Tarai in particular cannot be protected'. It went on to claim that 'the illegal settlers in all areas destroy a large area of forests every year'[13] (*Gorkhapatra*, 27 August 1978). However, this claim is also disputable.

Firstly, it must be remembered that a large area of forest in the Tarai was cleared for the planned resettlement itself. For example, if one were to compare the forest area cleared for the planned resettlement with that cleared by the 'illegal'settlers in the Nawalparasi district (an area containing very many official as well as unofficial, illegal settlements), the forest area under the former type of resettlement was significantly larger than that of the latter type. It has been shown in chapter three that between 1965 and 1985, 6,957 ha of forest area were cleared for planned resettlement, whilst the total area of land used by 'illegal' settlers who were legalized by the government during the same period was 1,940 ha; and it is also estimated that by the late 1980s, not more than 2,244 ha of forest area (1,591 ha settled by the sukumbasis and 653 ha occupied by the profit-seeking settlers) were under encroachment. This suggests that the total amount of forest land used by illegal settlers as a whole by 1987 was only 4,184 ha.

Secondly, numerous studies have established that it is cattle grazing and fuel-wood gathering that have resulted in the serious over-use and exhaustion of forests in many parts of the country. One study, for example, argues that because of this 'the forested areas are losing tree crown cover at a rate equal to about 50,000 hectares per year' (Nield, 1985 quoted in LRMP, ibid: 56). Such seemed to have been the situation especially in the Hill areas; and the evidence indicates that 'between 1965 and 1979, there was no change in cultivated area in the Middle and High Mountain Regions' (LRMP, ibid:46). This suggests that the above process was occurring in large part independent of new cultivation by the sukumbasis.

Lastly, some mention should be made of the substantial deforestation that was caused by excessive felling of trees for commercial timber sales. Ever since the early nineteenth century, India has been a highly lucrative market for the export of timber from Nepal. Although legally only limited timber-sales to India were licensed (only in Kailali, Kanchanpur and Bardia in the far west and Jhapa in the far east), illegally a great deal of wood and timber was being smuggled into and sold in India through the existing river, road and human transport systems (Tarai-DFC Seminar, 1987; Ghimire, 1988:2). Additionally, in recent years, the growing urban demands for fuel and construction created a similar prospect of profitable timber-sales within Nepal. The construction of the East-West Highway, in particular, which ran across the Tarai from east to west, provided those elements with vested interests in commercial timber with the infrastructure for cheaper transportation of wood and timber to urban centres. However, as the price of wood and timber across the border in India was considerably higher than in Nepal (Tarai-DFC Seminar, ibid:5), the Indian market remained very attractive. As far as the Nawalparasi district was concerned, the illegal export of firewood and timber across the border continued without much restraint. During fieldwork, the local people commonly claimed that the forest officials and the district level administrators did not allow them to collect fallen trees and rotten wood for household use, whilst the same officials were involved directly or indirectly in illegal felling of trees and timber sales both within Nepal and in India.

In this context, it is also important to clarify that 'illegal' settlements were not being established in all areas of the forests. The common practice amongst the sukumbasis was to settle on the border of the forest, mostly in areas without any trees and in areas near to the old villages (for wage-employment purposes).

For example, amongst the 'illegal' settlements established in Nawalparasi district, especially amongst those developed after 1975,[14] very few of them cut standing trees. In fact, in areas where some trees were standing at the time of the settlement, the sukumbasis seemed to have grown crops by clearing only the undergrowth and without felling the standing trees. This was because the sukumbasis were very much aware that substantial cutting of trees would invite immediate repression by the government.

What emerges from the above discussion is that there was a clear tendency within the State's present land-use policies to over-emphasize the sukumbasis' negative impact on forest-conservation measures. These policies exhibited their unwillingness to promote land settlement and agricultural extension and their willingness to ignore the subsistence needs of the rural population lacking other viable means of production and income such as the sukumbasis. This attitude has led the State to adopt tougher forestry–protection legislative measures and to legitimize repressive activities by its officials against the sukumbasis. Although this has not stopped the sukumbasis from expressing their discontent, State policies are likely to further affect the socio-economic position of the sukumbasis in many critical ways. This situation will be examined in the following chapter, as well as in the conclusion.

Notes

1. This is not to say however that the Ministry was completely autonomous in relation to the rest of the State apparatus. Above the Ministry, the cabinet and the royal palace played a vital role in making crucial decisions with respect to forest and land-use policies. Some of these aspects will be discussed in chapter eight.
2. The control over and the use of marginal and waste lands by the FASC was attributed to the need for resettling approved settler-households (also involving the non-sukumbasi settlers such as the ex-servicemen and the repatriated Nepalese) (FASC, 1984:9). This was primarily because, since the early 1980s, the government not only stopped releasing forest areas for further resettlement, but also sought to remove settlers already settled within forest boundaries and relocate them in marginal and wasteland areas such as in Rewa Rehta.
3. Translation from Nepali to English by author.

4. Besides giving these bribes, many sukumbasis said that they were also obliged to pay various other 'middlemen' who claimed to have contacts with the senior government officials in Parasi, Butwal, or even in Kathmandu and would be able to help them in obtaining legal title to land.
5. In Chitawan, for example, Kaplan and Shrestha note that 'one man was beaten to death and others were seriously injured. It was later reported that a young child was lost in the jungle and never found' (Kaplan and Shrestha, 1982:82).
6. The sukumbasis from these areas claimed that the Road Department evicted them particularly during the royal visits or the visits of foreign dignitaries to Chitawan National Park (for recreation and game) and to Lumbini (the birthplace of Buddha) in order to give a good and positive image of the area.
7. By addressing letters to the king, firstly, the sukumbasis hoped that with the attention of the supreme authority in the land, they might just be fortunate to acquire legal title to their holdings; and secondly, this also implied their extreme distrust of government officials and the State institutions and at the same time a certain belief that 'the king remained beyond corruption and cared for the poor'. It may be added that this image of the king rested partly on the monarchy's traditional and spiritual role in Nepalese society, but this was largely the direct result of the introduction of the Panchayat system and a heavy flow of foreign aid for development programmes in rural areas for which the monarchy took most of the credit.
8. Translation from Nepali to English by author.
9. Translation from Nepali to English by author.
10. Translation from Nepali to English by author.
11. Translation from Nepali to English by author.
12. This 1,203 ha of land was located in: Kawasoti (23 ha), Makar/Dhanewa (160 ha) and Shankarpur areas (1,020 ha).
13. Translation from Nepali to English by author.
14. Since, until this time, the government itself was directly involved (i.e. through initiating resettlement schemes and through timber-exports to India) in large scale tree-clearing both within and outside resettlement project areas, felling trees for agricultural purposes was more often permitted.

7

Implications for the future

The existing economic condition of the sukumbasis was the most visible indicator in explaining the socio-economic dynamics and the future trends. The general production relations and the economic situation of the sukumbasis have already been discussed at length. In this section, only such aspects that would have a direct bearing on future economic changes will be examined.

INSECURITY OF TENURE

The most common problem that the vast majority of sukumbasis in Nawalparasi district faced was the insecurity of land tenure. This situation had arisen primarily because of the establishment of their settlements in areas not authorized by the government and their subsequent inability to secure legal rights of possession and cultivation. Because of the illegal nature of their settlement, the sukumbasis were permanently open to government eviction. In the event of such evictions, the sukumbasis were to become not only homeless and resourceless but they were also to lose their base for wage employment.

To a limited extent, the degree of insecurity of tenure varied according to the type of land on which the sukumbasis had settled. For example, the households settled on public 'waste' land were less liable to evictions than those settled in forest areas, NRC land and on the roadsides. But, as the vast majority of the sukumbasis were settled in areas designated as 'forests', they were very vulnerable to eviction. For example, 57 per cent of the total sukumbasi-households were settled within the forest boundary; and for reasons of forest protection, the government was particularly active in removing these households. A further 20 per cent were settled on NRC land, where the FASC and the NRC were determined to substitute new groups of settlers approved by them (mostly profit-seeking settlers) for the already-settled sukumbasis. Furthermore, an additional 5 per cent of the sukumbasi households who were settled on the roadsides were certain to be removed, since major road-extension works on the East-West Highway were already underway. Thus, as many as 82 per cent of the sukumbasis maintained very insecure holdings. It should also be added that the FASC was empowered to evict even the households settled on 'waste' land areas (who formed about 17 per cent of the total number of sukumbasi households), and resettle people of its own choice. This reflected the extreme insecurity of tenure experienced by the overwhelming majority of the sukumbasis.

It must be emphasized that security of tenure would not only have given the sukumbasis the legal protection needed for growing staple food-crops for subsistence, but it would also have encouraged them to undertake some degree of land improvement and pursue other productive investments. The phenomenon of ownership security affecting investment incentives has been noted in studies carried out in the Pacific and South East Asia, specifically Thailand (Acquaya and Crocombe, 1984; Feder and Onchan, 1987). These studies have stressed that the lack of secure, legal, individual ownership of land often prohibits settlers from using their holdings as collateral for loans from institutional sources and thus inhibits them from turning their holdings to more productive uses. This was precisely the case with the sukumbasis. Furthermore, in desperate circumstances, the legal title would have also allowed the sukumbasis to mortgage and sell their plots. Since the sukumbasis did not have title, it was not only difficult for them to sell the land but, if they did sell, the price received was very nominal.

In fact, what needs to be recognized is that, even if the sukumbasis were allowed to remain in their settlements and were provided with legal ownership certificates, it is possible that the economic position of most households would still have deteriorated. In this regard, it is important to look at some other aspects of the present economic conditions of the sukumbasis.

Marginal location and poor quality of soil

Most of the sukumbasi-settlements were situated in areas where land was marginal both in terms of location and quality. The households settled on roadsides and town/market areas occupied land just sufficient for homesteads, and their agricultural production potential remained nearly zero. It was more or less the same situation with the households settled on public lands such as those settled on school play-grounds. However, more than half of the settlements were located on recently cleared forest land and one would have thought that the sukumbasis in those areas would be cultivating fertile land. But as most of those settlements were located near the old established villages, most households occupied land usually left by the 'formal' farmers either because of its poor quality or because of the difficulties in protecting crops from wild animals and birds, or cattle from the village. To some extent, this also applied in the case of NRC land where the sukumbasis cultivated land usually rejected by the earlier settlers because of its inferior quality. Also, many settlements were situated near the riverbanks where soil was sandy and unproductive.

Even within the forest area settlements, however, much of the area consisted of dryland located in higher regions where irrigation was difficult. And most sukumbasi households lacked the economic resources to construct irrigation canals. Furthermore, because of the illegal nature of their settlement, they were unable to receive any financial assistance from the government or from international aid agencies. Also, the uncertainty of obtaining legal title to land largely discouraged them from initiating long-term irrigation schemes. It should be noted too that in areas where the prevailing water resources were already utilized by the earlier settlers and landowners, the sukumbasis were unable to demand a share of water because of their lack of legal status and their general powerlessness. At the same time, where water sources (i.e. a river or stream) existed near their settlement, the economic inability of sukumbasis to execute flood control measures not only led to an increasing deposit of silt in land during the monsoon, but often their houses and crops were damaged as well. The poor quality of land available for cultivation was such that even by working harder and for longer hours, the possibility of increasing production remained limited for most sukumbasis households.

Small farm size with large family

Another factor which limited the production possibilities for most sukumbasis was the small size of land per household. As Table 25 indicates, the average land-size per household amongst the sukumbasis was not more than 0.23 ha. With the average family size of 6.1 persons, each hectare of land supported as many as 26.5 persons. Given this situation and the poor quality of soil, together with the lack of irrigation, the average land-size was inadequate to meet household subsistence needs. The small size of land also meant that maintaining 'full' subsistence was difficult even if there were prospects for multiple cropping and intensification.

Since the land that the majority of the sukumbasis possessed was not capable of supporting the subsistence requirements of the present generation, there remained very little hope for future generations, particularly as the population continued to expand and few opportunities existed in other sectors of the economy. The growing numbers of people would not only consume more and leave less savings for investment, but this was also likely to lead to a steady fragmentation of land as married sons generally separated from the main household and sub-divided the family land. Such socially and legally sanctioned sub-divisions and the accompanying increase in new houses, cattleshades and foot-paths would also mean a decrease in the share of agricultural land. Thus, it was likely that each new sukumbasi generation would hold smaller plots of land, leading to a decline in food

Table 25 *Land-holding pattern and population scenario amongst sampled peasant settler households*

average land size	average household size	total population	% of population under 20 yrs	total male population	total potentially separable male population	average % of potentially separable male population per house hold
0.23ha	6.1	976	59	487	322	2

Source: personal interviews;
sample size: 160 households

production in absolute and per capita terms. This process seemed particularly inevitable as 59 per cent of the sukumbasi-population was under 20 years (Table 25), and nearly 33 per cent of them would probably leave the household within a few years[1]. Against this background, it was probable that the average land-holding amongst the sukumbasis would become less than 0.1 ha before the year 2000, especially if the State maintained its pressure in preventing land settlement in forest frontier areas.

High degree of indebtedness

In addition to the process of fragmentation of existing plots and the decline in the amount of agricultural land cultivated, considerable numbers of households were also likely to lose their land because of the high degree of indebtedness and the general economic vulnerability that prevailed.

Even if most households avoided borrowing money—and obtaining loans was often very difficult because of their lack of collateral—there existed a significant degree of indebtedness amongst the sukumbasis. It was observed during field research that once a sukumbasi household was settled in an area, and as long as the household was comprised of potential wage labourers, obtaining small loans from the local moneylenders was not too difficult. These moneylenders were mostly large landowners, i.e. the main employers in the area, who often willingly extended loans in order to secure labour during the peak season of cultivation. Therefore, many of these loans were used to reinforce a long-term patron-client or employer-employee relationship between the moneylender and the borrower.

Loans were taken by sukumbasis for various reasons. The purchase of food followed by clothes and consumer items was the main reason for borrowing (see Table 26). Due to the seasonal nature of agricultural employment they needed to borrow to meet their food requirements during the slack season. The data also indicated that over 94 per cent of the loans were obtained for consumption purposes and only the remaining 6 per cent were taken for production purposes, primarily for buying oxen.

Since loans were used predominantly for consumption purposes, and since employment was seasonal and they themselves

TABLE 26 *Level of indebtedness amongst peasant settlers*

TABLE 26a

extent of indebtedness	no. of households interviewed	% of households interviewed
no debt	86	54
less than Rs 500	37	23
Rs 501–1000	13	8
Over Rs 1000	24	15
total	160	100

TABLE 26b

main reason for borrowing	no. of households interviewed	% of households interviewed
initial settlement expenses	10	6.2
to purchase food	61	38.1
to purchase clothes and other consumer goods	32	20.0
to cover medical expenses	14	9.0
to finance marriage and cremation	10	6.2
to support festival expenses	13	8.1
to purchase farm-inputs	10	6.2
other	10	6.2
total	160	100

Source: personal interviews;
sample size: 160 households

produced very little, most of the sukumbasi households were unable to repay the original loan principal and additional amounts became necessary. This led many households into borrowing again and falling further into debt. What also made repayment of loans impossible for many households was the high rate of interest that was charged. There were two rates of interest in the area. Where the sukumbasis remained potential wage labourers, the moneylenders asked Rs 5 per month per Rs 100. But where such possibilities were limited, the moneylenders commonly demanded 50 *paisa* (1/2 a Rupee) per day per Rs 100 (i.e. Rs 15 per month) until the loan was repaid, a simple rate of 180 per cent per annum. These repayments were made in cash, kind or labour, with the latter being the most usual form. In some cases, one or two persons in the household worked for the moneylender/s exclusively for the repayment of interest. In such circumstances, the original principal remained intact. This often led some sukumbasis to enter into virtual or actual bonded labour arrangements. It should be noted though that where the primary aim of the employers was to secure labour, some room for manoeuvring existed on the part of the sukumbasis (i.e. occasional postponement of repayments) provided the household continued to supply labour. But where employment was not the primary relationship, moneylending employers were particularly harsh with the sukumbasis.

Moneylenders were protected by law and, in the event of failure to repay the loans, they were authorized to seize any tangible property that the sukumbasis held such as cattle, pots and ornaments. But as most households possessed few valuables, non-employing moneylenders ultimately aimed at their land. Table 26 shows that amongst the sampled households as many as 23 per cent owed money already exceeding Rs 500; and, many households would hardly have been able to save the equivalent amount in order to repay the loans. This was particularly so for the additional 15 per cent of the sukumbasis who had borrowed over Rs 1,000. These households were in danger of losing their minimal land-rights since, in order to repay their outstanding debts, providing labour amounting to that value was bound to prove difficult if not impossible.

Loss of Customary Occupations

Another factor which aggravated the precarious economic position of the sukumbasis was the continual displacement of customary specializations practised by a significant proportion of the sukumbasi-households. This had previously been an important source of supplementary income. It is essential therefore that some attention be given to this process.

How the penetration of market forces destroy caste/ethnicity-based customary occupations has been elaborated elsewhere. In particular, there exists a large body of literature along these lines on the Indian situation (e.g. Thorner, 1962; Frank, 1975; Streefkerk, 1985). In the case of Nepal also, Rose and Fisher, for example note how the breakdown of the extensive homespun cotton and textile industry, brass work, papermaking and mining and production of conventional armaments (in which often a particular caste or ethnic group was involved) took place from the beginning of the nineteenth century under the impact of British colonial rule in India (1970:129–30); and Blaikie et al. argue how this process has been reinforced by the later penetration of Indian industrial capitalism into Nepal and Nepal's 'peripheral' role to the Indian economy (1976: 2.50–1).

Indeed, the process of reduction of customary occupations under the influence of market relationships is not a new phenomenon in Nepal. Also the effects of this process were not limited merely to the artisans within the sukumbasi population. In this regard certain points should be made. Firstly, there was a high concentration of artisans among the sukumbasis. At least a quarter of the sukumbasi-households came from artisan and 'occupational' groups. This concentration was especially remarkable as within the 'formal' and 'legal' households these people constituted a considerably lower proportion. For example, in two selected Panchayats in Parasi and Nawalpur (i.e. Makar and Shiva Mandir), the people from artisan and occupational castes represented under 14 per cent of the total population (Malaria Eradication Dept., 1988). Secondly, among the sukumbasis the hereditary-based occupations were being disregarded while, at the same time, other economic alternatives were limited. Thus, the implications of this process were particularly critical amongst the sukumbasis.

In Nawalparasi district, the Viswakarmas, especially the Kamis, comprised one of the largest sukumbasi-artisan groups. They were principally engaged in metal-working, especially the manufacture and repair of agricultural tools and kitchen utensils for the local communities. However, cheaper mass-produced tools and utensils from India and China and from the urban centres of Nepal were steadily displacing their goods and services. This phenomenon was particularly pronounced in areas near the market centres. During the time of fieldwork, in most villages, their services were sought primarily for repair-work and not for the production of new tools or utensils. As a result, there was little chance of maintaining full employment. Many of the workshops run by the Kamis were open only occasionally and employment was available for one or two family members only. For example, out of the 25 households interviewed, only 3 were able to secure 'full' employment and an additional 8 maintained only partial employment (see Table 27). It was also interesting to note that there was a significant decline in the level of their involvement after their migration. For example, prior to their migration, only 9 households did not engage in their traditional occupation, whilst in the present location as many as 14 households had ceased (ibid).

The most severely affected artisan category were the Sarkis/ Chamars, whose specialization in leather-working had disappeared; Table 27 shows that as many as 22 households (out of 24) of the Sarkis/Chamars had had no involvement with their hereditary occupation even in their previous place of residence. Traditionally, people from these castes relied on leather-working, primarily shoe-making, but the gradual influx of mass-produced shoes, especially rubber slippers and trainers, manufactured in India and China and in Nepal itself led to a total disappearance of their customary occupation. The only leather-working that was observed in some parts of the Nawalparasi district was the production of leather-ropes for tying ploughs (*Hademlo*). But an increasing commercial market for shoe-making companies purchasing raw leather from the villages was resulting in a growing shortage of leather for such works. Thus there was very little self-employment.

Similarly, the influx into and the popularity of 'ready-made' garments in villages and the emergence of sewing machine-based tailoring enterprises in the market/urban centres led to an increasing loss of employment opportunities for rural tailors such as the Damains (cf. Macfarlane, 1976: 154–5). In rural areas,

TABLE 27 *Level of participation in artisan services of three major peasant settler-artisan groups*

category	total households interviewed	no. of households involved in artisan services					
		full-time		occasionally employed		no. of households not involved at all	
		before migration	after migration	before migration	after migration	before migration	after migration
Viswakarmas	25	4	3	12	8	9	14
Sarkis/Chamars	24	0	0	2	0	22	24
Damains	5	1	0	3	1	1	4

Source: personal interviews;
sample size: 54 households

people from this group also occasionally performed as local musicians, especially during weddings. However, as far as the Damain households within the sukumbasi populations were concerned, since many of them were settled away from the main villages and often near ethnic groups which did not use musicians at weddings (i.e. Tharus), such opportunities were very limited. The establishment of professional music-bands in urban areas further reduced demand. Additionally, most musical instruments used by the Damains were not produced in the area, so they were required to purchase from outside. This meant that many economically weaker households could not continue with their customary occupation.

But it was the loss of tailoring opportunities that affected the Damains the most. It is evident from Table 27 that none of the Damain households held full-time employment as tailors and only one household was occasionally employed in this way.

Apart from the above factors, many households also claimed that, because they could not afford the cost of sewing machines, they were unable to compete in the job-market.[2] In addition to this, they also lacked the professional training which would allow their garments to compete in design and quality with garments produced outside the village.

Similar conditions also prevailed in the case of the Kumals whose products and services were being increasingly displaced. In the place of clay-pots traditionally produced by these people, mass-produced utensils, especially aluminium and tin pots, and recently plastic buckets and containers, were made available in every corner of the district. As a result, the involvement of Kumals in their customary specialization could be found only in isolated cases.

The case of the Botes or Bins/Mallahas, however, presented an even more striking and recent example. As indicated in chapter three, these people previously earned their livelihood mainly from ferry-crossing and fishing. In recent years, the local administration had begun to give ferry-crossing rights on a contractual basis to people usually with wealthier backgrounds; also, from the late 1970s on, the National Park authorities in Chitawan had put restrictions on fishing in the Narayani river (which bordered the Park). These measures, which failed to give any consideration to the needs of the Botes and Bin/Mallahas, resulted in the sudden loss of traditional specialization and immediately made the economic position of these people extremely precarious.

Similarly, the government's recent intervention in the brewing and selling of alcohol, which gave these rights exclusively to big distilleries in the area and made any brewing and sales by individual households illegal, affected many Gurung and Magar sukumbasis, who had previously generated important supplementary earnings though brewing and selling alcohol either in their little *Bhattis* or at local fairs. In fact, some of these households claimed that the police, acting on behalf of the local distilleries often intimidated them or demanded bribes where they brewed just for home-consumption.[3]

The decline in the practice of their customary occupations was not exactly the same in each case but increasing intervention from outside did lead to a steady erosion of the traditional specializations of the sukumbasis.[4] The external forces were supported by the existing political and legal systems, and they were also often associated with new technology and lower unit costs; hence sukumbasi-artisans could not compete with them. This was particularly so as the vast majority of the sukumbasis retained a weak economic base and their capacity to invest, with a view to establishing competitive enterprises or transforming themselves into sustainable petty commodity producers, was almost non-existent.

In this context, what also needs to be stressed is that these people were not merely experiencing the displacement of their former means of livelihood (or a major part of it), but the avenues for non-agricultural and occupational change in other fields were strictly limited as well. In the following section, how the occupational choice and the socio-economic mobility of the sukumbasis were specifically restricted by inadequate formal education will be examined.

Lack of Access to Education

It is commonly believed that formal education provides greater possibilities for upward mobility. Many sociological studies show a close connection between education and occupational advancement and opportunities for social mobility (Barber: 1957; Coxon and Jones:1975). However, the existing level of education amongst the sukumbasis suggests that the prospects for any significant occupational advancement and upward social mobility were hardly bright.

The data on education showed that the average literacy rate amongst the sampled sukumbasi households was only 11 per cent. This figure was considerably lower than the existing national average literacy rate which, around this time, was believed to be about 30 per cent (CBS, 1987: 284). About 1 per cent of the sukumbasi adults seemed to have obtained a secondary education, but none of them achieved higher education. This suggested that 89 per cent of the adult sukumbasi population were totally unable to read and write.

What was also noteworthy was that within the current sukumbasi population there was also a lower percentage of school-age children attending schools than the existing national average school attendance rate. For example, it was claimed by the government that 83 per cent of the school-age children in the country attended schools by the mid-1980s (ibid). But among the sukumbasi school-age children only 8 per cent went to school.

The children of sukumbasis generally had little opportunity to go to school. Schools were non-existent in many frontier areas;[5] and the parents were often reluctant to send their children to school outside their settlement as this meant that the children would need to travel a long distance to go to school and would not be available to help in the household both in the morning and the evening. In most sukumbasi households, besides working in the field, children performed a number of tasks both within and outside the household such as baby-sitting, fetching water, collecting fodder and firewood and looking after cattle. Their weak economic status and the need to turn their children into wage-earners was such that many households did not consider schooling as being a high priority. Even amongst those who realized the importance of education, many did not have the economic resources to allow their children to go to school. For this reason, even if some sukumbasi children went to school, very few managed to progress. The cost of education and the burden of supporting families at a young age usually caused many of them to drop out even of the primary schools.

Since access to education was difficult and hence educational achievement was rare, it was hard to envisage any prospects for occupational change and economic improvement amongst the sukumbasis. Furthermore, as shall be discussed below, the inability to promote their interests politically was likely to further strengthen the process of socio-economic decline which was already underway.

Lack of Political Representation

It has been shown how landuse and resettlement and regularization programmes were overshadowed by the government conservation and forest protection measures. It is essential to note that, within this decision-making process, there was no political representation of the group interest of the sukumbasis. In addition to this, there was little likelihood of the sukumbasis acting themselves as an organized political force in order to press for their land-rights.

Although quite large in numbers, the sukumbasis in Nawalparasi district were politically unorganized. They were divided not only in terms of the type of land on which they were settled (i.e. forest, NRC land, marginal, public and roadsides), but they were also divided in relatively isolated settlements within each land-type. As the government's policy towards the sukumbasis differed according to the type of land on which they were settled and as their cases were dealt with in isolation on the basis of individual settlements, many sukumbasis tended to limit their actions only to their settlement. Besides this, the geographical distance between settlements and the lack of communication often restrained the sukumbasis from organizing together politically.

In chapter four, some level of group identification amongst the sukumbasis was observed. And, in chapter six, examples of sukumbasis' collective actions in response to the government's evictions and other punitive measures (i.e. surrounding and attacking of government officials, open protests and rallies) were discussed. However, these actions were largely limited to what one writer calls the 'we-they mentality' (Sandbrook, 1982: 173) and were sporadic and fairly short-lived. According to Sandbrook, such an ideology of populism 'can foster only riots or *jacqueries*, with little or no long-term political significance' (ibid).

The lack of continuity of the movements of the sukumbasis was largely the result of their inability to organize internally and develop an effective leadership in the face of determined repression. Additionally, they completely lacked outside political support. The significance of outside political organizations and parties in legally and politically aiding the demands of squatters (both rural and urban) has been examined in Latin American as well as in some Asian cases, e.g. Philippines (Collier, 1976; Epstein, 1973; Feldman, 1979). As political parties and trade unions were either banned or actively restrained in their activities in Nepal, such possibilities were almost non-existent for the sukumbasis. In fact, in some cases, the sukumbasis' open contacts with the opposition political groups seemed to have been detrimental to their interest in terms of registration of land. The authorities responsible for the legalization of the sukumbasis very often found the sukumbasis' contacts threatening, and this often led to stepped-up evictions. As a result of this situation, the sukumbasis usually preferred to appeal to the establishment of Pancha politicians, who could possibly influence government officials with regard to the local land registration, than to seek assistance from underground political groups.

The existing level of direct electoral political participation amongst the sukumbasis was very low. Owing to the absence of internal organizations and leadership and the lack of political support from the political parties, whatever political participation existed amongst the sukumbasis had evolved primarily at the individual level. At the local level, few sukumbasis contested elections and even fewer won but there was a relatively high level of participation in voting during elections. This was partly due to active canvassing by candidates, especially by the sitting MPs, but was largely due to the sukumbasis' expectations that these politicians would assist in getting their holdings legalized once they came to office. At the same time, past experience had taught them that these elections and the voting for particular candidates would not drastically alter their status in any tangible way. In fact, during casual conversations, many sukumbasis not only openly criticized the politicians for raising false hopes, but they also expressed their extreme apathy towards voting.

The problem facing the sukumbasis was not only the lack of direct political support from outside, but also the absence of any outside moral or ideological support. As has been noted, the government officials blamed the sukumbasis for the ongoing deforestation and environmental problems. The international aid agencies in general stressed the importance of forest conservation and consequently tended to overlook the subsistence needs of the sukumbasis. Then too, as the sukumbasis operated essentially outside the existing forest laws and were considered a politically sensitive group by the Nepalese government, foreign aid agencies avoided getting directly involved with the sukumbasis. This meant that no outside force represented the political interests and aspirations of the sukumbasis at the centre in a highly centralized State.

Prospects for the Future

The above discussion examined the prevailing economic and political condition of the sukumbasis. From this, it would appear that the sukumbasis were destined to experience further socio-economic decline in the future, and the possibilities of improving this situation were virtually nonexistent. Most of the sukumbasi-households possessed few moveable assets and they had no savings or significant sources of income outside of agricultural wage labouring. Hence, the land which they occupied and cultivated was an important economic resource available to them, particularly in the context of future economic improvement. Yet, the fact that they lacked security of tenure together with their marginal location, inferior quality of soil, and most importantly, their small size meant that they had limited prospects for producing food and generating income. Since the present generation already lived on the brink of destitution, future generations were bound to experience an even greater drop in their standards of living.

Population growth and the corresponding increased demand for food and other consumer goods, poor prospects for increasing agricultural production and irregular wage employment had already resulted in a high degree of indebtedness amongst the sukumbasis. This in turn was most likely to lead to further land dispossession, since mortgaging and selling of even limited land rights was the final solution for the repayment of debts. Similarly, the steady loss of customary occupations was to make many sukumbasi-households further vulnerable economically. At the same time, their low economic status inhibited many households from sending their children even to primary school. Hence, occupational choice and mobility did not seem any brighter for new generations. As a matter of fact, a lower percentage of sukumbasi children were attending schools than in the previous generation.

Socio-economic and political problems similar to those faced by the sukumbasis have been examined in studies focusing on the rural poor in many Third World countries (ILO, 1977; Esman, 1978; Chambers, 1983; Sinha, 1984; Griffin, 1985). Chambers, for example, stresses that this situation of 'the deprivation trap' has its roots in the physical weakness, isolation, poverty, vulnerability and powerlessness of the rural poor (ibid: 111–12). Indeed, the poverty which the sukumbasis faced has also been frequently experienced by much of the labouring poor in Nepal (e.g. Blaikie, Cameron, Seddon, 1979). However, the main difference between the sukumbasis and the other groups of poor stemmed essentially from the illegal nature of their settlement and the further vulnerability caused by this. This illegality made their present access to the means of production not only constantly insecure—thus discouraging them from improving existing production through self-help—but also created a lack of access to schooling, institutional loans and international development funds. Under these circumstances, any improvements in the existing socio-economic condition of most sukumbasi-households will depend upon the conditions in the wage labour market which is generally unpromising.

Notes

1. This percentage of the potentially separable population may be a very moderate estimate as, in addition to males, in some cases, female members of the household (i.e. divorced wives and unmarried daughters over 35 years age) may also separate and claim a separate parcel of household-land.
2. It may be mentioned that, in January 1987, a sewing machine in the area cost Rs 4,500. This amount was more than two years' wage earnings of an average agricultural labourer in the Tarai.
3. For example, during fieldwork, at Karamghari Village (Naya Belhani Panchayat) in Nawalpur, a sukumbasi belonging to the Gurung caste was arrested by the local police check-post for allegedly brewing and selling alcohol in his *Bhatti*. This individual claimed that he was required to pay Rs 150 to the police before being released (personal communication).
4. A similar process of decline in the customary specializations of various artisan groups involving 50 households in West Central Nepal (covering both the Hills and the Tarai) was also shown by a Rural Survey in 1974/5 (Seddon, Blaikie and Cameron, 1981). This survey observed that there was 'an overall reduction in the number of peasant households involved in the *bista* system —an annual contract of services between the artisans and the households seeking their services, primarily larger landowners—(author), a general reduction in the size of payments made by the remaining households, and a general shift from payments in kind to payments in cash, reflecting the increasing importance of "market" considerations in relations between peasants and rural artisans' (ibid: 84). However, with specific reference to the sukumbasi-artisans, most households experienced an immediate and total

breakdown in their former *bista* relationships when they out-migrated from their former place of residence. Also, for many of them establishing such contacts in a new place of residence was equally difficult both because of the physical isolation of their settlement and the general financial inability to establish new enterprises. Furthermore, a greater degree of market penetration in the Tarai, with the provision of products and services similar to those which they were able to offer, meant an increasing risk in starting such enterprises.

5. This was primarily because the government allocated school-quotas for formal or legal settlement areas only, and the sukumbasis lacked the financial resources to run schools on their own.

8

Conclusion

Summary of Major Findings

The study began by outlining the historical roots of the socio-economic inequalities which seem to have directly influenced the sukumbasis' present socio-economic conditions. The extension of the caste system in reinforcing a rigid division of labour, the gradual alienation of the indigenous Mongoloid people from their land by the dominant Hindu migrants and the privatization of large tracts of productive land by the ruling classes (viz. members of the aristocracy and nobility, royal priests, senior army and civil officials) were the historical conditions for economic and agrarian inequalities; and any alterations to this situation were largely negated because of the domination of these elements over the State machinery and political power and their ability to exclude others. It was also observed how, because of the monopoly over State power exercised by these ruling elements, land reform measures failed to provide land to the poor and the agricultural extension services mainly benefited the rich. Consequently, despite a heavy flow of foreign aid and a great deal of rhetoric about rural and agricultural development, the landless and the rural poor secured no significant access to productive resources and extension services in order to improve their economic condition.

The field survey covering 160 sukumbasi households showed that since the condition of landlessness had long been experienced, many households found access to new land difficult. The government resettlement projects which should have provided land to the landpoor and the landless in reality did not do so. Instead, ex-servicemen, politicians, repatriated Nepalese and other influential elements secured a significant proportion of the land that was being distributed. The high market value of land

and the growing economic prospects of the Tarai further witnessed an increasing desire for land within resettlement projects by individuals and social groups. In addition, there was severe competition for land due to the release of insufficient land for resettlement, especially in the face of the increasing degree of landlessness, immigration and the high demand for land in the Tarai. However, those with power and ability to influence government officials evidently managed to obtain land.

Whilst the possibilities of the landpoor and landless obtaining land in government resettlement projects were very limited, many of these households had no other significant sources of income apart from agricultural wage-employment. Yet, wage-employment in agriculture in the Tarai was highly seasonal; and the wages received were minimal, particularly in relation to the subsistence needs of the people. The wages were especially low under a tied or contract labour arrangement; so, in order to maintain some degree of independence from the employer and to present themselves as 'free' daily labourers on the wage market, sukumbasis first and foremost sought home-plots. Obviously, many initially looked for land within an established village, but since most of the vacant land within the village boundary was already occupied, they normally had no chance but to settle down on the edge of forests, where they could establish their huts and also hope to grow some staple food-crops. For legal reasons and for a degree of economic protection, registration of the land they held became their ultimate aim thus drawing these people into direct contact with the State.

But despite the intense pressure and the rising demand for land amongst the sukumbasis and other landless populations, the government's recent land-use policies have been to bring resettlement programmes to a complete end. Since the early 1980s, the government has stopped releasing new forest land for resettlement purposes; and it has shown a reluctance to register the tiny parcels cultivated by the sukumbasis—even where the settlement has been in existence for a considerable length of time and where no tree cover existed. In chapter six, the 'official' justification for these policies was carefully examined; this threw doubt on the claims that there existed no land in the country for resettlement schemes and that any initiation of such programmes would have caused excessive clearance of forests, leading to serious environmental deterioration. Available evidence suggested that both claims were debatable.

As to the availability of land for resettlement, there was the possibility of extending land area by two-thirds in order to double the present cultivated area in the country. In fact, with regard to the immediate provision of land for the sukumbasis, the field survey revealed that 94 per cent of the households already occupied some land which provided them with at least ground for shelter and a minimum support base for outside employment; thus availability of land for these people did not seem to be the problem. The immediate aspiration of many sukumbasi households was to obtain legal title to the land which they held, rather than to demand a new and larger plot of land.

With regard to the question of environmental degradation as a result of forest clearance and the extension of resettlement programmes, the sukumbasis in many respects were merely 'scapegoats'. Firstly, it should be stressed that both the demand for land for food production and the prospects for resettlement schemes were essentially located in the Tarai which constituted not more than 11 per cent of the total forest area in the country. [1] Secondly, much of the Tarai forest, particularly those areas outside of the national parks and wildlife reserves, lacked substantial tree cover and were not being used productively. Therefore, expanding resettlement programmes in such areas or at least regularizing the presently settled sukumbasi households would have caused no more environmental problems than already existed. Instead, it could have led to increased food, wood and other useful biomass production in the area. It should also be pointed out that various studies relating to sustainable and productive land and forest use suggest that under the systems of 'forest farming', 'farm forestry' and 'agro-forestry', and with active community participation both increased food production and better environmental management can be achieved (Douglas and Hart, 1976; Foley and Barnard, 1984; Munslow, Katerere, Ferf and O'Keefe, 1988), rather than letting land lie idle and unproductive. At this point in time, the social value of resettlement schemes can also be seen in relation to a growing national food shortage and the import of food grains into the country.[2] Thus, the obvious question remains: why should there be so much opposition to resettlement schemes?

The answer is not easy and straightforward. However, it needs to be recognized that although the adoption of forest conservation policies in many circumstances may be desirable, that in itself says very little about who actually formulates them, their real motives as well as the social costs involved. It is argued here that a closer look at these developments in Nepal will reveal the powerful economic and other interests of the socially dominant groups which lie behind the policy of forest protection and the consequent curtailment of resettlement projects on forest land.

Vested Interests in Tarai-forest Areas and Further Likely Restraints on Access to Land for Rural Poor

In examining the interest groups behind the present forest policies in Nepal, first and foremost, the interests associated with the protection and the commercial extraction of Tarai forests for the purpose of revenue-generation must be recognized. It is interesting to recall that timber has been one of the most important sources of revenue since the early nineteenth century. Evidence shows that by 1834, Nepal had been generating Rs 300,000 from timber sales and another Rs 100,000 from elephants, ivory and pasturage and sundries from the Tarai (Hodgson, 1934 quoted in Oldfield, 1974: 305). Over much of the Rana period (1848–1951), as British India sought to expand their railway systems across the border in Bihar and Uttar Pradesh thus creating a great demand for hardwood for railway sleepers, Nepal found a ready market for its Tarai-timber and generated a substantial amount of revenue which, together with the earnings from food-grains, is reflected in its large balance of trade surplus with British India during this period (Blaikie, Cameron, Feldman, Fournier, Seddon, 1983: 17–18). The Tarai timber has remained an equally important source of revenue in the post-1951 period, and the approach of the subsequent governments to the Tarai forests has basically been one of commercial extraction (Bajracharya, 1983: 233). The introduction of resettlement projects in the Tarai from the mid-1960s onwards was closely linked to the opportunities for timber exploitation, as timber removed from the resettlement areas could be sold in India. This is reflected in a steady increase in the amount of revenue earned from timber and forest products throughout the 1970s and the early 1980s, which rose from Rs 43 million in 1976/7 to Rs 105 million in 1985/6 (CBS, 1987: 202). As a matter of fact, in recent years the revenue from timber and forest products has been considerably higher than that from land-tax which amounted to only Rs 73 million in 1985 (ibid: 425).

It must be recognized that since the costs of maintaining a rapidly expanding bureaucracy and enforcing forestry laws are increasing, the monarchy and the royal administration are not in a position to risk any loss of revenue earned from timber and forest products.[3] This is particularly crucial as land revenue has been declining, i.e. from Rs 89.3 million in 1976/7 to Rs 73 million in 1985/6 (ibid); and there is little prospect for taxing the peasantry more heavily given its average consumption level, especially in the face of declining crop yields and growing population.

Additionally, as the present land-tax system is based on land size and as the sukumbasis hold only small land plots, the amount of land revenue that may be extracted by legalizing the sukumbasis is fairly insignificant. On the other hand, if settlers are not allowed to convert forest area into agricultural land, more revenue is likely to be generated by maintaining forests and using them for timber-extraction. This economic reasoning for the protection of forests, and against the extension of cultivation, is commonly expressed in official documents (e.g. CBS, 1987: 199).

The development of tourism is another important reason why the interest groups are seeking to protect forest, the intention being to turn them into national parks[4]. Evidence shows that by 1986, the national parks and wildlife conservation areas covered 1,023,890 ha, representing over 16 per cent of the forest area and nearly 7 per cent of the country's total land surface (CBS, 1987: 2&200). The national parks—especially those located in the Tarai—are considered by the government as one of the important sources of foreign exchange earnings. Similarly, commercial interests (both national and international), especially those involved with the tourist industry, consider national parks as highly lucrative commercial ventures. However, as the hotel, safari, transport and other money-generating businesses in and around the national parks are mostly controlled by either international companies (e.g. Tiger Tops) or wealthier people from the urban areas, there is probably very little direct benefit to the local people. In fact, the local people are often prevented from using these areas as passageways and from collecting wood and other forest products.[5]

Thirdly, the present 'forest protection measures' serve the interests of senior bureaucrats and forestry officials of various levels who are actually involved in organizing the management and commercial exploitation of forests. Since many of these people can decide in what manner the forest resources should be utilized and who should be entitled to exploit them, and since they also carry out the day-to-day management and exploitation of the forests, it often allows them to formulate policies which will fit their own private agenda. This has become especially convenient since the official revenue-generation and the other related interests in 'protecting' the forests are not contradictory to the personal interests of the government officials. In the first place, the expansion and strengthening of the bureaucracy has further consolidated their own position and power. Secondly, since the bureaucracy is responsible for the protection and the commercial extraction of the forests, this has ensured a direct role for government officials in issuing licences and in supervising timber extractions, thus allowing them to benefit from share-deals and bribes. The Nepalese newspapers frequently give illuminating instances of the corruption of bureaucrats and forestry officials (e.g. see *Nepal Post*, 1 September 1979; *Tarka*, 30 March 1981; *Bankeko Yugdhara*, 5 January 1984; *Saptahik Bimarska*, 1 March 1985). Moreover, the government officials in some circumstances are also able to generate considerable personal income through receiving bribes to ignore the illegal felling and smuggling of timber. Such illegal felling takes place both for household uses and for sales to nearby towns and to India. The involvement of the officials in the latter kind of sales seems particularly profitable as it usually involves bigger-scale operations. Against this background, it is no wonder that 'Forest Department, if not the Customs' is the common saying amongst government officials, indicating a greater desire to serve in the Department of Forest. Thirdly, in recent years, forestry-related projects have created many benefits for government officials such as additional projects allowances, better office, housing and transport facilities and overseas visits, especially in the case of foreign aid projects. Therefore, the formulation and execution of increasing numbers of projects relating to the protection and conservation of forests, which are generally accompanied by increasing bureaucratic control and tougher legislative measures, are clearly in the interests of the government officials. In short, what needs to be recognized is that, in general, government officials will gain very few or no immediate benefits by legalizing the sukumbasis, initiating further resettlement, or extracting the small bribes which the sukumbasis are able to pay. On the other hand, there are substantial personal advantages attached to the bureaucracy-controlled management of forests.

The fourth interest group benefiting from the present forestry policies is the group of industrial and urban consumers. Many industries such as plywood, match factories, saw mills and furniture companies, brick kilns and distilleries secure timber and other forest products as raw materials and fuel. The other urban wood consumers include hotels, restaurants, bakeries etc. and, most significantly, urban households. It should be noted that the industries and bulk urban users get preferential treatment, whilst urban households procure firewood and timber at subsidized rates—below the actual costs of extraction and transport (Wallace, 1981: 38–40).[6] The point to be stressed here is that the provision of timber and firewood for the industrial and urban consumers at cheaper rates has so far been possible because of the relative abundance of timber and its easy exploitation in the Tarai. Therefore, the legalization of the settlers and the encouragement of further resettlement in the Tarai-forests is not in the interests of these elements because it is feared that such developments will reduce the availability of timber and firewood, and extraction is likely to be more difficult and expensive as frontiers are moved further away.[7]

Finally, how the interests of the landed elements, especially the large landowners, are expressed within the present forestry policies are also worth recalling. In areas near the national parks, some large landowners, together with other middle and small farmers, have increasingly come into conflict with the State over the issues of grazing in and around the national park boundary, access to fodder and firewood and the protection of their crops from the wild animals coming from the park. To a lesser extent, they have also entered into conflict with the forestry officials over the restricting of collection of wood for household uses. But overall, the interests of the large landowners, in particular, are substantially supported in the government's present forest policies. As examined in chapter five, the opposition of the landed elements to sukumbasis settling in the area revolved mainly around their interest in extending cultivation into unclaimed adjoining forest land and around the question of access for grazing, wood, fodder and other useful forest products. Moreover, the high demand for land and the stopping of resettlement schemes have allowed the landed elements to benefit from substantial speculation in land and dispose of their surplus food-grain at higher rates in the local areas. Another indirect benefit stems from the continuous expansion in the size of the bureaucracy and the initiation of various forestry-related projects which have created very many suitable official positions for their children coming out of the university and other higher educational institutions.[8]

The social forces described above and their vested interests are summarized in Figure 4. A look at the socio-economic and political positions of these interest groups indicates that all of those who profit from the preservation and the State-controlled management and exploitation of forests belong to socially dominant groups. Owing to their powerful position, it is obvious that they would be capable of exerting influence over the people/institutions involved in decision-making. Therefore, it is not surprising that the interests of these dominant political forces are well represented in the new forestry regulations.

It is acknowledged by sociologists as well as by natural resource experts that when resources become scarce and their value increases, not only is intense competition likely to occur amongst various social groups but also the monopolization over such resources will be sought on the part of the socially dominant groups (Weber, 1967:342; Parkin, 1979:44; Fife; 1971:20–2; Shiva, Sharatchandra & Bandyopadhyay, 1983:58; IUCN 1980:1). Active intervention through the medium of the State becomes crucial in securing exclusive privileges and also in legitimizing these privileges by creating a situation whereby, according to a Common Property Resources writer 'some would have the right

FIGURE 4 *The Tarai forest areas and the various interest groups*

interest groups	source of power	principal interest involved	ways of achieving objectives
the monarchy	centralized means of coercion	revenue generation/ recreation	legislative, executive, judiciary procedures/foreign aid
government officials	administrative and supervisory	higher salaries, better office and transport facilities/ overseas visits/ commissions and bribes	use of the State apparatus
industrial interests	individual access to decision makers/ organizational pressures/financial back-up	raw material/ fuelwood/ construction materials	through licences and illegal means, i.e. bribes
urban households	lobbying/ publicity/ many hold official positions	subsidized wood with a steady supply	official coupon/ bribes
tourist agencies/ hotels	lobbying/publicity/ many hold official positions	commercial	government permits
landed elements	representation at local and sometimes at national level i.e. MPs/personal contacts with forestry officials	cultivation into unclaimed forest area/ easier access to grazing, wood, fodder, etc.	political representation; contacts with decision makers
sukumbasis	—	shelter, food production, livestock-raising and base for wage-employment	'squatting'; 'illegal occupation'.

to stay, while others would have a duty to stay out' (Bromley, 1986:11).

The occupation and use of a small part of the forest land in the Tarai by the sukumbasis illustrates the above situation. In other words, the sukumbasis and other landless populations would like to see themselves being able to bring some of the forest land in the Tarai into immediate social use by growing food, whereas for other groups it was paramount that the remaining unsettled land remained under forests. Evidently, the interests of the sukumbasis remain in opposition to the interests of every single social group defined above.

Against this background, an inescapable conclusion is that the sukumbasis' interests in terms of access to land in the Tarai are likely to be further thwarted in the future. Besides the intense competition and the varied priorities of the socially dominant groups, the closing-off of access to the remaining agriculturally suitable land in the Tarai is exacerbated because forest-protection has become a 'non-negotiable issue' of the State. The government's present forest policies are characterized by not only an opposition to further resettlement but also a strong determination to bring the 'encroached' areas back under forest by evicting the settlers, often fencing off the area immediately with barbed wire. Indeed, more and more areas designated under forest and in some cases even settled villages[9] are sought to be made into national parks and wildlife sanctuaries.[10] These areas are effectively guarded by the national army. Thus the long-term establishment of settlements by the landless people in these areas has become virtually impossible. In areas outside of national parks and wildlife sanctuaries where landless people would have possibly been able to establish their homes and grow some food crops, lease arrangements to powerful individuals and industrial enterprises are now the rule. It is stated under the Forest Lease Act that an individual is allowed to lease up to 17 ha and an industry up to 67 ha of the Tarai forest area (Ministry of Law and Justice, 1986b: 3–4). The Act further specifies that the areas granted under lease must be used exclusively for commercial and industrial purposes, and not for agricultural use (ibid), thus ruling out prospects of leasing out part of the forest land for food production by sukumbasis and the landless. Another interesting feature of this Act is that the fixed royalty for leased areas is considerably lower than other present rates of land tax, and the rights to transfer and sales are guaranteed by law (ibid: 5).

The provisions for leasing out forests for industrial and other powerful elements have now become quite significant. It illustrates the two conflicting interests with regard to the use of the remaining potentially arable Tarai forest-areas, i.e. whether they should be used for 'growing food' as desired by the sukumbasis or for 'growing wood' as asserted by the government.

Abandonment of resettlement schemes and the restraints in legalizing the holdings of the sukumbasis on the one hand and the provision for forest-area lease on the other clearly demonstrate a situation in which the sukumbasis' subsistence needs are denied and other socially dominant groups' interests are preserved and extended.[11]

There is little doubt that through resettlement schemes and the legalization of the holdings of the sukumbasis, a great degree of social benefit could have been achieved, as it would have increased food production and provided avenues for subsistence cultivation for many landless households. But, instead, frontiers are closed off against new settlements and agricultural expansion. This development has undoubtedly hurt the deprived groups the most.

Forest Frontier Relations and Future Implications for Landlessness

Forest frontier relations is one of the most important factors that will determine if the sukumbasis and other landless populations will have access to land, or face adverse consequences in the future. This forest frontier relations has two components:

(a) the existence of potentially farmable land in frontier areas and

(b) the institutional policies and the interests of other competing but socially dominant groups over forests.

The lack of availability of forest frontiers and its effects on landlessness in many respects are self-evident. So far, this correlation can be seen in Siraha, Saptari, Dhanusha and Mahottari districts. Much of the agriculturally suitable land in frontier areas in Siraha and Saptari were already used by the early 1960s, whilst Dhanusha and Mahottari experienced the same in the early 1970s. A recent study of Dhanusha district, for example, demonstrated that in the district as a whole 32.4 per cent of the population were totally landless (Gevers, Ghimire, Goodman & others, 1988:37–49). The interesting aspect was that the further the settlements were from the forest, the higher the proportion of landless people observed. For example, in Thadi Panchayat, an area adjacent to the Siwalik forests, only 21.1 per cent of the people were found to be landless, whereas in

Goth Koilpur, one of the Panchayats furthest away from the forest frontiers, as many as 42.7 per cent of the people were recorded as landless (ibid). This high degree of landlessness in the area had resulted in a severe competition for wage-employment and had frozen wage-rates for at least a decade; also, the lack of access to land to grow trees and the long distance to the forest for fuelwood had forced them to buy wood and other biomass on the open market (ibid: 49), thus subjecting them to further economic stress.

It is important to note that, where frontiers are closed off for reasons of 'forest protection', yet migration and population growth continue, a high rate of landlessness is likely to occur. For example, in Chitawan, where frontiers were closed in order to create a national park in the late 1960s, by 1981, 16.5 per cent of the district's population were completely landless (Conway & Shrestha, 1981: 216). This figure appears particularly striking since, during this period, a great many of the landless and migrants from Chitawan moved to Nawalparasi in search of land where frontiers were relatively open. But now, as a large part of the forest in the Nawalparasi district is included in the wildlife sanctuary, resulting in the clearing of many adjacent settlements, no such migration and land settlement prospects exist for the landless from Chitawan or for people from within the Nawalparasi district. Similar trends are also visible in other Tarai areas where national parks and wildlife sanctuaries have been established. But even in areas which are outside of the national parks and wildlife sanctuaries and are under the jurisdiction of the Department of Forest, increasing forest patrols, especially by armed forest guards, and the imposition of high fines on people attempting to settle have terrified the landless into not settling even in areas without any tree-cover. As a matter of fact, in many cases, forest guards vigorously patrol the treeless areas to ensure that the productive land remains unused, whilst the hungry masses of people in the area multiply.

It may be recalled that ever since the eradication of malaria, among other changes, the forest frontiers in the Tarai have provided an important refuge for the growing numbers of poverty-stricken rural people. The fortunate ones, especially the early migrants and the beneficiaries of the government's first few resettlement schemes, were able to secure land which at least guaranteed subsistence and some level of marketable surplus. The late migrants—principally those migrating to the area after the mid 1970s—obtained access (albeit many of them are still unregistered and suffer frequent evictions) to less land. Nonetheless, they were able to establish their homes and seek wage-employment in the area, which was supplemented by whatever little food they could produce.

In recent years, the forest frontiers in the Tarai are being steadily closed. Already over 216,990 ha of Tarai-forests are included in national parks and wildlife sanctuaries (CBS, 1987: 200), and proposals have been made to include additional forest areas in the Chitawan national park (from Chitawan and Nawalparasi district) and to create four more hunting reserves in the Tarai (NPC, 1975: 262). Whilst settlement and cultivation in frontier areas are now becoming extremely difficult, a large section of the peasantry continues to have declining yields, in the face of a rapidly growing population. A very likely consequence of this situation is that many of the middle peasant households will be reduced to poverty and the ranks of the poor peasants will grow considerably. Additionally, restrictions over the 'swidden cultivation' practised by a large number of marginal peasants in the Siwalik areas and the alienation of the land of the indigenous people in the Tarai (i.e. the Tharus etc.) by wealthier powerful elements both through legal purchase and through the falsification of ownership documents are likely to aggravate the process of landlessness even further. This situation is compounded by the lack of employment opportunities for the rural poor in the urban areas. Industrial growth in Nepal has been extremely slow, and industry has not been able to provide employment to the urban labour force, let alone the rural.

Employment in Indian cities as manual workers and recruitment in the British and Indian armies as 'mercenary' soldiers have been important sources of employment for a large section of the rural population. But recent evidence suggests that these prospects are also getting slimmer. A rising population and the growing unemployment in India are such that the Nepalese migrants, who in general are uneducated and unskilled, are faced with an increasing level of competition for employment there. Furthermore, recent political violence against 'foreigners' (including the second generation) in Assam and anti-Hindu campaigns by Sikhs in Punjab and other neighbouring states have discouraged the Nepalese poor from migrating into India. With respect to employment in the Indian Army, since many of the recruits are selected from amongst the Nepalese already residing in India (i.e. from Darjeeling, Dehradun) and since a certain level of education is also required, it has become extremely competitive, with the Nepalese rural poor having very little chance. Competition is even keener with regard to the British Army. Evidence reveals that since 1966, the British Army has cut down the number of Nepalese from 10,000 to 4,500 (Bolt, 1967: 120). As half of these men are based in Hong Kong, some predict that after the handover of Hong Kong by Britain to China, no Nepalese will be taken in the British Army after 1997 (*The Guardian*, 12 August 1986). Under these circumstances, the bulk of the rural poor will have very little alternative but to remain in Nepal's rural areas even in the face of underemployment and economic hardship.

From Unsuccessful Peasants to Agricultural Labourers

In the preceding chapters, it has been demonstrated how the sukumbasis' aspirations to land are related to their desire to be self-sustaining peasants. This is primarily because land in rural areas in Nepal represents the single most important means of production. The access to land is particularly crucial for households which lack opportunities for employment and income outside of agriculture. In such circumstances, land is necessary to ensure subsistence and, if possible, provide a measure of economic security. For landless and migrant populations such as the sukumbasis, access to land is also vital in terms of establishing a suitable base from where they can look for wage-employment in the area, thus allowing them in the process a greater degree of bargaining power with their employers with respect to the conditions of work and wage rates. But the continuous migration of landless people into the area and the high competition for wage-employment are giving rise to an extremely depressed labour market in the Tarai. It is in this context that the sukumbasis aspire to become peasants.

It is difficult, however, for most sukumbasis to fulfil these aspirations. Firstly, as has been indicated earlier, finding a suitable and safe place to settle is becoming extremely difficult because of the lack of vacant land available outside the forest boundary and the government's increasing control over illegal settlements within forest areas. Secondly, even if they are already settled, they are constantly liable to eviction by the government despite the ability to bribe officials occasionally. In the event of eviction, not only will their present de facto access to land be discontinued, but their base for wage-employment will also be endangered.

Under these circumstances, another major conclusion that may be drawn is that, despite the existence of a strong peasant ideology and their present 'semi-proletarian' nature, the sukumbasis are likely to experience a steady loss of whatever remaining means of production they currently control, eventually becoming landless labourers. Given the extremely small plot of land held and the average household size of 6.1 persons, even if they are allowed to remain in their settlements and their holdings are eventually registered, most of the sukumbasis will not be able to sustain their aspirations to become peasants. The sub-division of land amongst household members is such that the vast majority of households are likely to cultivate less land with time, and the prospects for maintaining subsistence on their 'own' land will also decline. Indeed, a great many sukumbasi-households were already engaged in agricultural wage-employment as the main subsistence activity and the crops grown by them only supplemented the annual household food requirements. In view of this reality, these people already looked much more like agricultural labourers than self-cultivating peasants.

It may be mentioned here that, in assessing the processes related to the differentiation of the Russian peasantry before the 1917 Revolution, Lenin considered the 'allotment-holding farm labourers' as the 'most typical representatives of the rural proletariat' because of their 'insignificant farming on a patch of land, inability to exist without the sale of labour power' and 'an extremely low standard of living (probably lower than that of the worker without an allotment)' (Lenin, 1899, ch. II, part XIII, in Harriss, 1984: 132). Owing to their insecure tenure and a weak production base, even those sukumbasi households who did not engage in wage labouring to any large extent during the period of fieldwork will have to sell more labour-power to maintain their

TABLE 28 *Peasant settlers' perceptions on how they would maintain their livelihood in the future*

perceived livelihood options	number of households	per cent of households
wage-employment	130	81
don't know yet	18	11
other	12	8
total	160	100

Source: personal interviews;
sample size: 160 households

livelihood in the years ahead. Many households were indeed able to foresee a shift in their position to agricultural labourers. Asked for views on their own future, 81 per cent of the sukumbasis responded that they would have no other alternative but to engage fully in agricultural wage-employment in order to maintain subsistence in the future (see Table 28).

It should be mentioned that the process of rural proletarianization characterized by the transformation of small peasants into wage labourers (Mintz, 1974: 292–3) must be seen in the light of the changing nature of social relations of production in agriculture. One of the most commonly noted forms of development in many Third World countries is that of the rise in capitalist farming with relatively large-scale units of production and the separation of poor peasants from their land, who are thus transformed into wage labourers (de Janvry, 1983; Harriss, 1982 and 1984). In this regard, much has been said about India (a very close example to Nepal), where the rapid pace of capitalist development in agriculture has been observed as a result of the introduction of new agrarian technology (i.e. associated with the popularly-known 'Green Revolution') and the various incentives given by the government (e.g. low taxation, high support prices and liberal provision of credit and subsidized inputs (Bardhan, 1982: 87). In 1971, agricultural labourer households in India already constituted 37.5 per cent of the population (Nayyar,

1977). In Bihar and Uttar Pradesh adjacent to Nepal's Tarai, there was an even higher percentage of landless people. By 1976, 43.7 per cent of the population of Bihar were landless agricultural labourers (Bose and Ghosh, 1976); and a recent study of land transfer in Uttar Pradesh indicated a similar trend, demonstrating that considerably more land was sold in the post-Green Revolution period and that a significant proportion of the land was being sold by those who subsequently became landless with the land passing into the hands of larger landowners (Shankar, 1988). These are some of the dynamics which clearly exhibit the process of proletarianization occurring in India.

The relatively low number of landless people in Nepal's Tarai compared to that in India can partly be explained by the lack of capitalist development in agriculture. The high number of land parcels (and the larger the land-holdings, the higher the number of parcels),[12] falling yields of most cereal and cash crops, the declining use of improved seeds and the minimal use of chemical fertilizers and of modern agrarian tools means that, unlike in India, there will neither be any substantial rise in forces of production (i.e. the emergence of capitalist farmers with corresponding growth in agricultural labourers) nor any increase in agricultural productivity needed for productive reinvestment and economic expansion. Moreover, where peasants had lost land due to social relations of production and exchange, most of them in the past were able to regain their peasant status by migrating into the Tarai and settling in the frontier areas. In some cases, this process was even repeated as many were able to move on to the other frontier areas and bring virgin land under cultivation. In this regard, assessing the transformation of the peasantry in Brazilian frontier areas, one writer asserted that the total transition from small peasants into wage labourers 'cannot occur on the frontier where there is always more land to take in production' (Foweraker, 1981:175). Therefore, the negligible degree of landlessness in Nepal's Tarai can be explained by the availability of land in the frontier areas despite the fact that many households are illegal. Regardless of the nature and degree of capitalist development in agriculture in the future, what is clear now is that the rate of landlessness is bound to rise at an accelerated pace because of the various political factors hindering access to land in frontier areas. This situation combined with the limited availability of cultivated land, the sub-division and mortgaging of land and the lack of outside employment and income will most likely result in more people joining the ranks of the rural 'proletariat'. It is therefore apparent that many sukumbasi and poor peasant households in the future will have little alternative but to eventually become full-fledged agricultural wage laboureres and follow the fate of their counterparts in India.

The dust however is unlikely to settle without further struggle, anguish and suffering. It appears that the agricultural labouring households in the Tarai will face at least two additional, but closely related, problems which will make their future even bleaker than that of their counterparts across the border.

First, the indications are that the creation of wage-employment in agriculture is retarded in Nepal's Tarai. Obviously, for the moment, the farmers with large holdings are the ones who will have to be seen as the main generators of employment. However, an Asian Development Bank agricultural strategy study in 1982 indicated that the absentee nature of most of the large landowners is such that very few resources are invested in land (ADB/HMGN, vol. I, 1982: 16); consequently, very little extra employment is created. As far as the medium size farms are concerned (i.e. 2.7 ha or just over this size of holdings), the population growth within this stratum has resulted in an increasing labour supply within their households, especially as farm-sizes continuously decrease due to sub-divisions within the family. Hopes were raised in the 1970s that the introduction of new HYVs, particularly of maize, wheat and paddy, and of double-cropping would create an intensification of agriculture, thus leading to a greater degree of employment opportunities in rural areas (FAO, 1974: 31; Berry et al., 1974: 110–25; ARTEP, 1974: IV–36–8). But as mentioned in chapter two, between 1975 to 1985 the use of improved seeds of maize and paddy actually declined and that of wheat increased only nominally. This factor combined with other factors such as the lack of necessary external, government-level support services is reflected in the declining yield of these cereal crops over this period. During this period, the production of most of the cash crops also stagnated or declined. As a result, very few opportunities, if any at all, existed for employment in agriculture. Indeed, there is scarcely any basis to assume that this trend will be substantially altered in the future.

Secondly, as farm-sizes decrease as a result of sub-divisions, and as forest frontiers are closed off, pressures on the rural job market will increase dramatically, since more sukumbasis will be obliged to seek wage-employment in agriculture. And, an increasing competition for existing agricultural wage employment is inevitable as both the natural growth in the size of the local population of agricultural labourers and the immigration of landless people from India in search of wage-employment continue. In fact, any further capitalist development in agriculture across the border is likely to create even more landless people, thus possibly leading to a greater flow of people immigrating and seeking wage-employment in Nepal's Tarai. Moreover, this situation would not only create competition for rural wage-employment, it would also tend to depress wage-rates. The growing immigration of Indian labourers combined with the rise in the local labour force have already led to sluggish wages in the Nawalparasi district. To worsen the situation, the availability of an Indian labour force which is more compliant and prepared to work for lower wages[13] has resulted in a preference on the part of the employers for Indian migrant labourers. During fieldwork it was often observed that many large landowners in the area employed landless labourers from India on a sharecropping and contract-labour basis since, unlike native labourers, they were not eligible to claim any tenancy rights. Given the similar conditions (i.e. open border, immigration of Indian labourers and the growth in the local rural labour force), a similar pattern is emerging throughout the Tarai. Indeed, the paucity and the seasonal nature of wage-employment combined with stagnant wages is such that one can easily expect to see even further decline in the standard of living of labouring households in the Tarai; and the present minor advantages gained by sukumbasis in some locations are undermined.

The conditions under which the Nepalese sukumbasis are becoming agricultural labourers, when compared to their Indian counterparts in India, appear even worse in the context of outside political support. There is at present a lack of political consciousness, internal organization and leadership amongst the rural poor, thus the necessary political and organizational support must come from outside. It is here that the role of the political parties, the trade unions and the professional organizations are seen as indispensable (Wolf, 1971: 277–302; Alavi, 1973: 291–337; Shanin, 1966: 5–27; Skocpol, 1976: 201–4). Rosenberg and Rosenberg for example note that, with the prohibition of party politics in Indonesia since 1971, overt organization of the rural poor appeared largely 'infeasible' (1980: 68). Similarly, Mitra and Vijayendra studying recent agrarian changes in Bihar suggest that where social movements of agricultural labourers lacked the help of political parties and organizations, their struggles were found to be 'local and chaotic, and often leading to failure' (1982: 112), a close parallel with the experience of the sukumbasis. Even though the 1980s saw increasing activities of the opposition political parties, students' unions and professional organizations (Baral, 1983:42–72), these activities have largely been urban-based and limited to major political and economic reforms; very little attention has been given to the problems of people settled in isolated rural areas such as the sukumbasis whose grievances are yet to be heard.

The lack of internal organization and outside political support to provide an organizational and leadership framework, and the rudimentary urban and industrial base means that the sukumbasis will have to look for political support from other groups in the rural areas. Yet in the rural areas they have very little support in their aspirations to become peasants. Thus, the transformation from 'peasant' (or from an unsuccessful attempt to be a peasant) to agricultural labourer is the dominant process.

In summary, it is unlikely that the sukumbasis—as members of the landless or landpoor community desperately trying to regain their peasant position by settling illegally on the fringe of the Tarai forests—will remain in existence as a 'separate' social category; they will most probably be transformed into impoverished landless agricultural labourers. The sealing of the agricultural frontiers and the subsequent termination of access to forest land in the Tarai are such that in-migration and the maintenance of a peasant status or the movement to such a status in the future are now inconceivable. There is little doubt that as this process accelerates, the rural areas in the Tarai in particular will experience a high degree of landlessness, underemployment, economic destitution and mass misery, thus nourishing social tension and political discontent. But how such responses will be translated into politically effective movements and become a part of the larger struggle in the future will have to be seen. For certain, much of this will depend not only upon the actions of the rural poor themselves but also upon the support of other social forces and upon the wider socio-economic changes taking place in the country. Indeed, for most sukumbasis, learning to survive as wage labourers is likely to be as painful as learning that being a land-owning peasant is not possible.

Notes

1. In fact, in the early 1980s, the land area under forest in Nepal was remarkably higher than in some of the neighbouring South Asian countries. For example, Bangladesh, India and Pakistan had only 10.2, 24.9 and 4.9 per cent of forest areas respectively (FAO, 1988), whilst Nepal was believed to have retained as much as 43 per cent of its land area under forests (LRMP, 1986).
2. The government source suggested that the food-deficit districts in the country rose from 26 in 1975 to 46 in 1980, and between 25 to 40 thousand m.t. were dispatched annually to relieve the deficit (K. .C., 1982: 111–12). It is also estimated that the food shortage was likely to increase from 93 thousand m.t. in 1980 to 932 thousand m.t. by 2000 (ibid). Until 1970 a cereal-exporting country, Nepal in recent years has been importing a considerable amount of cereals; evidence suggests that between 1974 and 1985/6 Nepal imported 30,000 m.t. cereal (World Bank, 1988).
3. This is crucial as the cost of law and order and most parts of salaries of civil servants are not covered by foreign aid and therefore will have to be financed through internal resources.
4. Besides tourism, the national parks have also remained as areas for sport and entertainment for the Nepalese aristocracy. Historical evidence suggests that the Ranas were able to impress their British counterparts by taking them hunting in the Tarai forests (cf. Bhandari, 1981: 283), and these areas still remain as one of the important centres for entertaining foreign dignitaries. Indeed, many national parks, particularly in Chitawan and Bardia, were initially developed in order to satisfy and protect the game and recreational interests of the aristocracy, rather than for wildlife conservation.
5. How the local people can be excluded from the use of national parks in the interests of the commercial hunting and tourist industry is particularly evident in the African experience. For example, one recent study of the

Luangwa Valley National Park, Zambia, showed that tourism and the attempts to regulate safari hunting have resulted in the prohibition of traditional methods of resource use by the local people, increased conflict between various interest groups and eventually contributed to rural poverty (Abel & Blaikie, 1986: 746–7).

6. It may be noted that due to administrative inefficiency and corruption, the real costs of institutional level wood and timber extraction and marketing have been much higher than the existing market rates. Also the government must be aware of the possible urban unrest if actual costs were sought.
7. It is argued that similar industrial and commercial interests have also led the Indian government to introduce a new Forestry Bill in 1980 which restricted tribals and other forest dwellers from using forests but at the same time sought to make available timber and other forest raw material to commercial and industrial enterprises 'on a guaranteed basis' (Gadgil, 1983: 123). It is further noted that in some cases these rates were highly subsidized; for example, Gadgil claims that in Himachal Pradesh fir trees were made available to the packing case industry at about Rs 50 per tree whose market value was over Rs 2000 (ibid).
8. However, as has been discussed in chapter five, the large landowners also benefit from the establishment of sukumbasi settlements in their areas for settlers provide a reservoir of cheap labour and often lend political support, especially during elections. These factors together with the restrictions which they also face in exploiting the forest resources often lead them to premeditate their moves.
9. For example, in the late 1960s hundreds of long-established villages were included in the Chitawan National Park and in the 1970s equally large areas were cleared to establish Rara National Park in Mugu district.
10. Evidence suggests that between 1976 to 1984, as much as 515, 490 ha of land were brought under national parks and wildlife sanctuaries (CBS, 1987: 200).
11. It may be noted that, in most respects, this forest-area lease arrangement resembles that of the Enclosure Acts, introduced in England in the sixteenth century and in Scotland in the nineteenth century, which allowed the landed gentry uncontrolled sheep-raising rights in the commons and avoided competition from other users (Moore, 1981: 20–9). The main stimulus behind the enclosure movements in England and Scotland was the high profits to be had from the wool-trade. An even better example is the promulgation of laws protecting forest-owners against the theft of wood by peasants in the Rhineland areas in Germany in the early nineteenth century. These legislative measures were introduced in view of the high market value of timber resulting from railway construction activities, the increasing demand for wood for machinery and the growing need for fuel (Linebaugh, 1976: 12).
12. The agricultural census 1981/2 of Nawalparasi district, for example,

indicates that households with above 10 ha of land operated as many as 20 average land parcels whereas households owning between 0.5–1.0, 1.0–2.0 and 2.0–3.0 ha maintained 4.1, 6.0 and 7.4 parcels respectively (CBS, 1985b: 1).

13. During fieldwork, quite a few cases were observed in which migrant Indian labourers were engaged in contract labour with wages substantially lower than the going rates. Asked why they would work for such low wages, one Indian labourer replied, 'even if I earn just enough for myself, at least the food which I would have consumed at home is saved' (personal interview, Narsahi V.P.).

Epilogue

Since this book went to the press, some interesting political changes have taken place in Nepal. Largely inspired by recent political developments around the world, popular spontaneous protest movements involving underground political parties, students and professional organizations as well as significant sections of both the urban and rural populace challenged the country's long-established absolutist royal administration. The inability of the industrial bourgeoisie to develop as an important socio-economic category and the failure of the landed upper classes to make any successful economic transition to commercial agriculture, which would have politically strengthened their class position vis-à-vis the crown, had meant that no serious opposition to the central position of the monarchy was forthcoming from within the dominant classes. The backward nature of the industrial and agricultural sectors in the country had also meant that the generation of wage-employment and the emergence of a strong working class—which might have constituted a challenge for power—were largely thwarted.

At the same time, the monarchy was able to draw upon a tradition of caste and Hindu philosophy which together had provided an excellent ideological framework for the legitimization of centralized and concentrated unequal power relations. This philosophy underpinned the Panchayat system indicating that many rural as well as urban dwellers had tended to accept many of the existing structural conditions and power relations without further questioning. Even where questions were raised, there was a tendency amongst many of these groups to separate the crown from other State institutions and government officials with the typical response: 'the king is right, but his men aren't'. However, worsening employment opportunities, a higher literacy rate (especially in urban areas) and greater degrees of contacts with the outside world combined with the regime's reliance on repressive measures to meet all popular protests brought into question the 'unlimited' and 'unsupervised' power of the crown. Fearful of having to relinquish the throne altogether, in 1990 the king agreed to reconcile himself to a 'constitutional role'. The Panchayat system was withdrawn (although the traditions of the caste system and Hindu philosophy governing property laws, gender relations and legitimised socio-economic inequalities have not been challenged); a thirty-year ban on political parties was lifted and six successive governments have been formed by 1997. Whilst multiparty democracy has now been established, effective political participation of the poorer sections of the population such as the sukumbasis to directly advance their interests is still low.

As far as the provision of means of production and livelihood to the landless is concerned, the question is whether pressures for genuine land reform will emerge. As has been pointed out, legal land ceilings for a landowner household in the Tarai are the highest in Asia (i.e. 17 ha of agricultural land plus home sites). In terms of lessening immediate economic vulnerability and decreasing the current rate at which landlessness is taking place, thereby reducing pressure on the forest area, the lowering of existing land ceilings for the Tarai and effective appropriation and just redistribution of excess land are likely to yield some worthy results. Long-term success will depend upon what social forces will eventually come to power. Understandably, if elements with vested interests in land gain sway, the regime is unlikely to undertake any genuine sweeping land reform measures. In Nepal's Tarai, the most prominent of the landed classes currently retain land mainly as a source of supplementary earnings (i.e. the major part of the income being derived from paid employment within the bureaucracy, urban business and property speculation), or for maintaining an electoral base rather than for productive use. Large tracts of these under-used areas have substantial wage-employment potentialities. One of the most common ways of operating these holdings has so far been to hire destitute Indian labourers and extract the maximum surplus from them. The other advantage for the employing landowners is that the Indian labourers are ineligible to claim tenancy rights, for these rights are sanctioned only for Nepalese nationals. The landowners are therefore in favour of migrant labour, despite the increasing availability of a local labour force. In fact, present labour relations in the Tarai work neither in favour of migrant labourers nor the local landless, but are certainly in the interest of the large employers. It can be argued that this situation has in large part resulted from the existing open frontiers between Nepal and India. Hence, future agricultural and rural employment policies must be accompanied by a serious re-evaluation of this border issue. Indeed, frontier relationships are crucial not only in terms of discouraging the 'northward movement' of people from the over-populated Indian plains seeking rural employment, land settlement and food (which is transported out in large quantities by the migrants), but also in terms of allowing local industries the opportunity to flourish since at present the free influx of cheaper mass-produced goods from India do not permit them to make any significant headway.

The other fundamental issue is the present land-use policy which is biased against small-holder land settlement of 'forested' land, thereby going against the subsistence needs of the landless. I firmly believe that substantial land settlement in the Tarai can continue without serious damage to the local environment, and that the possibility exists for changing land-use from an exclusive forest plantation system to combining forestry with food production activities. But, there are many strong vested interests surrounding forestry in the Tarai, including the monarchical Nepalese State itself.

An equally decisive factor in this respect is likely to be the increasing international pressure for forest conservation. In other words, as international attention focuses more and more on the need for environmental stability and the preservation of plant and animal genetic resources (note the recent growing concern in developed countries about global climate change which has been partially attributed to deforestation in developing countries), further 'clearance' of forests is unlikely to be welcomed anywhere in the Third World. At the same time, Nepal's overwhelming dependence on developed countries for foreign aid means that the bargaining capacity of the future government/s would be strictly limited; therefore, some sort of continuation of the present restrictive land-use policies would be nearly unavoidable with consequent negative implications for the sukumbasis.

Under these circumstances, it looks as if landlessness and cumulative pauperization will remain the dominant features of much of rural Nepal. Therefore, the future of the Nepalese peasantry, now declining rapidly to the status of sukumbasis, is unlikely to be fundamentally altered by current political changes.

Bibliography

Abel, N., and Blaikie, P., 1986. 'Elephants, People, Parks and Development: the Case of the Luangwa Valley, Zambia', *Environmental Management*, vol. 10, No. 6.

Acquaya, B. and Crocombe, R. (eds.), 1984. *Land Tenure and Rural Productivity in the Pacific Islands* (FAO/SAO/IPS).

ADB/HMGN, 1982. *Nepal Agricultural Sector Strategy Study*, vols. I & II (Kathmandu: ADB/HMGN).

ADBN, 1984. *Highlights on Small Farmer Development Programs in Nepal* (Kathmandu: ADBN).

Agrawal, R.C. et al., 1978. 'A Study of Fertilizer Use in Gandaki Zone of Nepal', Technical University of Berlin.

Alavi, H., 1973. 'Peasants and Revolution', in Gough, K. and Sharma, H.P. (eds.), *Imperialism and Revolution in South Asia* (New York: Monthly Review Press).

Amnesty International, 1986. *Nepal Background Briefing and Statement of Amnesty International's Concerns* (London: Amnesty International Secretariat).

APROSC, 1978a. *Agrarian Reform and Rural Development in Nepal* (Kathmandu: APROSC).

———, 1978b. *Socio-economic Survey of Kanchanpur and Bardia Resettlement Project Area* (Kathmandu: APROSC).

ARTEP/ILO, 1974. *The Challenge For Nepal Growth with Employment* (Bangkok: ILO).

Bajracharya, D., 1983. 'Deforestation in the Food/Fuel Context Historical and Political Perspective from Nepal', *Mountain Research and Development*, vol. 3, No. 3.

Bankeko Yugdhara, Kathmandu Weekly (January 5, 1984).

Baral, L.K., 1987. 'The Actual Sequence of Events Regarding Susta', mimeo (Tribenighat: SFDP).

Baral, L.R., 1983. *Nepal's Politics of Referendum* (New Delhi: Vikas Publishing House).

Barber, B., 1957. *Social Stratification* (New York: Bruce and Co.).

Bardhan, P., 1982. 'Agrarian Class Formation in India', *The Journal of Peasant Studies*, vol. 10, No. 1.

Basham, A.L., 1954. *The Wonder that Was India* (London: Sidwick and Jackson).

Basnyat, N.B., 1981. *An Appraisal of Settlement in Regional Rural Planning in Nepal*, unpublished MA Thesis (The Hague: ISS).

Beenhakker, A., 1973. *A Kaleidoscopic Circumspection of Development: Planning with Contextual Reference to Nepal* (Rotterdam: Rotterdam University Press).

Berry, M.J., Laurence, J.F., Makin, M.J., and Vaddams, A.E., 1974. *Development Potential of the Nawalparasi Area of Nepal* (Surrey: Land Resources Division).

Bhandari, D.R., 1981. *Nepalko Aetihasik Bibechana* (Kathmandu: K.K. Devi).

Blaikie, P., 1983a (July). 'What Does the Nepalese State Do and Why?', paper presented at the workshop on the State and Political Economy in South Asia at the School of Development Studies, Norwich.

———, 1983b. 'The Political Economy of Soil Erosion', *Progress in Resource Management and Environmental Planning*, vol. 4.

Blaikie, P. and Brookfield, H., 1987. *Land Degradation and Society* (London: Methuen).

Blaikie, P., Cameron, J., Feldman, D., Fournier, A., Seddon D., 1983. *Centre, Periphery and Access in Western Central Nepal: Approaches to Social and Spatial Relations of Inequalities*, Monograph (Norwich: School of Development Studies/UEA).

Blaikie, P., Cameron, J., Feldman, D., Fournier, A., Seddon, D., 1976. *The Effects of Roads in West-Central Nepal* (Norwich: School of Development Studies/UEA).

Blaikie, P., Cameron, J., Seddon D., 1979. *The Struggle for Basic Needs in Nepal* (Paris: OECD).

Bolt, V., 1967. *Gurkhas* (London: Weidenfeld & Nicolson).

Bose, S.R. and Ghosh, P.P., 1976. *Agro-Economic Survey of Bihar* (Patna).

Boserup, E., 1972. *The Conditions of Agricultural Growth, the Economy of Agricultural Change under Population Pressure* (London: George Allen and Unwin Ltd.).

Bromley, D.W., 1986 (April 18–25). 'On Common Property Regimes in International Development', a paper presented at workshop on Institutional Development for Local Management for Rural Resources, held in Gilgit, Pakistan.

Burghart, A., 1978. *The History of Janakpurdham A Study of Asceticism and Hindu Polity* (London: unpublished Ph.D. Thesis, University of London).

Cameron, J., 1987 (Spring). 'A Note on the History of the Sugar Sector in Fiji: Peasantisation under Capitalism', *Peasant Studies*, vol. 14, No. 3.

Caplan, L., 1967 (March). 'Some Political Consequences of State Land Policy in East Nepal', reprinted from *Man*, vol. 2, No. 1.

———, 1970. *Land and Social Change in East Nepal* (London: Routledge and Kegan Paul).

Caufield, C., 1982. 'Tropical Moist Forests: The Resources, the People, the Threat' (London: Earthscan).

CBS, 1974, *Statistical Pocket Book Nepal* (Kathmandu: CBS).

———, 1976. *Agricultural Sample Census 1971*, (Kathmandu: CBS).

———, 1982. *Statistical Pocket Book* (Kathmandu: CBS).

———, 1984. *Statistical Pocket Book* (Kathmandu: CBS).

———, 1985a. *National Sample Census of Agriculture 1981/82* (Kathmandu: CBS).

———, 1985b. *National Sample Census of Agriculture 1981/82: District Nawalparasi* (Kathmandu: CBS).

———, 1986. *Statistical Pocket Book* (Kathmandu: CBS).

———, 1987. *Statistical Year Book of Nepal* (Kathmandu: CBS).

Chambers, R., 1983. *Rural Development, Putting the Last First* (Essex: Longman).

Chapagain, D.P. 1983. *Agricultural Productivity Pattern in Nepal and its Regional Variations* (Kathmandu: HMG/USAID).

Chayanov, A.V. 1925 in Shanin, T. (ed.), 1971. *Peasants and Peasant Societies*, (Middlesex: Penguin).

Collier, D., 1976. *Squatters and Oligarchies* (Baltimore and London: The John Hopkins University Press).

Conway, D. and Shrestha, N.R., 1981. *Causes and Consequences of Rural-to-Rural Migration in Nepal* (Indiana: Indiana University Press).

Coxon, A., and Jones, C., 1975. *Social Mobility* (Suffolk: Penguin).

Dandekar, V.M., and Rath, N., 1971 (January). 'Poverty in India', *Economic and Political Weekly*, 6:1.

Dasgupta, B., 1977. *Agricultural Change and the New Technology in India* (Geneva: UNRISD).

De Janvry, A., 1983. *The Agrarian Question and Reformation in Latin America* (Baltimore and London: The John Hopkins University Press).

Department of Information, 1974. *Mechi Dekhi Mahakali*, vol. III, (Kathmandu: Dept. of Information).

Department of Resettlement (RD), 1974. *Punarbas Ra Abyabasthit Basobas Niyantran Sambandhi Yojana Ra Karyakram* (Kathmandu: RD).

Devkota, M.N., 1986 (May 21–2). 'Perspective Land Use Plan', a paper presented at the seminar on Perspective Land Use Plan, Perspective Plan for Agriculture and Long Term Food Plan, Kathmandu.

Douglas, J.S. and Hart, R., 1976. *Forest Farming* (London: Watkins).

Eckholm, E., 1975. 'The Deterioration of Mountain Environments', *Science*, vol. 189.

Elder, J., Ale, M., Evans, M. et al., 1975. *Planned Resettlement in Nepal's Tarai: A Social Analysis of the Khajura/Bardia Purnavas Projects* (Kathmandu: INAS).

Epstein, D., 1973. *Brasilia, Plan and Reality* (Berkeley and Los Angeles: University of California Press).

Esman, M.J., 1978. *Landlessness and Nearlandlessness in Developing Countries* (Ithaca: Cornell University).

FAO, 1974. *Perspective Study of Agricultural Development for Nepal* (Rome: FAO).

———, 1988. *An Interim Report on the State of Forest Resources in the Developing Countries* (Rome: FAO).

FASC, 1984. '*Jilla Ban Chhetra Sudhridhikaran Adhikar Sampanna Samitiko Doshro Gosthi 2041*', mimeo (Kathmandu: FASC).

Feder, G. and Onchan, T., 1987 (May). 'Land Ownership Security and Farm Investment in Thailand', *American Agricultural Economics*, vol. 69, No. 2.

Feldman, D. & Fournier, A., 1976 (July). 'Social Relations and Agricultural Production in Nepal's Tarai', *The Journal of Peasant Studies*, vol. 3, No. 4.

Feldman, K. D., 1979. 'Sociohistorical Factors and the Growth of Squatter Settlements: Mindanao, Philippines, 1950–72', *Urban Anthropology*, vol. 8(1).

Fernandes, W. and Kulkarni, S., 1983. *Towards a New Forest Policy* (New Delhi: Indian Social Institute).

Fife, D., 1971 (April). 'Killing the Goose', *Environment*.

Foley, G. and Barnard, G., 1984. *Farm and Community Forestry* (London: Earthscan).

Fournier, A., 1976. 'Government Resettlement Schemes in Nawalparasi', mimeo, Nepal Library/UEA.

Foweraker, J., 1981. *The Struggle for Land* (Cambridge: Cambridge University Press).

Frank, A.G., 1975. *On Capitalist Underdevelopment* (Bombay: Oxford University Press).

Fürer-Haimendorf, C.V., 1967. 'The Position of the Tribal Populations in Modern India', in P. Mason (ed.), *India and Ceylon: Unity and Diversity* (London: O.U.P.)

Gadgil, M., 1983. 'Forestry With a Social Purpose', in Fernandes, W. & Kulkarni, S. (eds.), *Towards a New Forest Policy* (New Delhi: Indian Social Institute).

Gaige, F., 1975. *Regionalism and National Unity in Nepal* (Berkeley and Los Angeles: University of California Press).

Galeski, 1963, quoted in Shanin (ed.), 1971. *Peasants and Peasant Societies* (Middlesex: Penguin).

Gevers, E., Ghimire, K., Goodman, J. and others, 1988. *Dhanusha District Sustainable Woodfuel Strategy and Action Plan* (Leusden: ETC Foundation).

Ghimire, K., 1983. *Underdevelopment and Class Structure in Nepali Society*, unpublished IRDP research paper (The Hague: ISS).

——— 1988. 'Understanding People's Views on Deforestation Issues: A Village Perspective of Nepal's Central Tarai', research report submitted to Nuffield Foundation, London.

Gibbs, C., 1982. 'Institutional Obstacles to Effective Forestry for Local Community Development in Asia', USAID Conference on Forestry and Development in Asia, Bangalore.

Gill, L., 1987 (April). 'Frontier Expansion and Settlement in Lowland Bolivia', *The Journal of Peasant Studies*, vol. 14, No. 3.

Gorkhapatra, Kathmandu daily (20 May 1964, 18 September 1977, 27 August 1978 and 21 May 1979).

Griffin, K., 1985. 'Rural Poverty in Asia: Analysis and Policy Alternatives', in Islam R. (ed.), *Strategies for Alleviating Poverty in Rural Asia* (ILO/ ARTEP Bangkok and BIDS, Dhaka).

Gupta, R., Banerji, P. and Guleria, A., 1981. *Tribal Unrest and Forestry Management in Bihar* (Ahmedabad: Indian Institute of Management).

Harrison, M., 1975. 'Chayanov and the Economics of the Russian Peasantry', *The Journal of Peasant Studies*, vol. 2, No. 4.

Harriss, J., 1982. *Capitalism and Peasant Farming* (Bombay: Oxford University Press).

——— (ed.) 1984. *Rural Development: Theories of Peasant Economy and Agrarian Change* (London: Hutchinson University Library and Hutchinson Library for Africa).

Hitchcock, J.T., 1966. *The Magars of Banyan Hill* (New York: Holt, Rinehart and Winston, Ins.).

Hodgson 1934, in Oldfield, H.A., 1974 (reprint). *Sketches from Nepal* (Delhi: Cosmo Publication).

Höfer, A., 1978. 'A New Elite in Central Nepal', *Himalayan Anthropology*, J.F. Fisher (ed.) (The Hague and Paris: Mouton Publishers).

Hunt, D., 1978. 'Chayanov's Model of Peasant Household Resource Allocation and its Relevance to Mbere Division, Eastern Kenya', *The Journal of Peasant Studies*, vol. 15, 1.

ILO, 1977, *Poverty and Landlessness in Rural Asia* (Geneva: ILO).

Islam, R., 1984. 'Poverty and Income Distribution in Rural Nepal', in Khan, A.R. and Lee, E. (eds.), *Poverty in Rural Asia* (Bangkok: ARTEP).

International Union for Conservation of Nature and Natural Resources (IUCN), 1980. *World Conservation Strategy* (Gland: IUCN).

Joshi, B.L., and Rose, L., 1966. *Democratic Innovation in Nepal* (Berkeley and Los Angeles: University of California Press).

Kansakar, V.B., 1973/74. 'History of Population Migration in Nepal', *The Himalayan Review*, vol. VI, No. 5–6.

——— 1979. *Effectiveness of Planned Resettlement Programme in Nepal*, vol. I (Kathmandu: CEDA).

Kaplan, P. and Shrestha, N.R., 1982. 'The Sukumbasi Movement in Nepal: The Fire from Below', *The Journal of Contemporary Asia*, vol. 12.

Katwal, B.B., 1986 (July). 'Wages and Welfare: The Case of Attached Vs. Casual Labour in the Nepal Tarai', HMG-USAID-GTZ-WINROCK Project, Research Paper Series No. 31, Kathmandu.

K.C., R.B., 1984. 'Trends in Land Distribution and Landlessness in Nepal and their Implications for Agrarian Reforms', mimeo., undated, quoted in Islam, R, 'Poverty and Income Distribution in Rural Nepal', in Khan, A.R. and Lee, E. (eds.), *Poverty in Rural Asia* (Bangkok: ARTEP).

———, 1982. *Facts about Nepal* (Kathmandu: Department of Information).

———, 1980. 'The Quest for Agrarian Reform in Nepal', *Planning for Basic Needs and Mobilization of Resources* (Bangkok: ILO).

Kirkpatrick, W., 1811. *An Account of the Kingdom of Nepaul* (London: William Miller).

Kunstadter, P., Champman, E. and Sabhasri, S., 1978. *Farmers in the Forest, Economic Development and Marginal Agriculture in Northern Thailand* (Honolulu: East-West Center).

Ladejinsky, W., 1977. 'Too Late to Save Asia', in Walinsky, L.J. (ed.), *The Selected Papers of Wolf Ladejinsky Agrarian Reform as Unfinished Business* (New York: Oxford University Press).

Lappé, F.M., Collins, J., Fowler, E., 1977. *Food First, Beyond the Myth of Scarcity* (Boston: Houghton Mifflin Co.).

Lenin, V.I., 1899 in Harriss, J., 1984. *Rural Development: Theories of Peasant Economy and Agrarian Change* (London: Hutchinson University Library and Hutchinson Library for Africa).

Linebaugh, P., 1976 (Fall-Winter). 'Karl Marx, the Theft of Wood and Working Class Composition: A Contribution to the Current Debate', *Crime and Social Justice*.

Lipton, M., 1984. 'Why Poor Stay Poor', in Harriss, J. (ed.), *Rural Development: Theories of Peasant Economy and Agrarian Change* (London: Hutchinson University Library and Hutchinson Library for Africa).

LRMP, 1986. *Summary Report* (Kathmandu: Kenting Earth Science Ltd.).

MacAndrews, C., 1978 (October). 'Patterns and Uses of Land Settlements in South East Asia', *Land Development Digest*, vol. I, No. 2.

Macfarlane, A., 1976. *Resources and Population: a Study of the Gurungs of Nepal* (Cambridge: Cambridge University Press).

Maharjan, B.L., 1984. *Small Farm Development Problems* (Kathmandu: Shiva Narayan).

Malaria Department, 'Population Census in Makar and Shiva Mandir Panchayats', mimeo., 1988.

Manshard, W., 1974. *Tropical Agriculture* (London: Longman).

Martens, J., 1982. 'Forests and Their Destruction in the Himalayas of Nepal', *Plant Research and Development*, vol. 15.

Matribhumi, Kathmandu Weekly (28 March 1964).

McCoy, A., 1971 (Winter/Spring). 'Land Reform as Counter-Revolution, U.S. Foreign Policy and the Tenant Farmers of Asia', *Bulletin of Concerned Asian Scholars*, vol. 3, No. 1.

McDougal, C., 1968. *Village and Household Economy in Far-West Nepal* (Kathmandu).

Mellor, J.W., 1976. *The New Economics of Growth* (Ithaca and London: Cornell University Press).

Messerschmidt, D.A., 1976. *The Gurungs of Nepal* (Warminister: Aris and Phillips Ltd.).

Mihaly, E.B., 1965. *Foreign Aid and Politics in Nepal: A Case Study* (London: Oxford University Press).

Ministry of Forest and Soil Conservation (MFSC), 1980. '*Suchana*', mimeo (Kathmandu: MFSC).

Ministry of Law and Justice, 1986a. *Nepal Aien Sangraha*, vol. VII, *Kha*, (Kathmandu: Ministry of Law and Justice).

———, 1986b. *Kabuliyat Ban Niyamawali 2035 Ra Niji Ban Niyamawali 2041* (Kathmandu: Ministry of Law and Justice).

Mintz, S.W., 1974. 'The Rural Proletariat and the Problem of the Rural Proletarian Consciousness', *The Journal of Peasant Studies*, vol. 1, No. 3.

Mitra, M. and Vijayendra, T., 1982 (April). 'Agricultural Labourers and Peasant Politics: Rural Proletarianisation in Purnea, Bihar', *The Journal of Peasant Studies*, vol. 9, No. 3.

Miyan, K. and Poudel, S.K., 1986 (May 21–2). 'Perspective Plan for Agriculture (1985–2005)', paper presented at the seminar on Perspective Land Use Plan, Perspective Plan for Agriculture and long Term Food Plan, Kathmandu.

Moore, B., 1981. *Social Origins of Dictatorship and Democracy* (Bucks: Penguin Books).

Morris, C.J., 1928. *The Gurkhas* (London: John Lane The Bodley Head Ltd.).

Munslow, B., Katerere, Y., Ferf, A. & O'Keefe, P., 1988. *The Fuelwood Trap: A Study of the SADCC Region* (London: Earthscan Publications Ltd.).

Myers, N., 1984. *The Primary Source Tropical Forests and Our Future* (Ontario: General Publication Co.).

National Planning Commission (NPC), 1975. *Panchaun Yojana* (Kathmandu: NPC).

———, 1984a. *Social Aspects of Rural Development* (Kathmandu: NPC).

NPC/Task Force on Population, 1983. *Internal and International Migration in Nepal: Summary and Recommendations* (Kathmandu: NPC).

NPC/Task Force on Resettlement, 1984b. *Sataun Yojanama Punarvas Bikas* (Kathmandu: NPC).

Nayyar, R., 1977. *Poverty and Inequality in Rural Asia* (Geneva: ILO).

Nepal Australia Forestry Plan (NAFP), 1976. *Nepal's National Forestry Project* (Kathmandu: NAFP).

Nepal Post, Kathmandu weekly (1 September 1979).

Nepal Rastra Bank (NRB), 1980. *Agricultural Credit Review Survey* (Kathmandu: NRB).

NRC Dhanewa Project Office, 1986. 'Progress Report of Nawalparasi Project', mimeo (Dhanewa: NRC Project Office).

Ohja, D.P., 1982. *Planned and Spontaneous Land Settlement in Nepal: A Study of Two Settlements in the Kanchanpur District* (Ithaca: unpublished Ph.D. Dissertation, Cornell University.).

Paige, J.M., 1975. *Agrarian Revolution* (New York & London: The Free Press).

Pant, Y.P., and Jain, S.C., 1969. *Agricultural Development in Nepal* (Bombay: Vore and Co Publishers).

Parkin, P., 1979. *Marxism and Class Theory: A Bourgeois Critique* (London: Tavistock Publications).

Paudel, N.B., 1979. *Nepal Resettlement Company An Introduction* (Kathmandu: Aadarsha Chhapakhana).

Pinstrup-Andersen, P., and Hazell, P., 1985. *The Impact of the Green Revolution and Prospects for the Future* (Washington: International Food Policy Research Institute).

Pokhrel, B.K. et al., 1983. *Nepali Brihat Shabdakosh* (Kathmandu: Nepal Royal Academy).

Poudyal, S., 1983. *Planned Development in Nepal* (Kathmandu: Educational Enterprise).

Pradhan, M.B., 1979. *Nepalma Bhumisudharko Shabparichha* (Kathmandu: Pradhan Publication).

Pyakhuryal, K.N., 1978. *Impact of Rural Development Programmes on Income, Employment and Output of Small and Big Farmers* (Kathmandu: CEDA).

Rana, P.S., 1973. 'Trade', *Nepal in Perspective*, Rana and Malla (eds.) (Kathmandu: CEDA).

Regmi, M.C., 1971. *A Study of Nepali Economic History 1768–1846* (New Delhi: Manjushri Press).

———, 1973. 'Land Tenure', in Rana and Malla (eds.), *Nepal in Perspective* (Kathmandu: CEDA).

———, 1976. *Landownership in Nepal* (Berkeley: University of California Press).

———, 1978. *Thatched Huts and Stucco Palaces: Peasants and Landlords in the 19th Century Nepal* (New Delhi: Vikas Publishing House).

Rieger, H.C., et al., 1976. *Himalayan Ecosystems Research Mission Nepal Report* (Heidelbourg).

Rose, L.E. and Fisher, M.W., 1970. *The Politics of Nepal* (Ithaca and London: Cornell University Press).

Rosenberg, J. and Rosenberg, D., 1980. *Landless Peasants and Rural Poverty in Indonesia and Philippines* (New York: Cornell University).

Sainju, M.B. et al., 1973. *Revisit to Budhabare* (Kathmandu: CEDA).

Samai, Kathmandu daily (24 May 1980).

Sandbrook, R., 1982. *The Politics of Basic Needs* (London: Heinemann).

Sanwal, B.D., 1965. *Nepal and the East India Company* (Bombay: Asian Publishing House).

Saptahik Birmarsha, Kathmandu weekly (1 March 1985).

Scholz, J.T., 1977. *Policy Processes and Rural Development: A Study of Land Reform in Nepal*, unpublished Ph.D. Thesis (Berkeley: University of California).

Schultz, T.W., 1964. *Transforming Traditional Agriculture* (New Haven: Yale University Press).

Scott, J.C., 1972 (November). 'The Erosion of Patron–Client Bonds and Social Change in Rural Southeast Asia', *Journal of Asian Studies*, vol. XXXII, No. 1.

———, 1985. *Weapons of the Weak: Everyday Forms of Resistance* (New Haven & London: Yale University Press).

Seddon, D. with Blakie P.M. & Cameron, J., 1981. *Peasants and Workers in Nepal* (New Delhi: Vikas Publishing House).

Seddon, D., 1984. *Nepal -A State of Poverty–the Political Economy of Population Growth and Social Deprivation*, monographs in Development Studies, No. 11 (Norwich: University of East Anglia).

Shah, P.B. and Schreier, H., 1985. 'Agricultural Land Evaluation for National Land-Use Planning in Nepal: A Case Study in the Kailali District', *Mountain Research and Development*, vol. 5, No. 2.

Shah, R., 1982. *Essays in the Practice of Government in Nepal* (Delhi: Manohar, Publications).

Shanin, T., 1966. 'Peasantry as a Political Factor', *Sociological Review*, vol. 14, No. 1.

Shankar, K., 1988 (July 23). 'Land Transfers in Uttar Pradesh', *Economic and Political Weekly*.

Shiva, V., Sharatchandra, H.C. and Bandyopadyay, J., 1983. 'The Challenge of Social Forestry', in Fernandes, W. and Kulkarni, S. (eds.), *Towards a New Forest Policy* (New Delhi: Indian Social Institute).

Singh, M.L., 1984. *A Comparative Evaluation of Planned and Unplanned Resettlement in Nepal* (Kathmandu: CEDA).

Sinha, R., 1984. *Landlessness: A Growing Problem* (Rome: FAO).

Skocpol, T., 1976 (April). 'A Structural Analysis of Social Revolutions', *Comparative Studies in Society and History*, 18.2.

Srinivas, M.N., 1962. *Caste in Modern India and Other Essays* (Bombay: Asia Publishing House).

Stiller, L.F., 1968. *Prithivinarayan Shah in the Light of Debya Upadesh* (Kathmandu: Published by the author).

Streefkerk, H., 1985. *Industrial Transition in Rural India* (London: Sangam Books).

Tarai DFC Seminar, 1987 (August 18–21). '*Tarai Chhetrako Banma Samrachhan Baybasthapan tatha Sadupayogka Samasyaharu*', Kathmandu.

Tarka, Kathmandu (10 July 1978, 30 March 1981).

The Guardian (12 August 1986).

The Military Balance, 1977/8 and 1986/7 (London).

Thorner, D. and Thorner, A., 1962. *Land and Labour in India* (Bombay: Asia Publishing House).

Turner, R.C., 1980. *A Comparative and Ethnological Dictionary of the Nepalese Language* (London: Routledge and Kegan Paul Ltd.).

UNESCO/UNEP, 1983. *Swidden Cultivation in Asia* (Bangkok: UNESCO Regional Office).

Uprety, T.P., 1981. *Rural Settlements and Policy Processes: A Comparative Study of Government Planned and Spontaneous Settlements in Nepal* (Berkeley: unpublished Ph.D. Thesis, University of California).

Wallace, M.B., 1981. *Solving Common Property Resource Problems: Deforestation in Nepal* (Harvard: unpublished Ph.D. thesis, Harvard University).

Weber, M., 1967. 'Politics as a Vocation', in *From Max Weber: Essays in Sociology* (eds.), Gerth, H.H. and Mills, C.W. (London: Routledge and Kegan Paul Ltd.).

———, 1958. *The Religion of India* (eds.), Gerth, H., and Martindale, D. (Glencoe: The Free Press).

Wolf, E., 1971. *Peasant Wars of Twentieth Century* (London: Faber and Faber).

Wolf, E. and Mintz, S., 1957 (September). 'Haciendas and Plantations in Middle America and the Antilles', *Social and Economic Studies*, 6.

World Bank, 1981. *Nepal Staff Appraisal Report of the Agricultural Extension and Research Project* (South Asia Projects Dept., Report No. 3104-Nepal).

———, 1988. *World Development Report* (Washington DC: Oxford University Press).

Yadav, S.R., 1984. *Nepal Feudalism and Rural Formation* (New Delhi: Cosmo Publications).

Yugdhara, Kathmandu weekly (19 March 1983).

Zaman, M.A., 1973. *Evaluation of Land Reform in Nepal* (Kathmandu: Ministry of Land Reform).

Index